MYSTERIES OF THE BIBLE

Exploring the Secrets of the Unexplained

Timothy J. Dailey, Ph.D.

Consultant:
David M. Howard, Jr., Ph.D.

Publications International, Ltd.

Timothy J. Dailey earned his doctorate in theology from Marquette University and studied at Wheaton College and the Institute of Holy Land Studies, Jerusalem. He has taught theology, biblical history, and comparative religion in the United States and Israel including at the Biblical Resources Study Center, Jerusalem, and Jerusalem Center for Biblical studies.

David M. Howard, Jr., is professor of Old Testament and Hebrew at New Orleans Baptist Theological Seminary and holds a Ph.D. in Near Eastern Studies from the University of Michigan. He is the author of *Fascinating Bible Facts, An Introduction to the Old Testament Historical Books, The Structure of Psalms 93–100* and his writing credits include contributions to *The International Standard Bible Encyclopedia, Anchor Bible Dictionary,* and *Peoples of the Old Testament World.* He is a member of the Society of Biblical Literature.

Editorial assistance: **Loren D. Lineberry**

8 7 6 5 4 3 2 1

ISBN: 0-7853-3238-3

Libary of Congress Catalog Card Number: 98-68133

CONTENTS

CHAPTER THREE
Old Testament: Historical Books.

CHAPTER EIGHT
New Testament: Acts 246

THE HOLY BIBLE

A Most Remarkable Book

*T*he Bible is one of the most fascinating books ever written. No other book frames the same expanse of time or the vast assembly of peoples and cultures found between its covers. Composed of 66 books and written by more than 40 authors, the first of the Hebrew Scriptures were recorded around 1400 B.C. The New Testament was written over the course of 50 years, finishing at the end of the first century A.D. In all, the writing spans 16 centuries.

Mysteries of the Bible draws on events and stories beginning with Creation, continuing through the Revelation to St. John on the Isle of Patmos. It also extends to the Dead Sea Scrolls, the Shroud of Turin, and other recent archaeological findings, presenting some of the most intriguing questions raised by the Bible—questions that have occupied the attention of scholars and students throughout the centuries.

Beginning with Abraham in ancient Mesopotamia, the story of the Bible moves around the fertile crescent of the Middle East to the land of Canaan. From there, the setting moves to Egypt, which rivaled Mesopotamia as the great center of civilization and culture in the ancient world. One incredible chapter after another tells the story of 40 years spent wandering in the desert, culminating in the collapse of the walls of Jericho and the conquest of the Promised Land. Now, thousands of years later, can we be sure that Abraham did exist? And with virtually no substantiating proof, should we believe that the Israelites were enslaved in Egypt or that Moses parted the Red Sea?

The Bible makes manifest the stories of Hebrew judges and kings, prophets and warriors. Some stories are exciting.

Synopsis of Biblical History

2100–1900 B.C.	1900–1550 B.C	1550–1200 B.C.	1200–586 B.C.
INTERMEDIATE BRONZE AGE	MIDDLE BRONZE AGE	LATE BRONZE AGE	IRON AGE
Abraham	Isaac, Jacob, Joseph Israel in Egypt	Exodus, Judges	Saul, David, Solomon Divided Kingdom Isaiah, Fall of Israel

Many are innately intriguing. *Mysteries of the Bible* adds depth to these stories by including information gathered recently through high-tech imaging or low-tech digging.

History confirms that God's promise to Abraham was fulfilled, and Israel became a great nation. But refusing to heed the cries of the prophets, 10 tribes of Israel stumbled to destruction, followed in the next century by the fall of Judea. Seventy years of captivity ensued before a remnant of the Israelites returned to their native land. The temple was modestly rebuilt and the walls of Jerusalem restored, but the time of greatness passed. Mysteries, puzzles, enigmas—call them what you will—are strewn throughout Israel's early history, involving countless people and places.

When Rome entered the picture as the master of the known world, self-styled Herod the Great ruled as King of Judea.

The mysteries and wisdom of the Bible have held the attention of scholars around the world.

586–539 B.C.	539–332 B.C.	332–63 B.C.	63 B.C.–324 A.D.
BABYLONIAN PERIOD	PERSIAN PERIOD	GREEK PERIOD	ROMAN PERIOD
Jeremiah, Fall of Judea, Exile	Jews return under Cyrus Ezra, Nehemiah, Esther	Hasmonean kingdom	Herodian dynasty New Testament First and Second Jewish revolt

Having great confidence in Moses' obedience, God entrusted him with the Law, as depicted here by French artist Claude Vignon.

But the advent of another king was at hand, as a mysterious light in the sky led wise men from the East to a manger in Bethlehem. The very appearance of that star is fraught with theories—both astronomical and miraculous.

Through the Gospels we learn about the life of Jesus, witnessing his miracles and listening to his revolutionary teachings. But unlike the stories of other faiths, the Gospels do not end with the master in his tomb. Christ's resurrection transformed his downcast band of disciples into powerful evangelists who began boldly preaching the message of Christ. Their journeys took them far beyond the area around Galilee and Capernaum. *Mysteries of the Bible* discusses who among them died martyrs' deaths, offering curious bits of evidence regarding those thought to have died as old men in foreign countries.

The Bible brought moral and spiritual transformation to Rome, and from there to Western civilization. It is the story of God reaching down and touching all, a process that began with the people of Israel and, millennia later, continues to extend to the whole world. Today, millions of people throughout the world consider it a living book and the sacred word of the one true God. The issues raised in *Mysteries of the Bible* will stir your interest, and perhaps your spirit, regarding the Scripture. Possibly it will lead you to a greater appreciation of the Bible and of the God who caused it to be written.

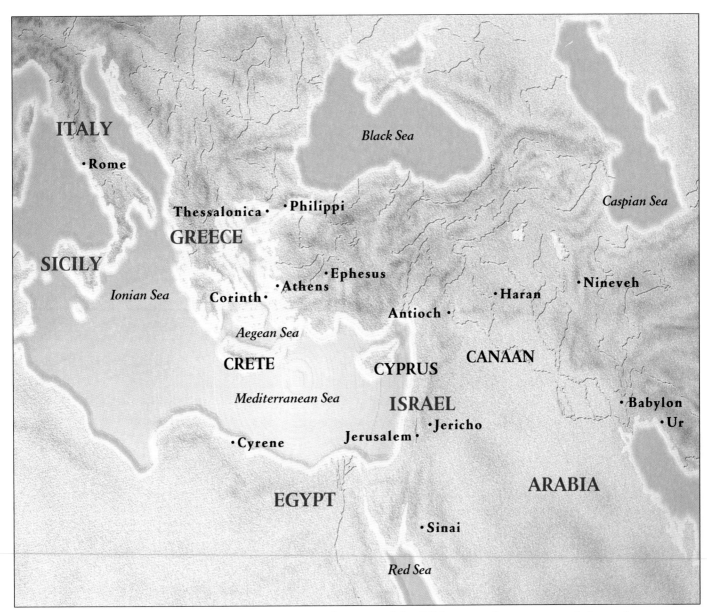

Beginning with Abraham in ancient Mesopotamia, the story of the Bible moves from western Asia to the Middle East, and from there to Southern Europe.

CREATION

*D*id the Garden of Eden really exist, or is it
simply a fanciful legend meant to be interpreted
symbolically? And what of the Great Flood? Is there
any scientific verification that such a monumental
catastrophe actually occurred? Attempts to answer
these and other questions based on readings of the
Old Testament often raise more issues than they resolve,
but the debate provides valuable insights into the divine
inspiration of the Bible and the very meaning of faith.

*A stained-glass depiction of Noah's Ark in the First Presbyterian
church of Fargo, North Dakota.*

BACKGROUND TO THE OLD TESTAMENT

The Garden of Eden

*I*s the Garden of Eden merely a fanciful legend? If so, it is curious that the geographic description of it found in Genesis is more detailed and specific than most other biblical locations. This observation has aroused the interest of scholars and adventurers through the ages.

According to the Bible, the first humans dwelled in a garden located "in Eden, in the east" (Genesis 2:8). A river flowed from the garden and divided into four head streams. Many scholars have felt that if the identity and location of

Intentionally or not, this portrayal of the Garden of Eden painted by Jan Brueghel the Elder resembles a view of a medieval Flemish countryside.

The Serpent

Given the role that the mysterious serpent of Genesis played in humanity's downfall, we should not be surprised to find its telltale tracks in the sand of other cultures of biblical times. And indeed this is the case.

The figure of the serpent appears as a supernatural creature throughout the ancient world, and it is not surprising to discover that the serpent was generally regarded with a respect mixed with fear and loathing.

A serpent appears in one of the oldest Mesopotamian creation myths, the Babylonian *Epic of Gilgamesh*. In a story that reveals distant parallels to the biblical account of the fall of humanity, Gilgamesh is directed to a "plant of life" that is to be found on the bottom of the sea. He

The common artistic rendering of a legless snake tempting Adam and Eve is inaccurate in that the curse "upon your belly you will go" was pronounced only after the disobedience in the Garden was discovered.

manages to obtain this plant, but it is stolen from him by a serpent.

The serpent was often depicted with the gods and goddesses of the ancient Near East, where it was often a symbol of sexuality. For the Canaanites, it was pictured with the fertility deity Baal and his consort Asherah.

In the Bible, the serpent is identified with Satan, a transliteration of a Hebrew word meaning "adversary." The first time Satan is called by name is in 1 Chronicles. "Satan stood up against Israel, and incited David to count the people of Israel" (1 Chronicles 21:1). The Bible hints that Satan fell from his once exalted position in Heaven because of his excessive pride.

---

these rivers could be established, the Garden of Eden could not be far beyond.

There is little question about two of the rivers mentioned in the text, the Tigris and Euphrates. Both exist today, located in Iraq and Iran. A third river flowing from Eden

was referred to as the Gihon, which "flowed around the whole land of Cush" (Genesis 2:13).

The mention here of Cush has puzzled Bible scholars because it usually refers to the area south of Egypt now known as Sudan. In Genesis, Cush is associated with Nim-

Cherubim and Seraphim

According to the Bible, there are beings known as cherubim that are neither human nor divine.

The cherubim of the Bible are powerful, mysterious creatures, not to be confused with the chubby winged infants of medieval art. One of their functions seems to be that of guardians, and it is in this capacity that we find them first mentioned after the fall of man: "He drove out the man; and at the east of the Garden of Eden he placed the cherubim, and a sword flaming and turning to guard the way to the tree of life" (Genesis 3:24).

One might infer here that the cherubim are intended not only to guard but to conceal the location of the Garden of Eden from humanity, which is no longer able to enter it. If so, it is tempting to speculate that this is one reason why the Garden has been lost to history.

The next mention of cherubim is when these angelic creatures are represented in the Tabernacle that God commanded the Israelites build during their wanderings in the wilderness. Golden cherubim adorned the Ark of the Covenant, located in the Holy of Holies, the inner sanctuary of the Tabernacle. Cherubim were also depicted in the woven tapestry of the curtain in front of the Holy of Holies.

Raphael's rendering of Ezekiel's vision of mysterious beings known as cherubim, often pictured in the Bible as attending the throne of God.

The cherubim on the Ark are similar to beings depicted elsewhere in the ancient Near East. Together they form a throne, with their backs serving as armrests and their wings forming a backrest. The idea of a cherub throne is indicated in other biblical texts as well.

In the vision of Ezekiel, the description of cherubim closely resembles that of beings called seraphim. The word literally means "the burning ones." Such creatures are known from ancient Egypt, where they were depicted as winged serpents that decorated the thrones of pharaohs.

In the Book of Isaiah, seraphim are depicted as marvelous creatures that utter perpetual praise to God: "In the year that King Uzziah died, I saw the Lord sitting on a throne, high and lofty; and the hem of his robe filled the temple. Seraphs were in attendance above him; each had six wings: with two they covered their faces, and with two they covered their feet, and with two they flew. And one called to another and said: 'Holy, holy, holy is the Lord of hosts; the whole earth is full of his glory'" (Isaiah 6:1–3).

What are we to make of such creatures? Scholars have sought in vain to explain them. The reason may be because cherubim and seraphim are by their nature beyond human comprehension.

rod, the founder of Babylon, which would put Cush in the region of the four rivers. One possible location is what is now a dry gully in Iran called Wadi Karun, which joins the Tigris and Euphrates rivers at the head of the Persian Gulf.

Scholars have long been curious about the last of the four rivers mentioned in Genesis, the Pishon. The text tells us more about the Pishon than any of the other rivers. We learn, for example, that "it is the one that flows around the whole land of Havilah, where there is gold; and the gold of that land is good; bdellium and onyx stone are there" (Genesis 2:12).

Havilah has been identified with the Arabian peninsula because the region—and particularly Yemen—was the historic source for highly prized fragrant resins such as frankincense and myrrh.

The reference to high-purity gold has prompted scholars to look for evidence of ancient mines in the peninsula. Only one site in Arabia fits the description: the famous Mahd edh-Dhahab, or "Cradle of Gold." The mine is located approximately 125 miles south of Medina near the Hijaz Mountains and is known to have been operating in ancient times.

Other intriguing evidence has recently come to light regarding the location of the Pishon River mentioned in Genesis. For some time, scholars have suspected that a dry riverbed in Iraq called Wadi Batin might be associated with the biblical Pishon. Wadi Batin runs directly into the head of the Persian Gulf at the junction of the other three biblical rivers, and satellite photos have confirmed the presence of an underground river running below it. An analysis of the geo-graphical features illuminated by the photos extends that underground river to the mountains of Hijaz.

Is this underground river a remnant of the Pishon River of Genesis? The fact that it leads to the gold of the Hijaz Mountains and the aromatic spices of Yemen lends support to that hypothesis. And if the four rivers running out of Eden can be identified, perhaps the location of the primordial garden paradise will also be revealed one day.

Unfortunately, if that day ever comes, deep-sea diving equipment may be required to view it. Some believe that the garden lies hidden underneath the headwaters of the Persian Gulf, not far from where the four rivers empty into it.

Drama in the Garden

The Bible doesn't tell us how long Adam and Eve were in the Garden of Eden before they succumbed to temptation and they lost favor with God.

Actually, very little is known of their life in the Garden, though the text does mention one fascinating detail: They apparently enjoyed fellowship with God "walking in the garden at the time of the evening breeze" (Genesis 3:8).

Into this pleasant existence comes the serpent, later identified as Satan. Deliberately exaggerating God's prohibition against eating from the tree of knowledge, the serpent asks: "Did God say, 'You shall not eat from any tree in the garden'?" (Genesis 3:1).

This painting by F. Curradi depicts Adam and Eve being cast out of the Garden of Eden after their disobedience, clothed in animal skins provided for them by God.

This is not what God had said, but Eve is put on the defensive. She replies, "We may eat of the fruit of the trees in the garden; but God said, 'You shall not eat of the fruit of the tree that is in the middle of the garden, nor shall you touch it, or you shall die'" (Genesis 3:3). The prohibition against touching the fruit is apparently a minor embellishment by Eve.

At this point, the serpent tells Eve she will not die, "for God knows that when you eat of it your eyes will be opened, and you will be like God, knowing good and evil" (Genesis 3:4–5). Tricked by the serpent, Eve eats from the tree and gets Adam to do likewise.

The first and greatest loss that Adam and Eve experienced after eating the forbidden fruit was the loss of fellowship with God, symbolized by their expulsion from the Garden of Eden. But not before Adam demonstrates his own self-deception by blaming *both* Eve and God: "The woman whom *you* gave to be with me—*she* gave me fruit from the tree, and I ate" (Genesis 3:12, italics added). For its part, the serpent—which up until that time apparently walked upright—was condemned to crawl on its belly and eat dust all the days of its life.

The Lord curses the evil serpent, adding a cryptic prophecy: "I will put enmity between you and the woman, and between your offspring and hers; he will strike your head, and you will strike his heel" (Genesis 3:15).

Theologians through the ages have taken this verse as the first hint of the eventual triumph of God over the forces of evil. The "he" spoken of here is thought to refer to the coming Messiah, who will crush the power of the Evil One.

The phrase "you will strike his heel" speaks of a lesser blow delivered against the Messiah at his crucifixion.

The Scarlet Thread

The fourth chapter of Genesis tells of the birth of Adam and Eve's first two sons, Cain and Abel. In a few short verses a story of a savage jealousy unfolds, ending with one brother killing the other.

The first sign of trouble comes when we read that "Abel was a keeper of sheep, and Cain a tiller of the ground." One day the brothers brought offerings to the Lord. Abel brought "the firstlings of his flocks, their fat portions," while Cain brought "the fruit of the ground." The offerings did not meet with equal acceptance. The Lord "looked with favor on Abel and his offering" but had no regard for Cain and his offering (Genesis 4:2–4).

Why was Abel's animal offering pleasing to the Lord while Cain's offering from his fields was not? Other biblical references to this story shed little light on the reason, but only confirm that Cain "was from the evil one" and murdered his brother because "his own deeds were evil and his brother's righteous" (1 John 3:12).

In trying to explain this story, some have theorized that it refers to the age-old tensions between farmers and nomadic shepherds, with the former seeking to protect their crops from the latter's flocks. But with the earth as yet unpopulated and there being more than sufficient space for both

flocks and fields, it is unlikely that such tensions would have arisen. Also, this theory does not explain the superiority of one offering over the other.

Other scholars see a thread in this story that begins in the Garden of Eden and runs throughout the Bible, that of the necessity of blood sacrifice. The first inklings of this theme  occur when Adam and Eve are cast out of the Garden of Eden for their disobedience. To cover their nakedness, Adam and Eve "sewed fig leaves together and made loincloths for themselves" (Genesis 3:7). However, this was apparently not sufficient, for we read that the Lord God "made garments of skins for the man and his wife, and clothed them" (Genesis 3:21).

When Cain's offering of vegetables was rejected by the Lord in favor of Abel's blood sacrifice, Cain slew his brother. As punishment, he was made a wandering vagabond.

What was wrong with the clothes that Adam and Eve fashioned for themselves? It is suggested that the killing of animals to provide covering for Adam and Eve is the first indication of what is later stated in the Book of Hebrews: "Without the shedding of blood there is no forgiveness" (Hebrews 9:22).

The theme of blood sacrifice is developed in the Book of Leviticus, which details various types of animal offerings. The massive Altar of Sacrifice, upon which animals were slaughtered for the sins of the people, would later be a prominent feature of the Jewish Temple.

According to the Book of Hebrews, the scarlet thread of blood atonement for sin throughout the Bible culminates in the sacrificial death of Jesus Christ on the cross: "How much more will the blood of Christ, who through the eternal Spirit offered himself without blemish to God, purify our conscience from dead works to worship the living God!" (Hebrews 9:14). Thus the "unblemished" sacrifice of the Son of God is foreseen in Abel's sacrificing the "firstborn of his flock" to the Lord.

Cain was filled with jealousy toward his brother when his own offering was rejected, despite the counsel of the Lord: "If you do well, will you not be accepted? And if you do not do well, sin is crouching at the door; its desire is for you, but you must master it" (Genesis 4:7).

Cain's response is made clear in the next verse. He invites his brother out into the fields and murders him. As punishment, Cain was no longer able to till the ground and was condemned to be a "wanderer on the earth" (Genesis 4:12).

Adam and Eve are depicted here mourning the death of their son Abel after he was murdered by his brother, Cain.

AFTER THE FALL

Did Giants Roam the Earth?

*D*id mysterious spirit beings intermarry with the human race at some point in earth's hoary past?

According to some, this is the meaning of one of the most mysterious and disputed texts of the Book of Genesis, where we read that, "When people began to multiply on the face of the ground, and daughters were born to them, the sons of God saw that they were fair, and they took wives for themselves of all that they chose" (Genesis 6:2).

Those who hold to this interpretation claim that the "sons of God" refers to angelic creatures who married women. Further support for this view is found in a following verse, which states: "The Nephilim were on the earth in those days—and also afterward—when the sons of God went in to the daughters of humans, who bore children to them" (Genesis 6:4).

Ancient rabbinic teaching held that a race of giants once roamed the earth. Although it was thought that most of these perished and were now in a place called Sheol, scattered references to giants are found in the biblical text.

The view that Nephilim were giants comes from a reference in the Book of Numbers. When the spies led by Joshua and Caleb returned from their incursion into Canaan they reported: "All the people we saw in it are of great size. There

Slain by David, the Philistine warrior Goliath was one of the "giants of Gath" mentioned in the Hebrew Bible. Goliath's height was "six cubits and a span," or more than nine feet tall.

Where Did Cain Get His Wife?

*I*n the fourth chapter of Genesis, we read that two sons, Cain and Abel, were born to Adam and Eve. We also learn in the same chapter that, after the murder of Abel, "Cain knew his wife, and she conceived and bore Enoch" (Genesis 4:17).

Presumably, Cain married one of his sisters. Close intermarriage was not forbidden then. It was not until the time of Moses that the sanction against brother-sister marriages was spelled out.

Still, the question of where Cain got his wife is not quite solved, for it is not until after the birth of a later son, Seth, that we hear mention of daughters: "The days of Adam after he became the father of Seth were eight hundred years; and he had other sons and daughters" (Genesis 5:4).

Is this text saying that daughters were born only later to Adam and Eve? And if so, we return to our original question of where Cain got his wife.

The likely answer lies in the nature of ancient patriarchal society, which very often excluded women from genealogical lists, since men were viewed as the originators of the family line. It is not surprising, then, that there would be no daughters of Adam and Eve mentioned in the text that speaks of Cain getting married. In fact, the names of the daughters of Adam and Eve aren't mentioned anywhere in the biblical text.

It is also evident that the biblical text is compressing huge amounts of time. Adam is said to have lived to be 930 years old. Since, according to the text, he was already 130 years old when Seth was born, he could have had numerous daughters by that time.

A great deal of fascinating history must have gone unrecorded, at least in the biblical text. Although the record is silent regarding the identity of Cain's wife, it is clear that she has her place in the early history of the human race.

---

we saw the Nephili . . ." (Numbers 13:32–33). Other races mentioned in the Bible, such as the Anakites and Rephaites, are described as people of extraordinary size who are related to the Nephilim.

A similar idea of primordial giants occurs with the Titans of Greek mythology, who challenged the ruling gods of Heaven and earth. The biblical story implies that the Nephilim were rebellious creatures, provoking divine judg-ment in the form of the flood. In the same passage we read: "The Lord saw that the wickedness of humankind was great in the earth, and that every inclination of the thoughts of their hearts was only evil continually. So the Lord said, 'I will blot out from the earth the human beings I have created'" (Genesis 6:5,7).

This interpretation is rejected by many biblical scholars because of the theological difficulties it raises. Did the members of this supposed half-angelic and half-human race of people possess souls? It would seem that their spiritual origin would confer immortality upon them—and if so, why is this race of giants no longer inhabiting the earth? What happened to these primordial giants?

Other scholars prefer to interpret the term "sons of God" as the righteous line of Seth, the God-fearing third son of Adam. The "daughters of men," on the other hand, is a reference to the rebellious descendants of Cain. According to this view, instead of remaining true to their righteous her-

itage, the descendants of Seth—the "sons of God"—were enticed by the beauty of ungodly, yet attractive, women—the "daughters of men." This tragic loss of spiritual heritage led to the moral degeneration that resulted in mankind being destroyed in the flood.

The term Nephilim need not refer to spiritual beings. There were people of great height in ancient times, just as there are today. There is no evidence that the giants reported in the Bible—notably, Goliath and his relatives—were considered to be half-angelic beings.

THE GREAT FLOOD

Summoning the Rain

The Bible tells us that, a mere 10 generations after the creation of Adam and Eve, the wickedness of their descendants was such that "the Lord was very sorry that he had made man on the earth, and it grieved him to his heart" (Genesis 6:6). Calling on the rain, he decided to destroy humankind with a massive flood so that he could start all over again.

The Lord found an exception in righteous Noah, deciding to spare him and his family, along with thousands of animals. The ark Noah was instructed to build was actually a huge wooden barge. With a length of 450 feet, a width of 75 feet, and three interior decks reaching a height of 45 feet, it

would have been the largest seagoing vessel known before the twentieth century. Interestingly, its dimensions are remarkably similar to that of modern ships.

Scholars are divided as to the extent of the biblical flood, many taking the view that it may have been a local event limited to the Mesopotamian floodplain. The Bible, however, is unequivocal in stating that "all the high mountains under the entire heaven were covered" (Genesis 7:19).

Archaeologists have attempted to find evidence of such a flood in Mesopotamia. Their efforts have thus far proved inconclusive. The first evidence came to light in 1929, when English scientist Charles Leonard Woolley was excavating a Sumerian burial pit at Ur on the Euphrates River. His workers came upon a layer of silt more than eight feet thick containing relics of a more primitive culture.

The Book of Genesis states that "all the high mountains under the entire heaven were covered" by the flood, and that all of the human beings, plants, and animals on the earth perished.

Woolley came to the conclusion that a great flood had occurred in the region sometime around the fourth millennium B.C. However, flood deposits discovered at other sites in Mesopotamia were dated to later historical periods, and Woolley's theory was dismissed.

In 1872, the scholarly world was rocked by the publication of the text from a cuneiform tablet from Nineveh on which was written an ancient Babylonian account of a great flood. The text is part of the classic *Epic of Gilgamesh*. The hero of the story is Utnapishtim of Shuruppak, who is warned that Enlil, the chief god of the Babylonian pantheon, would soon destroy mankind with a flood. Utnapishtim was instructed to build an ark for himself and his family and "the seeds of all living things."

Unlike the biblical account of Noah's flood, in which the rains and floods continued for 40 days and nights, the floods in the *Epic of Gilgamesh* lasted only six days and nights. There are, however, a number of striking similarities between the two accounts.

Utnapishtim and his ark also come to rest on a mountaintop. Like his biblical counterpart, Utnapishtim opens a window and releases a series of birds to find out if the surface of the earth has dried sufficiently. In yet another parallel, Utnapishtim's first act upon leaving the ark is to build an altar and offer a sacrifice. Since the discovery of the flood story in the *Epic of Gilgamesh*, at least two other Mesopotamian flood stories have come to light, both containing the same central features.

Scholars have long pondered the relationship between the Mesopotamian flood stories and the biblical narrative. Some have suggested that each of these accounts refers to the same cataclysmic flood. If so, then we should expect to find flood stories in other ancient cultures in other parts of the world. And this is exactly what ethnologists have discovered.

James Frazer, a well-known student of religions around the world, has collected numerous flood stories—from places as diverse as Greece, the South Pacific, and the Americas. Such evidence presents at least the possibility that, at some time in prehistory, a worldwide flood of cataclysmic proportions occurred, surviving today only as a dim memory in the cultural traditions of peoples around the world.

Was Noah's Ark Big Enough?

*T*he Bible says that God directed Noah to make an ark with the following dimensions: "the length of the ark, three hundred cubits; its width, fifty cubits, and its height thirty cubits. Make a roof for the ark, and finish it to a cubit above; and put the door of the ark in its side; make it with lower, second, and third decks" (Genesis 6:15–16).

Scholars have tried to ascertain the feasibility of such a vessel in the light of our present-day knowledge of both shipbuilding and zoology. The Hebrew cubit was approximately 18 inches long, which meant that the ark would have been 450 feet long, 75 feet wide, and 45 feet high. The length-to-width ratio of six to one is considered ideal, and this proportion would have provided excellent stability for the ark on the open seas.

Interestingly, by comparison, the boat in the Babylonian account of the Great Flood is described as a perfect cube with nine decks and extending 120 cubits on each side. Such a vessel would be hopelessly top-heavy, and a boat with these dimensions would have spun slowly and continuously in the water.

The next question is whether the ark would have been large enough to fit all the animals that would have needed to go inside. The floor space would have been more than 100,000 square feet, or more than in 20 basketball courts. With a volume of 1,518,000 cubic feet, it would have had a capacity equal to 569 modern railroad cars.

Noah's ark was constructed of "gopher wood," thought to be a variety of cypress. It is a hard, fragrant wood that was commonly used for furniture in ancient times.

It has been calculated that the dimensions of Noah's ark would probably have provided sufficient space for breeding pairs of all land animals.

But how many of the earth's animals would have had to be taken aboard the ark? Of the more than one million species of animals in the world, the vast majority can survive in water and would not have been brought aboard. These include 21,000 species of fish; 1,700 species of tunicates (marine chordates such as sea squirts); 107,000 species of mollusks (mussels, clams, oysters); 10,000 species of coelenterates (corals, sea anemones, jellyfish, and hydroids); 5,000 species of sponges; and 30,000 single-celled protozoans.

Aquatic mammals—whales, seals, and porpoises—and reptiles would have been excluded as well. The more than 838,000 arthropods—including lobsters, shrimp, crabs, and barnacles—would have survived outside the ark, as would many species of worms and insects.

What does this leave? Some scholars estimate that perhaps no more than 35,000 individual animals would have needed to go into the ark. Others, pointing out that the biblical term "created kinds" is more general than the modern term "species," believe that as few as 2,000 animals would have been aboard the ark. Many scholars—even conservative ones—also allow for "micro evolution," meaning that the dozens of species of horses, dogs, etc., could have been represented on the ark by a single ancestral pair.

Assuming that the larger animals could be represented by young (and therefore smaller) specimens, it is reasonable to assume the average size of all the animals to be that of a sheep. Returning to the boxcar comparison, a typical double-deck car can accommodate 240 sheep. On that basis, three trains hauling 69 cars each would have sufficient space for 50,000 animals—and that would only take up about one third of the capacity of the ark.

That would leave 361 cars for all the food and baggage, plus Noah and his family.

The Search for Noah's Ark

According to the Bible, Noah's ark came to rest on "the mountains of Ararat" (Genesis 8:4). The biblical Ararat is known in ancient sources as the land of Urartu, located north of Mesopotamia in the area of Lake Van. Today this geographical region is occupied by Turkey, Iran, and Armenia.

After the flood, the ark disappears from the pages of Scripture. Later biblical writers gave no indications that its location was known. Throughout history, however, there have been numerous reports of a large boat sighted in the mountains of the region. The earliest references, dating to the third century B.C., suggest that the ark was still clearly visible on the mountain.

Early Christian tradition began designating a 17,000-foot peak in northern Turkey as Mt. Ararat. At least two monasteries shaped like boats were built on the peak during the Middle Ages, and pilgrims were attracted to the area.

In the past century there have been aerial photographs taken of unusual structures on the mountain, reports of visits to the ark, and even the recovery of wooden timbers. The suggested location of the ark is above the snow line, and it has been theorized that only during exceptionally warm sum-

Genesis 8:4 states that Noah's ark found its resting place on "the mountains of Ararat," as depicted by Italian painter Vittorio Bianchini.

mers do the snow and ice recede sufficiently for the ark to be seen. Complicating visits to the site is the fact that Mt. Ararat has until recent years been a sensitive border region between Turkey and the former Soviet Union.

Nevertheless, during the past two decades dozens of expeditions have explored Mt. Ararat in hopes of finding evidence of the ark's existence. Perhaps the most famous were those organized and led by former NASA astronaut James Irwin. Unfortunately, these efforts have not been successful.

One of the most electrifying developments in the search for the ark occurred in 1955, when a French explorer named Fernand brought down a five-foot-long wooden beam from just beneath the glacial cap of Ararat. Finally, it seemed, indisputable proof of the ark had been discovered. But excitement turned to bewilderment when radiocarbon dating determined the wood to be no more than 1,200 years old.

Yet how could that be? What about the eyewitness reports of explorers visiting an ark-like structure? And how could the reports of people entering the structure be explained? The probable answers to such questions are found by calculating the time period that the wood was dated to. It was the same time period as that of the boat-shaped monasteries that were built on the mountain. The presence of more than one such monastery may also explain the conflicting reports about the ark's precise location on the mountain.

This does not mean that Mt. Ararat holds no secrets. It is also possible that the exploration of other peaks in the Ararat range will be undertaken, as explorations continue to find evidence of what may have been the most calamitous event ever to occur on this planet.

The Tower of Babel

*T*he barren desert sands of southern Mesopotamia are the backdrop for one of the most mysterious Bible stories, that of the Tower of Babel. Its construction is said to be the reason why so many different languages are spoken in the world today.

The text of Genesis 11 states that "the whole earth had one language and the same words. And as they migrated from the east, they came upon a plain in the land of Shinar and settled there" (Genesis 11:2).

It wasn't long before they imagined a grandiose scheme: "Come, let us build ourselves a city, and a tower with its top in the heavens . . . otherwise we shall be scattered upon the face of the whole earth" (Genesis 11:4).

The description of the building materials they used lends some authenticity to the text, for "they said to each other,

'Come, let us make bricks and burn them thoroughly.' And they had brick for stone, and bitumen for mortar" (Genesis 11:3). Interestingly, in ancient Israel, where the text originated, the use of fired bricks was unknown. Buildings were constructed either of stone or sun-dried bricks. But the use of fired bricks is well-documented throughout Mesopotamia. The use of tar instead of mortar to cement bricks is another detail confirmed by archaeology.

But what exactly was the Tower of Babel, and what was the offense of the people who built it? Archaeology has given us clues to solving this mystery. Scholars believe that the "tower" of Babel was actually a ziggurat, a pyramid-like structure that played an important role throughout Mesopotamian civilization. Nearly 30 ziggurats have been found—and nearly as many theories exist as to what purpose they served.

What is known from ancient texts is that ziggurats were typically dedicated to a city's patron god or goddess. Beyond this, scholars disagree as to their specific purpose. It was once thought that ziggurats were the tombs of kings or the gods, based upon the obvious similarity in shape to the early Egyptian step-pyramid tombs. But the step-pyramids have been shown to be more recent structures, having been built more than a millennium after ziggurats began to dot the map of early Mesopotamia.

Others believe that ziggurats were actually towering altars whose great height protected against flood and plunder. But this can hardly explain the massive size and height of some of the structures. The ziggurat dedicated to the god Marduk, which once stood in the center of the city of Babel, reached the height of a 30-story building.

One intriguing Bible story is that of the Tower of Babel. The mystery of the tower lies not in how it was built, but why it was built and why it offended the Lord.

A more plausible theory is that a ziggurat served as the dwelling place for the local god or goddess, who passed through the entrance door to the earthly plane. This is reflected in some of their names. The ziggurat at Larsa was known as "The Temple That Links Heaven and Earth"; the one at Sippar was "The Temple of the Stairway to Pure Heaven."

If the theory is correct, this indicates that the ziggurats served a profoundly religious purpose. They were an attempt to draw the gods down to earth. And here we have a clue about what may have been so objectionable to God about the Tower of Babel. It represented an attempt to reduce the deity to the level of human beings. The people's trust in themselves had surpassed their trust in God.

Are there any references to the "confusion of languages" beyond those described in the Bible? Some scholars see a cryptic allusion in the Sumerian epic, *Enmerkar and the Lord of Aratta:*

> *Once upon a time there was no snake,*
> * there was no scorpion,*
> *There was no hyena, there was no lion,*
> *There was no wild dog, no wolf,*

> *There was no fear, no terror,*
> *Man had no rival.*
> *In those days, the lands of Subur (and) Hamazi,*
> *Harmony-tongued Sumer, the great land of the*
> * decrees of princeship,*
> *Uri, the land having all that is appropriate*
> *The land Martu, resting in security,*
> *The whole universe, the people in unison*
> *To Enlil in one tongue spoke.*
> *(Then) Enki, the lord of abundance (whose)*
> * commands are trustworthy,*
> *The lord of wisdom, who understands the land,*
> *The leader of the gods,*
> *Endowed with wisdom, the lord of Eridu,*
> *Changed the speech in their mouths, brought*
> * contention into it,*
> *Into the speech of man*
> * that (until then) had been one.*

Does this ancient Mesopotamian text, dating from the fourth millennium B.C., allude to the same dramatic event described in the biblical text? Only time and further study—and perhaps discoveries yet to come—will be able to shed further light on the mysterious Tower of Babel.

OLD TESTAMENT: THE PENTATEUCH

The Pentateuch consists of the first five books of the Scriptures: Genesis, Exodus, Leviticus, Numbers, and Deuteronomy. Together, they tell the story of how God's pledge to Abraham and the Israelites—that "I will make of you a great nation, and I will bless you, and make your name great"—was finally fulfilled after years of bondage and wandering in the wilderness. The books establish God's authority over his people, but also show his mercy through their rise, fall, and ultimate redemption.

The patriarch Abraham, sometimes called "the father of many nations," as depicted in St. Mary's Basilica in Minneapolis, Minnesota.

THE AGE OF THE PATRIARCHS

Ur of the Chaldeans: Abraham's Hometown

*T*he Book of Genesis tells us that Abraham's father, Terah, took Abraham (then called Abram), Sarah, and Lot, and "they went out together from Ur of the Chaldeans to go into the land of Canaan" (Genesis 11:31).

Ur, the city of Abraham's birth, is one of the most ancient cities of southern Mesopotamia. Dating to 4000 B.C., its ruins are located in what is now southern Iraq, near the port of Basra.

Ur means "fire oven" and is the name of one of three major population centers in ancient Sumer and Babylonia in lower Mesopotamia, the others being Kish and Uruk. It is identified with modern Tel el-Muqayyar, approximately 220 miles southeast of Baghdad.

Ur formerly stood on the banks of the Euphrates River until the river shifted its course 10 miles to the east. The loss of river transportation and water for agriculture spelled doom for the city.

The most important modern exploration of Ur was conducted by the English archaeologist Charles Leonard Woolley between 1922 and 1934. Woolley's excavation revealed that Ur was settled around 4000 B.C. and continued to be occupied for 5,000 years.

Woolley stirred up controversy with his discovery of a thick layer of silt, which he initially took as evidence of the Great Flood. Other scholars, however, have shown that the layer was nothing more than deposits from local flooding.

The most valuable discovery of the excavation was the royal cemetery, with its 16 large tombs containing jewelry, gold artifacts, wheeled vehicles, and the bodies of the kings of Ur and their attendants.

The royal tombs tell us something about the religious atmosphere during the time when Abraham was called by God. The male and female attendants, as well as a large number of animals, were killed so that they could accompany the

In this painting by Italian Renaissance artist Raphael, Abraham receives three visitors, one of which is the Lord himself. Soon the trio will embark to destroy Sodom and Gomorrah.

ruler on his journey to the netherworld, where he would continue his reign. This worldview is similar to that of Egypt and other ancient Near Eastern cultures, which considered the king to be a divine being.

Woolley also uncovered a three-story, pyramidlike ziggurat dedicated to the moon god and containing chambers for the high priestess on its summit. Religious structures, ziggurats

served as a symbol of the people's ascension to the heavens and their proximity to the patron gods of the city. This intention is stated by the builders of another ziggurat, the famous Tower of Babel: "Come, let us build ourselves a city, and a tower with its top in the heavens" (Genesis 11:4).

We know nothing of how Abraham came to worship Yahweh, the true God, putting aside all the other deities common to Mesopotamia at that time. His conversion from the polytheism of his upbringing to monotheism was nothing less than a revolutionary change.

Abraham in History

Some scholars believe that Abraham, Isaac, Jacob, and Joseph existed only in the pious imaginations of later Hebrew writers. However, others feel this judgment is unwarranted.

Those who believe that the patriarchs are rooted in history say it is unreasonable to expect sources beyond the Bible to confirm events in the lives of Abraham and his sons. The fact that a tent-dweller such as Abraham is an important figure in the Bible does not mean he merits attention in ancient Near Eastern historical records.

Nevertheless, archaeologists have uncovered what some believe is just that—a reference to the Hebrew patriarch in a nonbiblical record. It comes from the reign of Pharaoh Sheshonq I, whom many scholars equate with the biblical Shishak.

In the Book of 1 Kings we read of a campaign against Palestine by Shishak: "In the fifth year of King Rehoboam, King Shishak of Egypt came up against Jerusalem; he took away the treasures of the house of the Lord and the treasures of the king's house; he took everything. He also took away all the shields of gold that Solomon had made" (I Kings 14:25–26).

The Book of Chronicles gives a fuller account of the extent of Shishak's campaign, stating that it involved 1,200 chariots, 60,000 horsemen, and countless troops. We read that Shishak "took the fortified cities of Judah and came as far as Jerusalem" (2 Chronicles 12:4), where disaster was averted when Rehoboam handed over the temple treasures.

If Pharaoh Sheshonq is to be equated with the biblical Shishak—and scholars are not agreed on this—we have an interesting parallel in an inscription in the Temple of Amun in Karnak. Throughout Egyptian history, whenever pharaohs returned from a victorious military campaign, they would usually record their triumph for posterity. At Karnak, archaeologists have deciphered a stela, or standing stone, on which Pharaoh Sheshonq describes his triumphant campaign against Israel.

Most of the perhaps 150 names on the stela have eroded and are unreadable. Of those that remain, perhaps 70 names come from the Negev, a desert in southern Israel. One of those has been identified by Egyptologists as the equivalent of the Hebrew "Abram." The phrase where the name occurs reads: "The fort [or fortified town] of Abraham."

Is the "Abram" of Fort Abram the biblical patriarch? Possibly. After all, the biblical Abraham lived in the Negev where this "Fort Abram" was located. Such an outpost may have been built in the time of David or Solomon as part of a line of fortifications against Egyptian intrusion. It would not be unusual for the fort to be named after some national hero or revered personage such as the patriarch.

Other scholars suggest that Fort Abram is actually Beer-sheba, a city founded by Abraham (Genesis 21:32–33).

The exchange between Abraham and Melchizedek has long puzzled students of the Bible. Melchizedek is a curious biblical figure who appears "out of nowhere."

Beersheba is not mentioned elsewhere in Pharaoh Sheshonq's list of victories. Since it was a prominent city in the Negev, its omission is inexplicable, unless, perhaps, it is the very same city that is called Fort Abram by the Egyptians.

If so, the connection with the biblical patriarch becomes probable, and it constitutes evidence that Abraham was indeed a real person.

Abraham and the Philistines: An Anachronism?

*T*he Book of Genesis relates that Abraham secured the rights to the well at Beersheba by making a covenant with the king of Gerar, after which "Abimelech, with Phicol the commander of his army, left and returned to the land of the Philistines" (Genesis 21:32). Later, during a famine, Abraham's son Isaac is said to have gone to Gerar, to "King Abimelech of the Philistines" (Genesis 26:1).

Many scholars say these verses cannot be historical for one inescapable reason: The Philistines, they say, did not exist in Palestine at this time, and only arrived many hundreds of years after the time of Abraham.

The earliest reference to the Philistines is in the Egyptian records of Pharaoh Ramses III, who describes a naval engagement that took place in the Nile around 1175 B.C. The participants of this battle included the "Sea Peoples," whose name in Egyptian hieroglyphics resembles that of the Philistines.

The Egyptian account indicates that these Sea Peoples were ejected from Egypt and then settled on the southern coast of Canaan, which became known as Philistine territory. This, it is claimed, was the first Philistine presence in the Promised Land.

This theory is based on the absence of any earlier reference to the Philistines inhabiting Canaan in any other literature. It is an argument that would be easily overthrown with the introduction of new evidence.

This was the case regarding the biblical cities of Sodom and Gomorrah, which some critics dismissed as legendary because there is no proof of their existence.

However, with the discovery of the cuneiform library at Ebla in northern Syria, that theory has been severely challenged. The Ebla tablets, dated as early as the twenty-fourth century B.C., mention commercial relations with two cities that some scholars equate with the biblical Sodom and Gomorrah.

Further excavation of the Philistine cities may also shed more light on the question of when they came to the land of Canaan. The earliest evidence uncovered at the Philistine city of Ashdod, for example, dates at least to the seventeenth century B.C., which approaches the time of the biblical patriarchs. Similarly, inscribed Egyptian seals found at Gaza, another Philistine city, bear the names of pharaohs of the patriarchal era.

Thus the Philistine cities were occupied long before 1175 B.C., when the Philistines were said to have migrated to Canaan. The question remaining is whether these early peo-

Mysterious Melchizedek

We read in the Book of Genesis of a mysterious encounter that occurred after Abraham rescued his nephew Lot from an attack by a coalition of kings from the East.

Upon his return he was met by a certain Melchizedek, king of Salem, who is called "a priest of the most High God." Melchizedek brought bread and wine and blessed Abraham: "Blessed be Abram by God Most High, maker of heaven and earth; and blessed be God Most High, who has delivered your enemies into your hand" (Genesis 14:19–20).

Curiously, we also read that Abraham gave him a tithe of one-tenth of all his goods. Who is this Melchizedek, who seemed to command the reverence of Abraham?

The mystery of Melchizedek's identity deepens when the Book of Hebrews provides further information about him. We learn first that his name means "king of righteousness" and "king of peace." And then comes an intriguing description of Melchizedek: "Without father, without mother, without genealogy, having neither beginning of days nor end of life, but resembling the Son of God, he remains a priest forever" (Hebrews 7:3).

Little is known about Melchizedek, depicted here greeting Abraham with bread and wine as the patriarch returns from battle.

The fact that he is spoken of as having no mother or father, or beginning or end of days, has led some to wonder if he was some kind of divine or superhuman personage. Most theologians, however, reject this possibility because it would ascribe to another being that which properly belongs only to God—that is, his eternalness. In the Judeo-Christian worldview all creatures—even the angels—had a beginning.

So why does the Bible speak about Melchizedek in such terms? Many theologians believe that Melchizedek is used by the biblical writers as a "type" of Christ, someone who in some respects resembled the divine figure of the Messiah. And indeed, Melchizedek was an unusual figure who did seem to come "out of nowhere."

Nothing is known about Melchizedek's origins, and so in this respect he is like the Messiah, who comes from God. To emphasize his divinity, Jesus is described in Hebrews as being "according to the order of Melchizedek," rather than being of the order of the earthly Aaronic priesthood. For the same reason, Psalm 110 speaks of the coming Messiah as being forever a priest in the "order of Melchizedek" (Psalm 110:4).

ples were Philistine or another people that the Philistines replaced.

One possibility is that the Philistines migrated in waves, over a long period of time, to the fertile agricultural lands along the coast of Canaan, and that they were indeed present in Abraham's day. Another possibility is that the "Philistines" in Genesis were not truly blood ancestors of the later ones, but that both groups had a common place of origin by the Aegean Sea.

It is hoped that archaeological excavation will one day solve the question of how early to date the Philistine presence in Canaan.

A Wandering Aramean

The Book of Deuteronomy instructs the Israelites to prepare an offering celebrating their first harvest in the Promised Land and to recite a prayer of thanks that begins: "A wandering Aramean was my ancestor; he went down into Egypt and lived there as an alien, few in number, and there he became a great nation, mighty and populous" (Deuteronomy 26:5).

Aram was a confederation of cities in what is now Syria. Its reach extended to Babylonia, which was the birthplace of

An illustration depicting the ruins of the Philistine city of Ashdod as they appeared to nineteenth-century English artist David Roberts.

Abraham. The Bible describes numerous territorial conflicts between Israel and Aram from the time of King Saul.

Aram became a great military power, expanding into Assyrian territory and defeating Assyrian kings Tiglath-pileser I and II and Ashur-rabi II. Under Saul, however, the Israelites defeated King Hadadezer of Syria and conquered Aramean territory from Damascus to Hammath in the north.

David also had great success against Aram, demanding tribute from Hadadezer and marrying Maacah, the daughter of Talmai, the Aramean king of Geshur. It was Absalom, the son born to David by Maacah, who brought grief to his own father and nearly succeeded in overthrowing him.

Late in the reign of Solomon, Rezon established an Aramean kingdom hostile to Israel. This enmity continued into the period of divided kingdoms, when the Aramean kings Ben-hadad I and II led numerous attacks upon the northern kingdom of Israel.

The biblical record also describes times of wary cooperation between Israel and Aram. When Ben-hadad of Syria was captured on the battlefield, King Ahab of Israel refused to kill him. Instead, he called Ben-hadad "my brother" and negotiated an agreement with him.

In another curious incident during this same period, the king of Aram sent Naaman, the commander of all his forces,

In M. Merisi da Caravaggio's "Conversion of Saint Paul," the young persecutor of the church is struck down by a blinding light while traveling to Damascus, the ancient capital of Aram.

to Israel to be healed, along with a letter and gifts of gold and silver. The text records that, when the king of Israel read the letter, "he tore his clothes and said, 'Am I God, to give death or life, that this man sends word to me to cure a man of his leprosy? Just look and see how he is trying to pick a quarrel with me'" (2 Kings 5:7).

Aram eventually declined in power until it was brought to an end by the Assyrian king Tiglath-pileser II in 732 B.C., ten years before the northern kingdom of Israel would suffer a similar fate.

Although Aram disappears from history, the Bible records one more footnote concerning the kingdom, which is now in modern Syria. The zealous persecutor of the early Christians, a young man by the name of Saul, was on his way to the Syrian—and ancient Aramean—capital of Damascus when he was struck down by a blinding flash of light from heaven.

The words "Saul, Saul, why do you persecute me?" initiated the conversion of the greatest apostle of Christendom.

Sodom and Gomorrah

*I*n the Book of Genesis we read that Abraham looked up from the entrance to his tent "by the oaks of Mamre" at Hebron and saw three strange men standing nearby. Keeping with Middle Eastern customs of hospitality, he invited the men inside his tent while a meal was being prepared for them.

We soon learn that two of the men were angels, while the third was the Lord himself. This is one of the rare occurrences in the Old Testament of what theologians call a theophany—a visible appearance of God.

It seems Abraham's guests had a dual purpose for their visit. The first was to announce that Sarah, then nearly 90 years old, would bear a son, a prediction that would be fulfilled with the birth of Isaac.

Nothing is said about the second purpose until the men get up to leave. Then, looking down from the hill country of Judea to the Dead Sea, the Lord said: "How great is the outcry against Sodom and Gomorrah, and how very grave their sin! I must go down and see whether they have done altogether according to the outcry that has come to me" (Genesis 18:20–21).

What follows is a fascinating exchange in which Abraham tries to find out how few righteous people in Sodom would be required to save the city from destruction. First he inquires whether the Lord would spare Sodom if 50 righteous people could be found there. Then he lowers the stakes to forty people, to thirty, and then to twenty. Finally, Abraham musters the courage to ask: "Oh, do not let the Lord be angry if I speak just once more. Suppose ten are found there?" The Lord answers: "For the sake of ten I will not destroy it" (Genesis 18:32).

Unfortunately, Sodom lacked even a bare quorum of ten. The story reads like an adventure, with moments of high drama in which the angels show themselves to be bold and fearless beings worlds apart from the innocent cherubs of religious art.

to lose. The angels urged Lot and his family to leave the city at once. In a curious footnote to the story, we read that "Lot's wife, behind him, looked back, and she became a pillar of salt" (Genesis 19:26).

The Bible speaks of Sodom and Gomorrah as being among the five "cities of the Plain," which were likely located in the Valley of Siddim, adjoining the Dead Sea. Some scholars have suggested that Sodom and Gomorrah are located under the shallow southern end of the Dead Sea, where the water is less than ten feet deep in many places. However, aerial photographs of the area have shown no traces of ancient settlement.

The desolate region of the Dead Sea flanked by the mountains of Moab was the possible site of the biblical cities of Sodom and Gomorrah.

The climax of the narrative comes when the men of the city come to Lot's home in the night demanding the men who came to him that night: "Bring them out to us, so that we may know them" (Genesis 19:5). Lot feebly offers his two daughters in exchange, which only enrages the men of the city, who order him to get out of their way.

As they surge forward to break down the door, two angels move quickly. They pull Lot back into the house and shut the door. "And they struck with blindness the men who were at the door of the house, young and old, so that they were unable to find the door" (Genesis 19:11). There was no time

More recent investigation has focused on two sites directly bordering the Dead Sea to the east and south. The modern name for these sites are Bab edh-Dhra, thought to be Sodom, and Numeira, thought to be Gomorrah. Excavations have revealed a three-foot-thick layer of debris, with indications that both places were destroyed by an immense conflagration. A problem with this identification is the dating of the cities, which would have existed several centuries before the usually accepted dates for Abraham. Further refinement of dating methods may solve this puzzle.

But what could have brought about such devastation? The description found in Genesis tells us that "the Lord rained on Sodom and Gomorrah sulfur and fire." The answer to the mystery may be found in the Dead Sea, one of the most unique bodies of water on the earth's surface.

As Lot and his family fled Sodom, his wife looked back at the destruction and "became a pillar of salt." Today, imaginative tour guides point out pillars of calcified salts said to resemble Lot's wife.

Geologists have long suspected the presence of oil underneath the Dead Sea because of the many reports throughout history of petroleum-based substances, such as bitumen, found in and around the body of water. Bitumen often contains a high percentage of sulfur, prompting some geologists to suggest that an earthquake in the area could have released huge quantities of subterranean gases and other flammable substances into the atmosphere. Once ignited, these substances could have created a conflagration of biblical proportions. Interestingly, geologists have discovered that both Bab edh-Dhra and Numeira are located on a fault line extending along the eastern side of the Dead Sea.

Did an earthquake cause the fiery devastation that consumed Sodom and Gomorrah? No one knows for sure, but at the close of the Bible story, we read that Abraham, looking down toward the two cities, "saw the smoke of the land going up like the smoke of a furnace." The description is suggestive of a petroleum-based fire.

Israel's Ancient Foe Unearthed

*I*n the Negev desert of southern Israel are numerous Israelite fortresses that puzzled archaeologists for the longest time. What enemy were these military installations designed to protect against? Recent evidence indicates that the fortresses were a frontline defense against Edom, Israel's ancient foe.

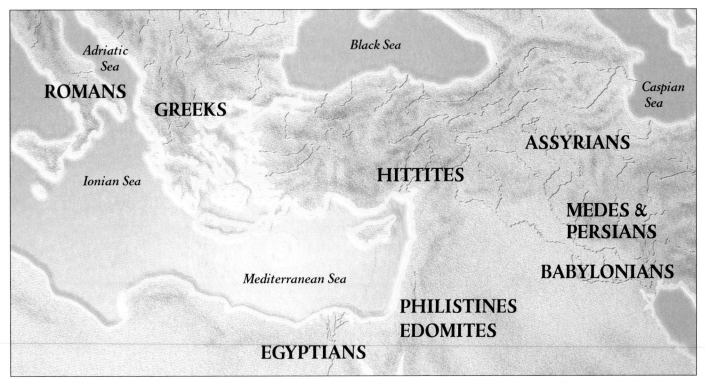

Throughout the centuries, various nations laid claim to middle eastern territories. As the Israelites traveled to the Promised Land, the Edomites denied them permission to travel through Edom along a major trade route known as the King's Highway. Later, the Israelites would conquer Edom and make it part of their kingdom.

The biblical story of Jacob and Esau is one of sibling rivalry that foreshadows the continuing strife in the Middle East. While the two brothers were still in the womb of Rebekah, she was told by the Lord:

"Two nations are in your womb,
and two peoples born of you shall be divided;
the one shall be stronger than the other,
the elder shall serve the younger."
— *(Genesis 25:23)*

Esau, the firstborn, was tricked by his brother Jacob into surrendering his birthright for a mess of pottage. Then, with Rebekah's connivance, Jacob deceived his dying father Isaac into giving him the blessing usually reserved for the firstborn son. Eventually, Esau took Canaanite wives and settled in the hill country of what today is southern Jordan—but which was then known as Edom.

Until recently, little was known of the nation that figured so prominently in Israel's early history. It was the Edomites who, despite assurances by the Israelites, refused to allow them to pass through their territory on their way to the Promised Land. The route that the Israelites desired to take was an ancient trade route known as the King's Highway. Edom would later pay for its hostility when it was attacked by King Saul and conquered by King David.

Archaeologists were surprised to discover evidence of Edomite cities in the Negev region of southern Israel. Some scholars think these cities date to the seventh century B.C., a time of great political upheaval in Judea. The northern kingdom of Israel had fallen to the dreaded Assyrians, and the Babylonians were encroaching ever deeper into the southern kingdom of Judea.

The large number of ritual artifacts—including idols, incense altars, and cultic shrines—uncovered at the Edomite sites stand in marked contrast to the strict monotheism of the Israelites. The considerable religious and cultural differences between the two nations ensured that they would remain perpetually at odds, and it may explain the reason for the line of Judean forts in the Negev.

Edom was destined to fade from history, but not before making its mark once more in the form of one of its most infamous descendants. By the fourth century B.C., the Edomites in the Negev were called by another name: Idumeans. The mother of Herod the Great was an Idumean who married a Judean. And so the two peoples were symbolically reunited in the turbulent person of Herod, a ruler legendary for his cruelty and insecurity.

The Sacrifice of Isaac

After the exiling of his son Ishmael in obedience to the Lord, Abraham would again be shaken by the prospect of the death of his son Isaac—at Abraham's own hand.

We read that the Lord "tested" Abraham, saying: "Take your son, your only son Isaac, whom you love, and go to the land of Moriah, and offer him there as a burnt offering on one of the mountains that I shall show you" (Genesis 22:2). One can only imagine the horror that Abraham experienced upon being told to sacrifice Isaac—who was miraculously born to Sarah in her old age.

Scholars also have struggled to understand this inexplicable command. After all, Abraham and his descendants, the

An angel sent by God intervenes just as Abraham is about to obey God's command and sacrifice his son, Isaac.

Israelites, were told to follow the one true God, Yahweh, and to oppose the worship of pagan gods. However, pagan rituals included human sacrifice, which was observed among the peoples of the surrounding cultures.

And now Abraham was being asked to perform what to all appearances seemed to be a human sacrifice like that of his pagan neighbors. What do we make of this divine command? It seems evident that Abraham viewed the event as what the text says it was: a "test" from the Lord.

It was through Isaac that God would fulfill his promise to Abraham: "I will make of you a great nation, and I will bless you, and make your name great, so that you will be a blessing. I will bless those who bless you, and the one who curses you I will curse; and in you all the families of the earth shall be blessed" (Genesis 12:2–3).

Abraham knew that the fulfillment of this prophecy required an heir, a son through whom a "great nation" would come. That this was Isaac is made clear when Abraham sent Ishmael from his presence, after which the Lord comforts him: "Do not be distressed because of the boy and because of your slave woman; whatever Sarah says to you, do as she tells you, for it is through Isaac that offspring shall be named for you" (Genesis 21:12).

A doubtlessly bewildered Abraham went with his son to Mount Moriah with the Lord's promise regarding Isaac ringing in his ears. That he remained unswerving in his faith in God's promises is indicated when he instructed his servants who accompanied them: "Stay here with the donkey; the boy and I will go over there; we will worship, and then we will come back to you" (Genesis 22:5).

Abraham had full confidence that both he and his son Isaac would return after the sacrifice. When Isaac asks where the sacrifice is, Abraham replies: "God himself will provide the lamb for a burnt offering, my son" (Genesis 22:8).

The unswerving faith of Abraham shines through the text, up until and including the dramatic moment when the knife is poised above his son, who is tied to the altar. At the last moment, an angel intervenes, and a ram is sacrificed in Isaac's place. Indeed, it is Abraham's obedience that earns him a leading place in what is called the "hall of fame of faith" in the eleventh chapter of the Book of Hebrews. Abraham's faith is evident from the time he obeyed the divine command to set out for the land of promise, "not knowing where he was going" (Hebrews 11:8).

The Book of Hebrews gives another reason why Abraham was willing to sacrifice Isaac with confidence: "He considered the fact that God is able even to raise someone from the dead" (Hebrews 11:19).

It was the supreme trial to see whether Abraham would hold fast to the promises of God.

Rachel's Premature Death

One of the most moving love stories in the Bible is that of Jacob and Rachel. Jacob saw the lovely Rachel bringing her sheep to water and was instantly smitten. He would work seven years for her father Laban for the right to marry her, followed by another seven years because of Laban's craftiness in tricking him.

In one of the Bible's most poignant love stories, Jacob worked fourteen years for his relative Laban so that he could marry Rachel, only to lose her during childbirth.

The love they shared was made even more touching by the untimely death of Rachel during childbirth. From that time on, it is clear that Jacob favored Joseph and Benjamin, the two sons that Rachel bore him. When he is shown Joseph's bloody coat and believes him to be dead, Jacob is inconsolable. Later, he takes the unusual step of granting Joseph's two sons, Ephraim and Manasseh, equal inheritance rights as his other sons.

Jacob explains the reason he is doing this: "For when I came from Paddan, Rachel, alas, died in the land of Canaan on the way" (Genesis 48:7). Until the end of his life, Jacob was haunted by the death of his beloved Rachel. A startling reason has been suggested as to why Jacob was so troubled: He felt responsible.

To understand this, we must return to when Jacob and Rachel finally took their leave of Laban and set out for Canaan. Before they left, Rachel spirited away her father's household idols, probably because of the good luck she thought they would bring. When he discovered that his idols were gone, Laban pursued Jacob and accused him of theft. Unaware that his wife had taken the idols, an indignant Jacob vowed that "anyone with whom you find your gods shall not live" (Genesis 31:32).

Oaths were considered binding in biblical times, and they often had unintended effects. By pronouncing judgment upon the guilty—even though he was ignorant of Rachel's action—he unwittingly condemned her to death. Rachel herself was unaware of Jacob's oath. While he was speaking with Laban, she was in her tent, guarding the idols by sitting on them.

After leaving Laban, Jacob was commanded by the Lord to go to Bethel and build an altar. Bethel was an important religious site for the Hebrew patriarchs: It was here that Abraham "invoked the name of the Lord" (Genesis 12:8). Jacob had stopped at Bethel many years earlier on his flight from Esau. During the night, he dreamed of a ladder going up to heaven. The Lord spoke to him, confirming the blessing originally given to Abraham.

In preparing for his arrival at the holy site of Bethel, Jacob instructed his family and servants: "Put away the foreign gods that are among you, and purify yourselves, and change your clothes; then come, let us go up to Bethel" (Genesis 35:2–3). It was likely he was addressing the servants when he spoke about getting rid of idols and did not suspect that his wife Rachel would have idols in her possession.

Though the text does not specifically say that Rachel surrendered her idols at Jacob's command, it is reasonable to conclude that she did so. The text states that the people with him "gave to Jacob all the foreign gods that they had" (Genesis 35:4). Rachel likely complied with the others, not having heard Jacob's fateful oath to Laban and being unaware of any consequences that would follow.

But the tragic consequences would follow all too soon. With a heavy heart, Jacob left Bethel with his family. They did not get far, for we read that Rachel went into labor and died giving birth to her son Benjamin. Jacob buried her and went on his way, tormented by the fear that his hastily spoken oath may have been Rachel's death sentence.

The Dead Sea

The ancients were fascinated by the Dead Sea, and we find mention of it in the writings of Aristotle, Strabo, Pliny the Younger, Tacitus, and others.

This unique body of water lies on a giant crack in the earth's surface stretching from Ethiopia to Turkey. At 1,300 feet below sea level, it is the deepest depression on the planet. By comparison, the lowest inhabited location in the United States, California's Death Valley, is 300 feet below sea level.

The water level of the Dead Sea has declined in recent years, and it is now divided into two separate bodies of water. The northern portion is 1,300 feet deep, while the southern end is extremely shallow.

The sea is void of all life, except for a highly adaptive microorganism only recently discovered by scientists. The sea has no outlet, and the evaporation of water through the ages has gradually intensified its salinity. At present, the water is saturated with various salts to a maximum degree of about 30 percent.

Despite its inhospitable setting, the Dead Sea is surrounded by a richness of biblical history. At the southern end are the ancient settlements of Bab edh-Dhra and Numeira, which have been identified as the possible sites of Sodom and Gomorrah. Along the western side is the spectacular mountain fortress of Masada, built by Herod the Great and defended by Jewish Zealots during the First Revolt against Rome in A.D. 66–70.

North of Masada along the coast is the important oasis of En-gedi, where David hid from King Saul. Here also is where, during the reign of Jehoshaphat, a coalition of armies from the East assembled to attack Judah along the ancient route to Jerusalem.

Across the waters from En-gedi are the hot springs of Callirrhoe, where a grotesquely diseased Herod went in the vain hope of a cure during his last terrible illness. On the ridge above are perched the remains of the fortress of Machaerus. It is here where years later Herod Antipas reluctantly granted the request of the young Salome, instigated by her vengeful mother, and had John the Baptist beheaded. At the northern end of the sea lie the ruins of the Essene settlement at Qumran. Caves in the nearby cliffs mark where the renowned Dead Sea Scrolls were discovered in 1947.

The Dead Sea is the lowest inhabited place on earth. Modern settlements, as well as health spas and tourist facilities, cluster along the shores of this unique body of water.

In Roman times the sea was called the Lake of Asphalt because of the bitumen, a form of tar, that was collected from the surface. Bitumen was a valuable substance that had several uses in the ancient world. It served as a caulk for the timbers of boats and was used both as a component of plaster and as a cement for fired bricks. The Egyptians used bitumen in the embalming process. But the chief use of bitumen in ancient Israel was as an insecticide to protect orchards. A dressing of bitumen, sulfur, and olive oil was manufactured for smearing on the stocks of vines and trees to protect them from various pests.

Largely due to trade from bitumen and perfume from En-gedi, several ancient routes crossed the area of the Dead Sea. In Roman and Byzantine times—and during the Crusades—the sea carried heavy marine traffic. After that, however, trade languished, and it became known as the "Sea of the Devil." Superstitions arose that no bird could fly over it, nor any boat traverse it, because of toxic fumes. That notion was challenged in 1848 by the first scientific survey of the Dead Sea, conducted by the United States Navy.

THE EXODUS

Plagues: Past, Present—and Future?

*F*or people living in ancient and medieval times—and even up to the last century—the threat of plague was a terrifying reality. Several plagues are recorded in the Bible, and although we do not know the specific pathogens involved, they caused a great many fatalities.

We read in the Book of Numbers (25:3), for example, that 24,000 Israelites died because "Israel yoked itself to the Baal of Peor, and the Lord's anger was kindled against Israel." In the Book of Chronicles, a plague is sent upon the land as a result of King David's disobedience, killing an estimated 70,000 people. As the angel carrying out this mission was about to ravage Jerusalem, the Lord stayed his hand, sparing the city from harm.

It has also been suggested that a plague played a role in the mysterious destruction of the Assyrian army at the gate of Jerusalem in 701 B.C. The biblical text states that no less than 185,000 Assyrian soldiers died virtually overnight.

These may sound like impossibly high casualty figures from an infectious dis-

ease—but not to those who are familiar with the full scope of plagues throughout history.

Ancient cities were almost entirely lacking in any kind of sanitary precautions, and were thus at the mercy of deadly waterborne, insectborne, and other contagious diseases. People had little or no idea what caused such illnesses, blaming them on bad air, the position of the planets, or even the gods. Although the microscope was invented in 1674, the specific microbes that caused disease would not be identified for another two centuries.

This painting by Nicolas Poussin depicts the chaos caused by the plagues that erupted in the cities of the Philistines when they captured the Ark of the Covenant.

The typical peasant family of the Middle Ages lived in a one-room hovel with a hole in the roof to allow smoke from heating and cooking fires to escape. People slept on hay strewn on the floor—a haven for lice and vermin—and often drank contaminated water. Sanitary facilities for commoners were almost unknown; people rarely bathed, and sewage flowed in the streets. It was in conditions like these that the Black Plague was able to sweep across Europe, killing an estimated one third of the population.

Typhus is another highly contagious disease that is spread by lice dwelling in human feces. France's Napoleon Bonaparte, a brilliant soldier, is said to finally have been defeated by three generals: General Winter, General Famine, and General Typhus. Thousands of his men perished in Russia—as did the enemy when they caught the disease from Napoleon's men.

Typhoid fever causes symptoms similar to typhus, but is caused by a salmonella bacillus. In the Boer War of 1899–1901, the undisciplined British troops drank water straight from the rivers. Of 400,000 troops, 43,000 contracted typhoid.

In New York and Massachusetts, the disease appeared in the early 1900s, compliments of the infamous Typhoid Mary. A cook by the name of Mary Mallon, she worked for wealthy families and was known for her homemade ice cream. Unfortunately, her frozen desserts included a deadly ingredient—salmonella. Before she was tracked down, Mary may have been responsible for more than 1,400 deaths.

The Bible mentions different plagues that wreak havoc on the earth, causing fatalities in the thousands.

An Israelite House in Egypt?

Scholars have long been puzzled by the absence in ancient Egyptian records of any mention either of the exodus or even the presence of the Israelites in Egypt.

This is partly understandable in that the official annals of ancient kings were not so much concerned with accuracy as they were with casting the ruling potentate in a favorable light. So one could hardly expect to find an inscription detailing the loss of a pharaoh's army in pursuit of a conquered people such as the Hebrews.

The nature of the topography in the ancient land of Goshen, where the Israelites settled while in Egypt, also makes it difficult to find any conclusive evidence of their existence there. Archaeological remains are best preserved in dry ground, where there is little decay-causing moisture. Goshen, however, is located in the Nile River delta, where a high water level and waterlogged ground accelerate the destruction of buried artifacts.

For these reasons there has been comparatively little excavation in Goshen. However, archaeological excavations in other, drier areas have uncovered what could be evidence of the Israelite presence in Egypt. One fascinating piece of evidence has come to light in Thebes, the capital of Upper Egypt.

Like virtually every culture today, ancient civilizations had their own trademark styles of building. By examining the floor plan of an excavated structure, along with the pottery and other artifacts connected with it, archaeologists can usually determine which people constructed it and the approximate time period when it was built.

In the Holy Land, one particular house plan appears in hundreds of sites that were known to be occupied by Israelites. It consists of a four-room house containing one broad room with three smaller rooms extending from it. The center of the three long rooms is usually an open courtyard marked by a row of pillars. This style of house is so common in the central hill country of Canaan that it has come to be called an "Israelite house." Some archaeologists consider this type of architecture an ethnic marker—that is, whenever such a house is found, it indicates Israelite settlement.

Thus it was with extraordinary interest that scholars learned that a structure with obvious similarities to that of an "Israelite house" had been found in Egypt. The differences were relatively minor: The house in Eygpt had internal walls made of reeds and wood—common building materials along the Nile—instead of stone.

One theory is that the house was built by Hebrew slaves conscripted to work at a nearby temple. If so, it is the first archaeological evidence of an Israelite presence in Egypt.

Many of the 10 plagues, four of which are pictured here, demonstrate the power of Yahweh while mocking the gods of the Egyptians.

for a religious festival. The British army suffered 10,000 fatalities in the outbreak, and it has been estimated that several hundred thousand Indians died from the disease. Cholera raged along the trade routes as merchants from Europe and Russia carried the disease home with them.

The spread of the plagues of cholera, typhus, and typhoid fever were only checked when standards of public sanitation were widely adapted. The introduction of municipal water mains and sewer systems, as well as the discovery of effective treatments, also helped to reduce the incidence of such diseases.

Have we seen the last of the deadly plagues that have wreaked havoc on earth? In the Bible one of the mysterious four horsemen of the Book of Revelation is described in ominous terms by the apostle John (Revelation 6:8): "I looked, and there before me was a pale green horse! Its rider's name was Death, and Hades followed with him; they were given authority over a fourth of the earth, to kill with sword, famine, and pestilence . . ."

Another waterborne disease, cholera, strikes with devastating suddenness. The symptoms begin with diarrhea and painful cramps, then fever sets in and finally death—all within 12–48 hours. In 1817, cholera broke out in Calcutta, India, as pilgrims from around the country gathered

The Hardening of Pharaoh's Heart

Several times during the biblical account of Moses' confrontation with Pharaoh Ramses II, we read that "God hardened Pharaoh's heart." This peculiar phrase occurs at critical moments in the story, when Ramses is about to allow the Hebrews to leave Egypt.

Theologians have long sought to understand the meaning of God hardening someone's heart, anxious to dispel the notion that God appears to be compelling someone to do evil. This would violate the belief that individuals are able to choose between right and wrong, and are responsible for that decision. Today, new insights into Egyptian culture and religion bring a fresh understanding to the meaning of the expression.

It is evident that the biblical writer had a keen understanding of Egyptian religion. From beginning to end, Exodus is a story of confrontation between Yahweh and the gods of Egypt. This cosmic struggle is reflected in the plagues that God brought upon Egypt.

In the ninth plague, for example, the sun does not shine and instead darkness rules for three days. The chief deity in the Egyptian pantheon was the sun god Amon-Re, who was worshipped as the creator god. Rising each morning, Amon-Re represented the newness of life; in the evening, as he sank into the west, he was the symbol of death and the underworld.

In French painter James J. Tissot's "Plague of Flies," Pharoah and his helpers seek in vain to escape the swarms of flies sent by God as punishment.

Amon-Re presented a distinct challenge to Yahweh, the God of Israel: "On all the gods of Egypt I will execute judgments: I am the Lord" (Exodus 12:12). The ruling pharaoh was included in this indictment because, in Egyptian religion, a pharaoh was the incarnation of the son of Amon-Re. This belief, known as "divine kingship," was common throughout the ancient Near East.

The attributes of a deity were ascribed to a pharaoh. He was considered to be eternal, the *ka* or "life force" of Egypt, the creator, and fit to be worshipped. In the afterlife, he ruled over his subjects, and offerings were made to him to ensure his good will. One ancient Egyptian text refers to the pharaoh as "a god by whose dealings one lives, the father and mother of all men, alone by himself without an equal."

Miracle at Rephidim

The Bible says that when the Israelites arrived at Rephidim there was no water available to them. This may have been because the Amalekites controlled the only spring in the area.

The disgruntled Israelites demanded of Moses: "Give us water to drink." We then read of a curious action on the part of Moses. He was commanded by the Lord to take his rod and go to the rock of Horeb: "I will be standing there before you on the rock at Horeb. Strike the rock, and water will come out of it, so that the people may drink" (Exodus 17:6).

While this action may be unimaginable to the modern mind, Bedouins of times past or present would realize exactly what happened. In the desert wadis of the Sinai, the scarce rainfall filters down and collects in porous layers of limestone. These layers are exposed at the base of the mountains, but the water cannot escape because of a thick build-up of limestone crust. Bedouins know how to look for these hidden water sources.

There are accounts of this phenomenon in recent times. In the 1930s, Major C. S. Jarvis, the British

Although the events at Rephidim and Kadesh are presented in the Bible as miracles, there is a possible scientific explanation for how Moses found water in the desert.

Governor of the Sinai, was leading a camel expedition through a dry wadi when his men came across a trickle of water coming out of the limestone rock. Trying to dig into the ground where he thought there might be a pool of water, one of his men by mistake struck the rock instead. To everyone's surprise and delight, the hard crust fell away and out of the crevice shot a powerful stream of water.

This method of obtaining water was employed by Moses on at least one other occasion. We read that, on the journey from Kadesh to Edom, "Moses lifted up his hand and struck the rock twice with his staff. Water came out abundantly, and the congregation and their livestock drank" (Numbers 20:11). On this occasion, Moses disobeyed by striking the rock instead of speaking to it as the Lord had commanded.

Perhaps God had intended to perform a miracle by having Moses speak to the rock instead of strike it. In any event, Moses' disobedience at Kadesh cost him dearly. He was denied the opportunity to personally lead the children of Israel into the Promised Land.

But there was one who appeared to be much more than a pharaoh's equal. When Moses addressed the Pharaoh Ramses he did so with the formulaic expression: "Thus says the Lord, the God of the Hebrews . . ." In so doing, Moses was indicating that, as Yahweh's messenger, he was relaying the divine pronouncement and issuing a direct challenge to the pharaoh.

But what does it mean that God "hardened" the pharaoh's heart? The answer may be found in the Egyptian concept of the heart as the *ib*, the inner spiritual center or essence of the individual. The condition of one's heart determined one's eternal destiny. After death, the soul of the deceased was weighed in the balance of truth, which represented judgment. On one side of the scale was the deceased's heart. On the other side of the scale was a feather, symbolizing the good. If the heart weighed no more than the feather, its owner would receive eternal life. But if the evil in one's heart caused it to outweigh the feather, the person would be devoured by the goddess Amenit.

The Hebrew word that has been translated as "hardened" can also mean "to make heavy." Thus, the phrase in question may actually mean "God caused Pharaoh's heart to become heavy"—another way of saying that he was dooming himself to eternal destruction, this because of the falsity of his religion.

According to the Bible, by hardening the pharaoh's heart, Yahweh was demonstrating that he alone was the true God of the universe: "I will harden Pharaoh's heart . . . so that I will gain glory for myself over Pharaoh and all his army; and the Egyptians shall know that I am the Lord" (Exodus 14:4).

The Parting of the Red Sea

*F*ew events recorded in the Bible capture the imagination as does the story of Moses parting the Red Sea.

For contemporary Americans, the sight of actor Charlton Heston raising his knurled staff over the waters in the epic Cecil B. DeMille film is a famous moment in film history. Two hundred years ago, Benjamin Franklin and Thomas Jefferson suggested that the official seal of the United States be a representation of the Israelites fleeing across the parted waters of the Red Sea to freedom.

Biblical scholars continue to be divided as to the meaning of the event. Did the Children of Israel cross a body of water that miraculously parted for them—or was it actually a marsh they crossed, which happened to ensnare the chariots of the pursuing Egyptians?

Part of the mystery involves the identification of the Hebrew words *yam suf*, which are translated in some versions of the Bible as "Red Sea." Scholars have long known that the word "red" does not occur in *yam suf*. A better translation of the Hebrew words would be "Reed Sea"—a rendering that opens the possibility that the Israelites crossed a swampy area to the north of the Red Sea. Accordingly, many historical maps trace the route of the Exodus through the marshy Lake Timsah or Bitter Lake region.

This solution is not as simple as it seems. It cannot be denied that some biblical references to *yam suf* clearly refer to the Red Sea. Complicating the problem is the fact that

In this work by the German painter Lucas Cranach, Moses and the Israelites look on as Egypt's army is engulfed by the Red Sea.

the parting of the Red Sea is not mentioned in any contemporary Egyptian texts. Some have taken this as evidence that the event is mythological rather than historical. Yet the omission is not surprising.

The royal chronicles of ancient times were notorious for ignoring events that might cast the ruling potentate in an unfavorable light. Not a single reference can be found in Egyptian records, for example, that mentions the humili-ating, century-long domination of Egypt by the Hyksos. Similarly, it would be hard to imagine any ancient potentate chronicling the loss of an entire army in pursuit of unarmed slaves.

But how could the Israelites have escaped unscathed while Pharaoh's army perished? One ingenious theory ties the events of the Exodus to a massive volcanic explosion that occurred in 1628 B.C. on the island of Thera in the Mediterranean. According to this theory, the volcano caused a gigantic tidal wave that initially drained the tidal plain over which the Israelites crossed. Then, as the Egyptians followed suit, it flowed back with devastating force, trapping the charioteers.

The theory that the Red Sea was parted by a volcano has interesting parallels with the 10 plagues of Egypt—for example, connecting the casting of the land under the pall of darkness with the gigantic sun-obscuring dust cloud accompanying the eruption. Unfortunately, the date of the eruption predates the earliest acceptable date of the Exodus by nearly two centuries.

Scholars continue to search for evidence that will shed light on this famous story.

THE GIVING OF THE LAW AT SINAI

The Language of the Decalogue

As the eminent Egyptologist and archaeologist Flinders Petrie was excavating the site of Serabit el-Khadem, he found fragments of stone tablets along with a statue of a crouching figure. Both had strange markings on them, which neither Petrie nor any of the other Egyptologists present could decipher.

Petrie realized that, since the writing was different from Egyptian hieroglyphics, it must have been the product of foreign workers hired by the Egyptians. But from where? Petrie concluded they came from nearby Canaan. He dated the inscriptions to 1500 B.C.

Petrie's theory ran contrary to the critical scholarship of the day, which held that writing did not appear in Canaan until around the ninth century B.C., some 600 years later than the date Petrie assigned to his inscriptions. For such scholars the story of Moses writing down the law at Sinai was an impossibility because there was no written language at that early date.

The only way to conclusively determine whether Petrie's inscriptions were of Canaanite origin was to decipher them. Unfortunately, despite the efforts of paleographers around the world, no one was able to translate them. However, one scholar, the brilliant Egyptologist Sir Alan Gardiner, managed to decipher one phrase of the text, which read "(dedicated) to (the goddess) Baalath."

This was all of the text that Gardiner was able to read, but it provided an important clue. Baalath was a female deity

The Arabian Peninsula and Africa are separated by the Red Sea. At the northern end, two branches define the Sinai Peninsula, which is pictured here.

who was venerated in the seaport of Byblos in northern Syria. From the inscriptions, it was clear that the temple at Serabit el-Khadem was dedicated to the goddess Baalath.

The Egyptians called her by another name—Hathor. The appearance at Serabit el-Khadem of the Canaanite and Phoenician Baalath meant that workers from those regions were working at the temple.

A crucial clue had come to light establishing that the people of Canaan possessed written language centuries earlier than many scholars had thought. The full importance of the discovery would not be made known until 30 years later, six years after Flinders Petrie's death.

In 1948, archaeologists finally managed to decipher the Serabit el-Khadem texts in their entirety. What they discovered was the ancestor of the Latin alphabet. Up until the time of its development, there were two primary modes of written language in the ancient Near East, Egyptian hieroglyphics and languages written in the cuneiform style of writing.

The language of the Serabit el-Khadem texts is called "West Semitic" by scholars. The West Semitic alphabet was adapted by the Greeks in the ninth century B.C., and from there it was passed to Rome, which spread it throughout the Western world.

The discovery and deciphering of the texts at Serabit el-Khadim have lent new credibility to the divine instructions given to Moses after the defeat of the Amalekites at Rephidim: "Write this on a scroll as something to be remembered" (Exodus 17:14).

The Roman Moses

The location of the traditional site of Mount Sinai is well known to students of the Bible and to tourists visiting the Sinai peninsula. Few, however, may be aware of the curious story of how a Roman emperor obsessed with his own visionary role as the new Moses identified the site that came to be known as the Sinai of old.

After the biblical record of the events at Mount Sinai, there are no later references in the Bible or in ancient Jewish literature that shed further light on its location. Beginning in

This arch was built in Constantine's honor at Rome. Constantine ascribed his successes to Christianity and divine inspiration.

The Emperor Constantine, represented on this Byzantine coin, transformed the Roman Empire in the early fourth century when he made Christianity the official state religion.

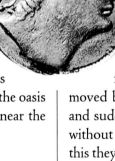

the second century A.D., however, Christian monks began settling in southern Sinai. These hermits attempted to identify the route of the Exodus and the exact site of Mount Sinai. Two sites were suggested at this early date: Jebel Sirbal, near the oasis of Firan, and Jebel Musa, 25 miles farther south near the tip of the Sinai peninsula.

Jebel Musa came to predominate, largely due to the presence of the Monastery of Saint Catherine at the foot of the mountain. The monastery was built in the fourth century by the Roman Emperor Constantine to commemorate what he believed to be Mount Sinai of the Bible.

The story of how Constantine arrived at this conclusion is a rather curious one. It seems that he was given to visions and dreams in which he placed great confidence in making decisions. The mystical side of the emperor who Christianized the Roman Empire can be traced to the famous battle at Milvian Bridge outside Rome. As the story goes, Constantine and his troops witnessed the sign of the cross in the heavens, along with the words, "By this sign conquer."

Constantine was profoundly affected by this vision, which seemed to bless him with success on the battlefield. He began to think of himself as a new Moses who was destined to lead the Roman Empire to new heights of glory. Before entering into battle he would retreat with his military advi-

sors into a special tent that he, like Moses, placed outside the camp. Inside the tent, which was constructed in the form of a cross, he would await divine counsel for the upcoming battle.

The early church historian Eusebius described what happened in the tent: "And making earnest supplications to God, he was always honored after a little while with a manifestation of His [God's] presence. And then, as if moved by a divine impulse, he would rush from the tent, and suddenly give orders to his army to move at once and without delay, and on the instant to draw their swords. On this they would immediately commence the attack, fight vigorously...and raise trophies of victory over their enemies" (*Life of Constantine*, II, 12).

Eusebius relates how these "divine impulses" came to dominate Constantine's life, noting that "a thousand such acts as these were familiarly and habitually done" (Ibid., II, 12,14). After becoming Emperor in 324, Constantine ordered the construction of churches throughout the Holy Land. This was in part a penance for the deaths of his wife Fausta and his son Crispus, who were executed at his command.

Constantine sent his 80-year-old mother to the Holy Land, charged with the task of locating the sites he had "foreseen" in his visions. In Jerusalem and Bethlehem, her task was made easier in that the exact location of the sites she sought had been preserved by an unbroken chain of historical records stretching back to the time of Christ.

However, in the deserts of Sinai there was little to check her imagination as she sought to determine where Mount Sinai was located. Perhaps bewildered by the vast possibilities offered by the expanse of the region, she accepted the mountain site that was suggested to her by monks living in the area. There, at the foot of Jebel Musa, she built a small chapel, which was enlarged to its present dimensions by the emperor Justinian in A.D. 527.

In Search of Sinai

*I*n the spring of 1904, archaeologist Flinders Petrie set out with a long camel caravan from the Egyptian city of Suez to the Sinai Peninsula. In addition to his own assistants, he was accompanied by a small army of scholars, surveyors, and Egyptologists.

Petrie was on a historic quest, to find the route that the Israelites took out of Egypt on their way to Mount Sinai. According to the Bible (Exodus 12:37), "about 600,000 men on foot, besides children" led by Moses journeyed into the desert after crossing the Red Sea. However, since few of the place names mentioned in the biblical text have been definitively identified, scholars are divided as to the route they took.

One possibility was a northern route that follows the Mediterranean coast up to Canaan. It was the shortest and most logical route, which would have taken them through the territory of the Philistines. But the Bible specifically states that the Israelites did not take that route: "When Pharaoh let the people go, God did not lead them by the way of the land of the Philistines, although that was nearer" (Exodus 13:17).

The reason is given in the text. God thought, "If the people face war, they may change their minds and return to Egypt" (Exodus 13:17). Until recent times, this reference to war puzzled scholars. After all, would not this northern route be the quickest way for the Israelites to escape into Canaan?

Archaeological excavations along the Sinai coast have provided the reason why the Israelites were warned against going in that direction. The route has been shown to be studded with Egyptian military fortifications. By going that way, the Israelites would have walked right into a trap.

Another possibility for the route of the Exodus would have been one of two trade routes leading through the Sinai. One of these led eastward across the desert, avoiding the southern mountains, in the direction of Beersheba. Some of those who suggest that the Israelites took this route point to a massive yellowish mountain called Jebel Yeleq as the possible Mount Sinai of the Bible. Another route went in a more easterly direction towards Ezion-Geber at the head of the Gulf of Aqabah.

Both of these "central" routes were virtually without water sources. They were frequented by caravan traders who carried sufficient supplies of food and water and who were conditioned to traveling long distances. These routes would hardly have been suitable for a slow-moving mass of people dependent upon regular and copious water supplies.

For these reasons, many scholars favor what is called the "traditional" route of the Exodus. It is this route that Petrie and his caravan attempted to trace as they followed an ancient trail that led to the Sinai mountains.

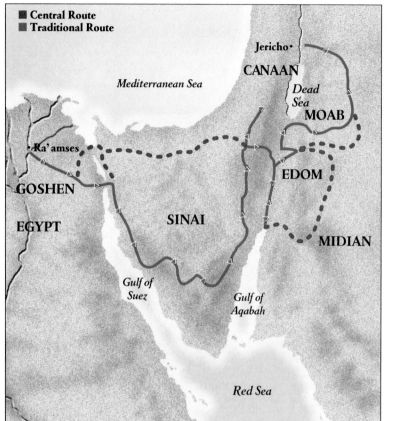

Central Route
Traditional Route

Mediterranean Sea

Jericho•

CANAAN

Dead Sea

MOAB

•Ra'amses

GOSHEN

EGYPT

EDOM

SINAI

MIDIAN

Gulf of Suez

Gulf of Aqabah

Red Sea

Attempts by scholars to trace the path of the Exodus have produced several alternative theories, as shown.

Petrie had good reason to believe that the old trail was the same one that the Israelites took. In ancient times, established routes were almost never changed, remaining the same for thousands of years. This is because they were the most convenient way of crossing whatever natural obstacles—such as mountains, rivers, and deserts—stood between the point of origin and the destination.

Petrie estimated that, on foot and traveling with their herds of sheep and goats, the Israelites could have managed around 12 miles a day. The Bible describes the first stop of the Israelites: "They went three days in the wilderness and found no water. When they came to Marah, they could not drink the water of Marah because it was bitter" (Exodus 15:22–23).

Trying to retrace this route, Petrie traveled along the ancient trail for 45 miles—or three days—before coming to a spring called Ain Hawarah by the Bedouins. The spring is little used by nomads in the area because the water is salty and sulfurous. Ain Hawarah appears to match the biblical description of the "bitter" waters of Marah, which the Israelites reached after a three-day journey.

Writing in the nineteenth century, explorer Charles Wilson writes of Ain Hawarah: "There is a stunted palm tree, or perhaps one might say a small thicket of stunted palms, shading a spring of brackish water on the slope of a ridge; and that is all." Hardly sufficient either in quantity or quality for vast numbers of thirsty Israelites.

The Bible then describes the next stop of the Israelites: "Then they came to Elim, where there were twelve springs of water and seventy palm trees; and they camped there by the water" (Exodus 15:27). In attempting to trace the Israelites' tracks, Petrie continued along the ancient route. Fifteen miles farther—about one day's march—his entourage came to Wadi Gharandel. There he found a fine oasis with shady palms and numerous springs, exactly as the Bible describes.

After Wadi Gharandel comes the plain of El Kaa along the shores of the Red Sea, which again corresponds with the biblical text: "The whole congregation of the Israelites set out from Elim; and Israel came to the wilderness of Sin, which is between Elim and Sinai" (Exodus 16:1). It is here that the Israelites complain about the lack of food and are supplied with quail and manna.

From Wadi Gharandel, the ancient track led Petrie and his caravan deeper into Sinai. After rounding a sharp bend in the hills, Petrie suddenly ordered a halt. Before them stood the remains of an Egyptian temple, with stela-shaped stones carved with hieroglyphics strewn on the ground. Petrie found the name of the great Ramses II inscribed on one of them and immediately identified the site as that of Serabit el-Khadem, where for more than a thousand years the ancient Egyptians mined copper and turquoise.

Serabit el-Khadem is likely the third stop mentioned in the Bible: "They set out from the wilderness at Sin and camped at Dophkah" (Numbers 33:12). Some believe the Hebrew word "Dophkah" is related to metal or smelting operations.

Petrie's caravan continued to Feiran, which he took to be the biblical Rephidim, where the Israelites stopped next. Here they were attacked by the Amalekites. Through extensive surveying of the area, Petrie believed he learned the reason why. Feiran is the only water source in the entire southern part of the Sinai massif. The nomads who lived there, including the Amalekites, were dependent upon the spring for their herds. Petrie concluded that the Amalekites must have been trying to defend Wadi Feiran from the foreign invaders.

After successfully repelling the Amalekites' attack, the Israelites camped at Rephidim before continuing their journey, unaware that some of the most momentous events of their history awaited them in the jagged mountains towering some 25 miles distant.

The traditional site of Mount Sinai is the 7,500-foot-high Jebel Musa, one of three granite peaks located near the southern tip of the Sinai Peninsula.

The Mountain of God

The location of one of the most important events of the Old Testament—the handing down of the Ten Commandments to Moses—remains unknown. Although the traditional site of Jebel Musa has been identified with Mount Sinai since at least the fourth century, numerous other possibilities have also been suggested.

Some scholars believe that Mount Sinai is located not on the Sinai Peninsula but in Arabia. We read in the Book of Exodus that when Moses fled Egypt, he went to the land of Midian, where he worked as a shepherd for Jethro, a priest of Midian.

After spending 40 years of his life in the desert, Moses was shepherding Jethro's flock near Horeb, "the mountain of God," when the Lord suddenly appeared to him in the burning bush (Exodus 3:1). There he is told: "When you have brought the people out of Egypt, you will worship God on this mountain" (Exodus 3:12). And indeed, after the Exodus, we find that Jethro, together with Moses' sons and wife, came to him while he was camped "near the mountain of God" (Exodus 18:5).

Some scholars have taken this to mean that the "mountain of God," known both as Horeb and Sinai, is in the former territory of the Midianites in Arabia. This view is reinforced by the reference by the Apostle Paul to "Mount Sinai in Arabia" in Galatians 4:25. "Arabia" here is taken to refer to what the Romans called *Arabia Petraea*, or Transjordan.

During the nineteenth century, an Englishman by the name of Charles Beke advanced the theory that

Raphael's depiction of the Israelites adoring the second set of tablets containing the Ten Commandments. The original set of commandments was smashed in anger by Moses.

Mount Sinai was an active volcano. The description in the biblical text appears to bear that out: "On the morning of the third day there was thunder and lightning, with a thick cloud over the mountain....The smoke billowed up from it like smoke from a furnace, the whole mountain trembled violently, and the sound of the trumpet grew louder and louder" (Exodus 19:16,18).

Beke set out for the Sinai Peninsula to prove his theory and identify Sinai. He returned to England disappointed after discovering that neither Jebel Musa nor any of the other mountains of Sinai are volcanic in origin.

However, on the western side of the Arabian peninsula—the traditional territory of Midian—vast lava and ash fields provide evidence of past volcanic activity.

There are many legends among the peoples of the area involving a sacred mountain in Midian. The first-century Jewish historian Josephus mentions this sacred mountain and identifies it with Sinai. He repeatedly mentions that it was the highest mountain in the area. Accordingly, attention has focused on Jebal el-Lawz, the highest peak in northwest Arabia, where ancient Midian was located. By comparison, the traditional site of Sinai, 7,400-foot-high Jebel Musa in the Sinai Peninsula, is not the highest peak in the area.

Despite this, the traditionally cited location of Sinai is not easily overturned. A location in the southern Sinai Peninsula fits better with the movements of the Israelites after the Exodus as recorded in the biblical text.

It appears that, like the events that transpired on it, the location of the "mountain of God" will remain hidden.

The Jebeliya Bedouins of St. Catherine's Monastery

Most of the present-day Bedouins of the Sinai desert trace their origins to the nomads of the Arabian desert. Fleeing drought, famine, and tribal conflict, they migrated in small groups to the Sinai Peninsula between 400 and 600 years ago.

Those extended families and others who joined them for protection grew into tribes that carved out territories for themselves. Although one seldom sees signs of tribal boundaries, the entire Sinai is divided between various Bedouin tribes. In each area, the ruling tribe owns exclusive rights to the grazing pastures, tillable land, and limited water resources.

One tribe, however—the Jebeliya—is distinct from all other Bedouins of the Sinai. They trace their lineage to the sixth century A.D. At that time a furious revolt by the Samaritans had left many churches and Christian villages destroyed. After the revolt was put down, the Byzantine Emperor Justinian decided to fortify a number of monasteries in Palestine against further attacks. One of these was the small church and monastery built at the foot of Mount Sinai on a site chosen by Queen Helena, mother of Emperor Constantine.

According to tradition, after the completion of the new fortifications, Justinian presented one hundred Roman and Egyptian slaves, along with their wives and children, as servants to the monastery. These servants lived outside the walls of St. Catherine's, tending to the fields and flocks. As

Jebeliya Bedouins still tend the fields and gardens of St. Catherine's Monastery, as they have for centuries.

their numbers increased, Islamic authorities began to view the Christian tribes in the Sinai as a threat and decided to force them to convert to Islam.

Many from the tribes gathered on the peak of Mount Sinai, prepared to resist. In the end, however, they yielded and renounced their faith, except for one man who refused to submit and prepared to throw himself over the southern cliff of the peak. The man's wife pleaded with him to kill her and their children—or to allow them all to jump with him—

rather than be forced to deny their faith. The tormented man finally relented, drawing his sword and slaying his family.

He then leaped over the cliff, but he survived. The tragedy so marked him that, until his death many years later, he wandered about in the mountains apart from the warmth of civilization. According to written accounts, as he approached the end of his life, he appeared at the doors of the monastery, where he received Holy Communion and was ministered to by the monks before dying peacefully.

The descendants of those tribes that converted to Islam are known as the Jebeliya—"the tribes of the mountain (of Sinai)"—and to this day they still tend the fields and gardens of St. Catherine's Monastery.

Count Tischendorf's Remarkable Discovery

Konstantin von Tischendorf taught theology during the nineteenth century at the University of Leipzig in Prussia. But Tischendorf was more than a professor. He had a burning ambition to discover ancient manuscripts of the Bible, and so he roamed the libraries of Europe and the Near East in search of worn, dusty parchments hidden away in back rooms.

In 1844, Tischendorf's journeys took him to St. Catherine's Monastery at Mount Sinai. There, as he warmed himself with the other monks, he was horrified to see that they were feeding the fire from a basket full of old parchments. He managed to save some of them, which upon examination turned out to be sheets from an ancient Greek version of the Old Testament.

Tischendorf had worked with many old manuscripts, but these were clearly the oldest he had ever seen. He was elated, and he asked if he could keep the sheets that he had saved. The head monks agreed, but later became suspicious and did not allow him to take any others.

Tischendorf spent the next fifteen years of his life trying in vain to gain access to other manuscripts. By 1859, the count had formed a friendship with the czar of Russia, which finally opened the doors for him to return to the Sinai. Since St. Catherine's was a Greek Orthodox monastery, his backing by the czar, the titular head of the Russian Orthodox Church, carried considerable weight.

Armed with his letter of introduction, Tischendorf once again went to St. Catherine's, only to be disappointed when day after day of his most careful searching turned up nothing. By this time he had given up, assuming that the parchments he was looking for had wound up in the fire.

On his very last evening at St. Catherine's, a dispirited Tischendorf happened to be talking with the steward of the monastery, who mentioned to him that he had an old manuscript in his possession. To the professor's utter amazement, the manuscript the steward produced was the very one he had been looking for. Tischendorf managed to compose himself so as not to give away his excitement. Almost indifferently, he asked if he could take the manuscript back to his room for a closer look. There he worked tirelessly throughout the night to read as much as he could of the priceless document.

His struggle to obtain the manuscript was not yet over, but after a long series of events he was finally able to obtain it as a gift to the czar. The manuscript remained in Russia until 1933, when Soviet authorities, more interested in money than in the Bible, sold what has come to be known as the Codex Sinaiticus to England for the then-princely sum of 100,000 pounds.

One of the most important manuscript discoveries of modern times, the document is now in the British Museum.

FORTY YEARS IN THE WILDERNESS

The Desert Wanderers

*F*rom the modern Arab nomads who make their home in the desolate yet stunningly beautiful wastelands of Arabia, Syria, and North Africa, we can glimpse the ways of the desert. The Bedouin are a fascinating people, enduring a scorching sun during the day and freezing temperatures at night. They have no written language, yet have preserved ancient customs that go back to biblical times.

The robes with which Bedouins clothe themselves are similar to those worn in ancient times. They would have been similar in style, if not in beauty, to Joseph's "cloak of many colors," as well as to the seamless garments that Jesus wore.

The Bedouin live in tents woven from the hair of black goats, the fibers of which expand when wet to provide a waterproof covering. During the long summer, the heat of the sun becomes unbearable when it is high in the sky, and we find the typical Bedouin, like Abraham before him, sitting "at the entrance to his tent in the heat of the day."

The Bedouin tent is divided into a main area where the men entertain guests and the women's section where food is cooked. Women are generally not invited to participate in the conversation, but are expected to prepare and serve the food. However, because the size of the tent makes for close quarters, the women miss little of the conversation. And so it was that Sarah was "listening at the tent entrance behind him" when she heard the news of her good tidings.

Nomadic Bedouin shepherds tend a herd of goats in Israel, much as their forefathers have done since time immemorial.

The scant rainfall allows the Bedouin to cultivate a meager field at best for a little winter wheat or beans, and he may succeed at this only once every few years. The grain and legumes pro-

Bedouin men partake of the ancient Arab custom of hospitality, according to which a needy traveler must be provided with up to three days and nights of accommodations and food.

duced are a major part of the Bedouin diet. The flat bread baked on coals is probably the same as that which the patriarchs ate.

We read in Genesis that "Abraham hastened into the tent to Sarah, and said, 'Make ready quickly three measures of choice flour, knead it, and make cakes'"(Genesis 18:6). The urgency with which Abraham is concerned to offer food to his guests has changed little through the centuries. The hospitality of Bedouins is legendary, and it would be a great offense for guests not to be offered something to drink and, if the visit is of any length, food as well. Esteemed guests can expect that an animal from the flock will be butchered in their honor, even when the host can scarcely afford the loss of a sheep or goat.

Women do most of the menial labor in Bedouin tribes, while men occupy themselves with buying and selling livestock, socializing, and protecting the family honor. Today, as in biblical times, women and girls water the flocks. When Abraham's servant set out for the town of Nahor in search of a wife for Isaac, he went to the well outside the city. There he found Rebekah, who offered to water his thirsty camels for him. This was no simple feat, given the fact that a thirsty camel can drink 20 or more gallons of water.

When he fled from Egypt into the desert, Moses came to the attention of his future father-in-law Jethro after helping his daughters at the well: "The priest of Midian had seven daughters. They came to draw water, and filled the troughs to water their father's flock. But some shepherds came and drove them away. Moses got up and came to their defense and watered their flock" (Exodus 2:17).

This gracious act began a friendship between Moses and Jethro that would endure throughout their lifetimes.

Ark of the Covenant

*T*he Ark of the Covenant was an elaborate container that symbolized God's presence among the ancient Israelites.

The Hebrew word for "ark" can be used interchangeably to mean "box," "chest," or "coffin" and was used to describe objects as diverse as the coffin of Joseph and the collection box in the temple. The word "covenant" refers to the original purpose of the Ark as a container for the Ten Commandments.

The Ark was constructed while the Israelites resided at Mount Sinai. After the original tablets of the law were broken by Moses because of the Israelites' idolatry, he made it out of of acacia wood as a container for the new tablets. The Ark was a rectangular-shaped box approximately four feet long, two-and-a-half feet wide, and two-and-a-half feet deep. It was designed with built-in handles for portability and was carried only by priests.

During the wanderings of the Israelites, the Ark was kept within the tabernacle. Moses addressed the Ark as if the divine presence were within: "Whenever the Ark set out, Moses would say, 'Arise, O Lord, let your enemies be scattered, and your foes flee before you.' And whenever it came to rest, he would say, 'Return O Lord of the ten thousand thousands of Israel'" (Numbers 10:35–36).

As the powerful symbol of God's presence, the Ark was routinely taken into battle. During the period of the Judges, the sin of the wicked sons of Eli led to the defeat of the Israelites by the Philistines. The Ark was captured by their mortal enemies.

This led to a series of adventures in which the Ark was passed from one Philistine city to another, bringing calamity to each one in turn. The Ark was placed in the temple of the Philistine god Dagon in Ashdod, after which we read: "When the people of Ashdod rose early the next day, there was Dagon, fallen on his face to the ground before the Ark of the Lord. So they took Dagon and put him back in his place. But when they rose early on the next morning, Dagon

A depiction of the Ark of the Covenant in a medieval manuscript. Carried by the Israelites throughout their desert sojourn, the Ark was a symbol of the guiding presence of God.

had fallen on his face to the ground before the Ark of the Lord, and the head of Dagon and both his hands were lying cut off upon the threshold; only the trunk of Dagon was left to him" (1 Samuel 5:3–4).

This was a sign of things to come, for we then read: "The hand of the Lord was heavy upon the people of Ashdod, and he terrified them and struck them with tumors" (1 Samuel 5:6). By this time the inhabitants of Ashdod had had quite enough of the Ark and passed it on to the next Philistine city. Once again, its inhabitants were tormented by tumors, until finally they decided to send it back to the Israelites.

The Hebrews rejoiced to see the Ark returning to them on an ox-drawn cart across the fields of Beth-shemesh. However, the sacredness and mysterious powers of the Ark would soon be impressed upon the Israelites. When a clan of Israelites known as the descendants of Jeconiah refused to celebrate the return of the Ark, 70 of them were struck down, causing a great mourning among the people.

Years later, when David became king, he brought the Ark up to Jerusalem. On the way, a curious incident occurred. A certain Uzziah "reached out his hand to the Ark of God and took hold of it, for the oxen shook it. The anger of the Lord was kindled against Uzziah; and God struck him there because he reached out his hand to the Ark; and he died there beside the Ark of God" (2 Samuel 6:6–7).

We read that David was angered because the Lord struck down Uzziah, and the divine action can perhaps only be understood as emphasizing the holiness of God, before whom no man can stand. Uzziah apparently disregarded the command not to touch the Ark and to respect its sanctity.

After this incident, David was reluctant to bring the Ark to Jerusalem for fear of what else might happen, and for three months it was entrusted to the care of Obed-edom the Gittite. It was during this time David and his household enjoyed great blessings from the Lord.

David's successor, Solomon, placed the Ark within the Holy of Holies of his temple. At this point, the Ark was said to contain Aaron's rod that budded and a pot of manna, along with the Ten Commandments. Hovering over the Ark in the darkness of the Holy of Holies were two golden cherubim, their solitude disturbed only by the annual appearance of the High Priest.

Most scholars believe the Ark of the Covenant was captured or destroyed by the Babylonians when Jerusalem fell in 586 B.C. Some believe that this mysterious object was not destroyed. The Ark, they say, remains hidden in a secret location, ready to be revealed at the ordained time.

In Search of the Biblical Manna

According to the Bible, the Israelites were nourished during their forty-year stay in the desert by a food that miraculously appeared each morning on the ground: "The house of Israel called it manna. It was like coriander seed, white, and the taste of it was like wafers made with honey" (Exodus 16:31).

Students of the Bible through the centuries have sought to identify what manna was, and pilgrims to the deserts of Sinai reported seeing and ingesting substances that resembled manna. In 1823, German botanist G. Ehrenberg offered an ingenious theory as to its origin. Ehrenberg

believed that the biblical manna was actually a secretion of tamarisk trees, which are found in the Sinai. The secretion is produced by two kinds of scale insects that feed on the sap of the tamarisk.

Tamarisk sap is rich in carbohydrates but poor in nitrogen. Large quantities of the sap are consumed by the insects in order to obtain sufficient nitrogen, and the excess carbohydrate is excreted in the form of a liquid containing three kinds of sugars and a jellylike substance known as pectin. This would account for the description of manna as sweet and tasting like honey.

The secretion dries quickly in the hot desert climate, leaving sticky droplets behind, once again prompting comparison with the biblical text, which states that "when the layer of dew lifted, there on the surface of the wilderness was a fine flaky substance, as fine as frost on the ground" (Exodus 16:14).

A hundred years after Ehrenberg proposed his theory, a "manna expedition" to Sinai was organized by scientists from the Hebrew University in Jerusalem. After several months of investigation, the expedition brought back photographic and other evidence linking the insect secretions with the biblical manna. In addition, the scientists discovered that the secretions are indeed approximately the size and shape of a coriander seed just as the Bible describes.

Opposite page: *"The Fall of Manna," as depicted by the Italian painter Gian Battista Tiepolo. Manna is described in the Book of Genesis as "a flaky substance, as fine as frost on the ground."*

The biblical text adds that the manna was white in color. Similarly, the insect secretions are initially white, but after lying on the ground they turn yellowish-brown. In tasting the secretions, the scientists reported that it resembled honey that has been left to solidify.

The local Bedouin Arabs call the insect secretions from the tamarisk sap *Mann es-Sama*—meaning "Manna from Heaven." They gather it early in the morning, just as the Israelites did, because when the sun rises, ants and other insects find and consume it. The Israelites also found that any unconsumed manna "bred worms and became foul" overnight (Exodus 16:20).

Would this manna be sufficient to feed the Israelites? In good years, according to reports, the Bedouins of Sinai can gather up to four pounds of it per day, enough to satisfy a grown man. Like the Israelites of old who ground the manna into a paste, they knead the *Mann es-Sama* into a puree to supplement their meager diet.

While an intriguing possibility, the identification of *Mann es-Sama* with the biblical manna is not wholly satisfactory. Questions remain whether such a substance qualifies as a basic foodstuff and whether it would provide sufficient nourishment over a long period of time.

Meat in the Desert

After the Israelites escaped across the Red Sea, their problems were far from over. After a month, their food was running out, and some people began to think perhaps their former life as slaves wasn't so bad after all. The

Manna: A Pilgrim's Account

The following account was written in 1483 by a German named Breitenback, identified as the Dean of Mainz, following his visit to the Sinai:

"In every valley throughout the whole region of Mount Sinai, there can still be found Bread of Heaven, which the monks and the Arabs gather, preserve, and sell to pilgrims and strangers who pass that way. This same Bread of Heaven falls about daybreak like dew or hoarfrost and hangs in beads on grass, stones, and twigs. It is sweet like honey and sticks to the teeth. We bought a lot of it."

For 40 years the Children of Israel were nourished in the desert by manna, which appeared on the ground on each morning of the week except the Sabbath.

Israelites complained to Moses: "If only we had died by the hand of the Lord in the land of Egypt, when we sat by the fleshpots and ate our fill of bread; for you have brought us out into this wilderness to kill this whole assembly with hunger." (Exodus 16:3).

We then read that the Lord heard the cries of the Israelites and promised that their needs would be met immediately: "At twilight you shall eat meat, and in the morning you shall have your fill of bread; then you shall know that I am the Lord your God" (Exodus 16:8).

To supply food for over a million people is no simple task in a desert environment. However, the text records that in the very same evening "quails came and covered the camp," providing the people with longed-for meat (Exodus 16:13). Is there any evidence to corroborate this incredible event?

Amazingly, there is. The great Israeli soldier and statesman Moshe Dayan spent years traversing the Sinai when Israel controlled the area militarily. Through his intimate knowledge of the area and his contacts with the Arab nomadic peoples known as Bedouin, he learned of a remarkable parallel to the biblical account.

Every autumn, birds from the northern hemisphere, including quail, migrate south. Their migration route takes them from central Europe south through Turkey. There the birds prepare for a difficult feat: crossing the Mediterranean in a single night, an effort made necessary by the absence of an intervening land mass for the birds to rest.

The flight pushes the birds to the very limit. They must cover a great distance and maintain a high speed of 50 miles per hour. Every year, untold numbers of birds give in to the rigors of the journey and fall into the sea.

The quails are already approaching the coast as the first rays of dawn are appearing on the horizon, illuminating the palm trees along the shore. Spurred on by the sight and at the very limits of their strength, the birds drop to an altitude of only a few yards above the water. Without losing speed they make for the trees and drop exhausted to the ground. There they lie in the sand, warming themselves in the autumn sun.

Unfortunately, many of them do not get the chance to complete their migration. Dreaming of tasty birds roasting in the embers of a campfire, the local Bedouins eagerly await the arrival of the quail. Fences of fish-netting are strung along the shore, trapping some of the fatigued birds as they prepare to land.

On their northbound return trip in the spring, the surviving birds faced another threat as they crossed the Red Sea and lighted on the shores to gather their strength for their flight over the mountains of Sinai. The Jewish historian Josephus describes the Bedouins catching the exhausted quails by hand.

Through the generations, Bedouins have been so successful at trapping the helpless, depleted quail that most of the vast migration flights have disappeared. In biblical times their numbers were likely far greater—perhaps even enough to provide flesh for the multitudes of Israelites to enjoy.

OLD TESTAMENT: HISTORICAL BOOKS

Containing the books of Joshua, Judges, Ruth, 1 and 2 Samuel, 1 and 2 Kings, 1 and 2 Chronicles, Ezra, Nehemiah, and Esther, the so-called Historical Books tell the story of the Israelites' conquest of the Promised Land, their defeat and exile by the Babylonians, and their eventual return to Judah to rebuild Jerusalem and restore their kingdom. Even though God's people repeatedly fell from grace through temptation and loss of faith, he forgave their transgressions and did not abandon them.

The anointing of Saul by the prophet Samuel, from the chapel of Quigley Seminary, Chicago, Illinois.

THE CONQUEST OF CANAAN

The Fifth Gospel

*I*srael has been called the "Fifth Gospel" because the land is the key to understanding the background of the Bible stories.

Packed into this relatively small country measuring approximately 150 miles by 50 miles is an amazing diversity that

few regions can match. The elevation varies from 9,200 feet on the snow-covered peaks of Mount Hermon to the barren deserts next to the Dead Sea at 1,300 feet below sea level. The vegetation at well-watered En-gedi along the shores of the Dead Sea is subtropical, but a few hundred meters above in the wilderness of Judea, only a few hardy plants can be found in the sun-washed desert.

Students of the Bible have wondered why the tiny land of Israel has commanded the attention of so many empires. Geography provides the answer. Israel is located on the land bridge between three continents: Africa, Asia, and Europe. For that reason, Israel has experienced both the cultures and the armies of these regions, whose presence in the Holy Land is recounted on the pages of the Bible and in many extrabiblical texts from antiquity.

The Assyrians and Babylonians came from Asia, the Egyptians from Africa, and the Greeks and Romans from Europe. They traveled along the same ancient trade routes that the biblical characters knew.

An Arab farmer plows his vineyard in much the same way as his forefathers, loosening the ground to soak up as much of the seasonal rains as possible.

The abundant flow from one of the headwaters of the Jordan River, located in northern Galilee in the foothills of Mount Hermon.

Unlike the great river cultures of Egypt and Mesopotamia, the land of Israel depends upon the seasonal rains for water. Rainfall can vary from up to 40 inches in northern Galilee to only a few inches annually in the southern deserts.

Since rain was not a dire necessity in Egypt and Mesopotamia, their chief deities, Amon Re and Marduk, respectively, were sun gods. By comparison, the chief god of Canaan was Baal, a god of rain and fertility often pictured with a lightning bolt in his upraised arm.

As the Israelites prepared to enter Canaan, the land was described to them: "For the land that you are about to enter to occupy is not like the land of Egypt, from which you have come, where you sow your seed and irrigate by foot like a vegetable garden. But the land you are about to enter is a land of hills and valleys, watered by rain from the sky, a land that the Lord your God looks after" (Deuteronomy 11:10–12).

In ancient Egypt, farmers irrigated their crops using pumps that brought the waters of the Nile into their fields. The inhabitants of Israel did not have the luxury of an abundant supply of water. As the text of Deuteronomy indicates, the Israelites were to look to the God of Heaven for their survival.

The drama of the Bible is played out against this relationship, and it is largely a tragic story, as Israel became increasingly rebellious rather than dependent upon God, as the land itself sought in vain to teach them.

The Merneptah Stela

References to ancient Israel outside the Bible are few. One that has been of considerable interest to scholars is an inscription found in an Egyptian temple at the end of the last century. It sheds light on an important event in Israel's early history.

The date of the Exodus and the Israelites' conquest of Canaan has been fiercely debated among scholars. One popular theory is that the biblical portrayal is an exaggerated account of what was actually a gradual process during which the Israelites emerged from peoples indigenous to Canaan.

According to this theory, the dramatic stories of the conquest of Jericho and other cities are merely religiously motivated fables with little historical basis. The development of the Israelite nation supposedly took place in the middle of the twelfth century B.C.—around 1150 B.C. That is more than 200 years later than the Bible indicates the conquest of Canaan took place.

In 1896, the great Egyptologist Flinders Petrie was excavating in the mortuary temple of Pharaoh Merneptah in Thebes when he discovered what has come to be known as the Merneptah Stela. A stela is a cut, standing stone with writing on it used in ancient times to chronicle important events in the reign of a king or pharaoh.

As it turns out, the Merneptah Stela preserves what is the most important mention of Israel outside the Bible and the only mention of Israel in Egyptian records. The stela is, in fact, a poetic eulogy to Merneptah, who ruled after Rameses the Great, from 1212 B.C. to 1202 B.C. At the end of the poem is a record of a military campaign into Canaan by Merneptah around 1210 B.C. It is here that we find the famous citation: "Israel is laid waste, its seed is not."

This text appears to pose a problem for the so-called gradual emergence theory, for it indicates that Israel was already a recognizable entity by 1210 B.C. instead of 1150 B.C. or later. Accordingly, the Merneptah Stela has been carefully analyzed by scholars attempting to harmonize it with the gradual emergence theory. It has been variously suggested that the word "Israel" actually refers to "Jezreel," the valley in the north of the country, or perhaps to "the wearers of the side lock," the Libyans.

These alternative renderings have not met with widespread acceptance. The word for Israel is accompanied in the Merneptah Stela with a special hieroglyphic indicator for people, not a geographic feature such as a valley. And the presence of Israel in a list of Canaanite peoples argues against identifying it with Libya.

Attention has also focused on the meaning of the word "seed" as it appears in the stela. There are only two possibilities, "grain" or "offspring." A comparison with the use of the term in other Egyptian texts affirms that it refers to grain.

While it would be unwise to attempt to draw too much from this overly scrutinized text, the evidence indicates that, by the late thirteenth century, a nation by the name of Israel not only existed, but was an important enough military power to be mentioned in the stela.

It also seems clear by the reference to grain that the Israelites were primarily agriculturists. The biblical text supports the fact that during this period the Israelites were primarily tillers of the soil. Grain storage pits are common to the hill country sites that they occupied.

The examination of teeth from tombs of the period also indicates that grain was a primary food source for the inhabitants. The worn state of the teeth is due to the fact that stone mills were used to grind the grain, which would therefore contain minute particles of stone.

The Cursing Prophet

Not all of the prophets mentioned in the Bible were from Israel. In the Book of Numbers we read that Balak, king of Moab, is alarmed at the presence of the Israelites camping on his border as they prepare to enter the Promised Land. Consequently, Balaam, son of Beor, is summoned, but he refuses to curse the Israelites.

Balaam is killed when the Israelites fight the Midianites, but that is not the last we hear of the prophet from Midian. In the Book of Numbers he is said to be the cause of the Israelites' sin of worshiping the Moabite god Baal-Peor. In 2 Peter, we learn that Balaam "loved the wages of doing wrong," and Jude speaks of the ungodly men following greedily after "Balaam's error." The "teaching of Balaam" is described in Revelation as having "put a stumbling block before the people of Israel, so that they would eat food sacrificed to idols and practice fornication."

These references to Balaam throughout the Bible indicate that he exercised a profoundly negative influence lasting for centuries after his death. But do any other ancient records mention him?

Interestingly, archaeologists have uncovered an inscription that appears to shed some light upon this mysterious figure. Discovered in 1967 at Deir Alla in Jordan, the inscription consists of 50 lines of text written on an ancient plastered wall that may have been damaged in an earthquake during the reign of King Uzziah and the prophet Amos around 760 B.C. The message, written in Aramaic and thought to have been composed much earlier, is titled, "Warnings from the Book of Balaam the son of Beor. He was a seer of the gods." The text relates a vision of impending divine judgment for Moab.

Scholars have found a number of parallels between the inscription and the biblical account. Deir Alla is located approximately 25 miles from where the Israelites were camped on the plains of Moab across the Jordan River. Some scholars have suggested that Deir Alla was in the same location as ancient Pethor, mentioned in the Bible as Balaam's home.

Balaam was known as the "cursing prophet" because he was summoned by Balak for the purpose of cursing Israel. The inscription indicates that he continued to be revered by the people of Midian for hundreds of years. For the people of God, he served as a warning against false religion.

The debate over the date of the Exodus and the conquest of Canaan continues, and this latest research will surely give biblical scholars something more to chew on.

When Did the Walls of Jericho Collapse?

*I*t was from the east that the Israelites converged upon the city of Jericho after camping "at Gilgal on the east border of Jericho" (Joshua 4:19). According to the biblical account, the Israelites marched around the city once a day for six days. On the seventh day, however, they encircled Jericho seven times, after which they blew their trumpets and shouted. The Bible records that the walls of the city collapsed, and the Israelites then rushed in and conquered Jericho.

Several major archaeological excavations of Jericho have been undertaken in the past century, each hoping to uncover some evidence related to the biblical story. In 1907 and 1909, an Austro-German team uncovered the base of the city and what appeared to be massive piles of bricks. It would take another half a century before those findings would be identified.

English archaeologist John Garstang worked at the site from 1930 to 1936 and stunned the scholarly world by announcing that the walls of Jericho had indeed fallen, sometime before 1400 B.C. However, archaeology was still in its infancy in Garstang's day (it is still considered a "young" science even today), and by modern standards his techniques were crude.

Another English archaeologist, Dame Kathleen Kenyon, overturned Garstang's conclusions regarding Jericho after excavating at Jericho between 1952 and 1958. Kenyon determined that the piles of bricks were from a city wall that had collapsed when the city was destroyed. She dismayed Bible enthusiasts by concluding that this destruction occurred at

The walls of Jericho fall after the Israelites march around it, blowing their trumpets. To the regret of archaeologists, the walls have eroded with the passage of time.

Tales of Ancient Teeth

A burial cave at Khirbet Nisya, eight miles north of Jerusalem, has yielded a wealth of information about the ancient Israelites.

Dating from the time of the Israelite Judges in the twelfth century B.C., the tomb contained almost no intact bones, though it did contain teeth, which is not unusual, considering that teeth are the hardest bone substance in the body and therefore remain intact the longest. What is unusual at the 3,200-year-old tomb is that archaeologists found complete sets of teeth for 51 individuals—792 teeth in all.

The burial site at Khirbet Nisya was a natural limestone cave that was enlarged and used as a tomb for approximately 200 years. At the time, it was common practice that, when a new body was placed in the tomb, the remains of the previous inhabitants were simply pushed to the side. The deceased were simply laid on the floor, along with various personal or household objects.

The teeth provided a wealth of information about the lives of the ancient Israelites. That it was a difficult existence is indicated by the fact that nearly one quarter of those buried in the tomb were children. Almost half of the population of the tomb died before the age of 40 and only four of them had attained the age of 60.

The wear patterns on the teeth indicated that during this period the Israelites had a very stable and uniform diet. The degree to which the teeth were worn was typical of a coarse diet of wheat and barley. Additional staples included olives, figs, and other fruits. Dental analysis showed the positive benefits of such a diet: Little evidence of decay was found in the teeth of older individuals.

Although the worn teeth indicated a diet that contained little meat, archaeological evidence from ancient houses in the area suggests that sheep and goats were kept as animals, but primarily for milk, cheese, yogurt, and wool. Scholars believe that meat was consumed only a few times a year, at religious feasts and other special occasions.

The Jewish belief system required periodic animal sacrifices, and the family was often allowed to partake of the remaining meat after the priests had taken their share. The availability of roasted meat doubtlessly contributed to the joyous nature of such occasions.

the end of the Middle Bronze Age, around 1550 B.C.—well before the generally accepted date for the Israelites' arrival into Canaan. Since the walls had fallen long before Joshua's time, there was, in effect, no city for the Israelites to conquer.

Kenyon's conclusions had a significant influence on biblical studies for decades to follow, as skeptics used her findings as a prime example of what they claimed was the historical unreliability of the Bible. Nevertheless, the question of the walls of Jericho continued to dog scholars, some

The excavated ruins of et-Tell are thought to be the location of the biblical city of Ai, which was destroyed by Joshua during the initial phase of the conquest of Canaan.

of whom turned their critical attention to Kenyon herself. She died in 1978 without ever having published a formal excavation report.

A reexamination of her original data has led some scholars to question her conclusions. It is clear that she found evidence of massive destruction: walls and floors blackened by fire, and rooms filled with fallen bricks and burnt timbers. But when did this destruction occur?

The likely answer came when scientists carbon-dated a piece of charcoal from the debris layer to 1410 B.C., with a margin of error of plus or minus 40 years. This date coincided with other evidence ignored by Kenyon, such as Garstang's

The Damming of the Jordan

After their spies returned from Jericho, the Israelites prepared to cross the Jordan River and enter the Promised Land. Even then, before modern irrigation siphoned off much of its water, the Jordan scarcely deserved to be called a river during much of the year.

However, we are told that "the Jordan overflows all its banks throughout the time of harvest" (Joshua 3:15). This is the grain harvest in late spring, when the snows of Mount Hermon at the headwaters of the Jordan begin to melt. The river is transformed into a swiftly flowing, churning tide that greatly enlarges its banks, making it impossible to cross.

Even in modern times, the river has proved difficult to manage. In 1917, on its way to attack Amman, the British Army lost a number of soldiers to the swift currents before it managed to secure guide ropes across the river.

As the priests bearing the Ark of the Covenant came to the Jordan, "the waters flowing from above stood still, rising up in a single heap far off at Adam, the city that is beside Zarethan, while those flowing toward the sea of the Arabah, the Dead Sea, were wholly cut off. Then the people crossed over opposite Jericho" (Joshua 3:16).

The placid Jordan River shortly after exiting the Sea of Galilee. Here the famous river begins its twisting, 100-mile journey south to the Dead Sea.

The biblical account of the crossing of the Jordan is often assumed to be fanciful. But there is interesting historical data that lends some credibility to the story. Scholars have discovered that, over the past 2,000 years, the region has experienced at least 30 earthquakes. Interestingly, ten of these resulted in the temporary damming of the Jordan River by mud slides.

The most recent of these occurred in 1927 at a ford known as Damiyeh, some 25 miles upstream. An earthquake loosened great masses of earth from overhanging cliffs, which fell into the river and choked the narrow ford. The flow of water was completely stopped for 21 hours.

The river was stopped up by an earthquake three years earlier, in 1924, as well as in 1906. In the latter case, the river bed at the lower reaches of the Jordan was completely dry for 24 hours.

There is little doubt that for an earthquake to occur just as the Israelites were preparing to cross the Jordan—and at the very time of year when the river's water level was at its highest—is at the very least highly remarkable. But what the skeptic labels as coincidence can be a miracle through the eyes of faith.

discovery of a continuous sequence of Egyptian scarabs (decorative beetle-shaped carvings) at the site.

As if that weren't enough to cast serious doubts about the validity of Kenyon's work, Garstang also recorded large amounts of pottery fragments dating to the same period. If the destruction of the walls of Jericho actually occurred around 1400 B.C., this would support the traditional date of the fall of Jericho indicated by the Bible.

This latest evaluation of the evidence from the excavations at Jericho remains hotly debated among archaeologists, and only time will tell whether Kenyon's conclusions will stand up—or collapse like the walls of Jericho.

THE JUDGES OF ISRAEL

A Fateful Oath

*J*ephthah, one of the judges—or tribal leaders—of Israel, lived a life marked by tragedy. He was born to a harlot in Gilead and was rejected by his family, who disowned him and drove him from their midst. Growing up in the land of Tob, he joined a band of outlaws who made him their leader.

Some time later, after Jephthah had begun raising a family, the Ammonites invaded Gilead and Judah. The Israelites were in sore need of a leader to bring an end to their oppression. Jephthah had made a reputation as a fighter, and his countrymen turned to him for help in ridding the country of the Ammonites.

Jephthah quite understandably balked at the request, reminding them: "Are you not the very ones who rejected me and drove me out of my father's house? So why do you come to me now when you are in trouble?" (Judges 11:7).

Nevertheless, he is persuaded to come to their assistance. He rallies the Israelites and musters an army. As he prepares to lead the Israelites against the Ammonites, he makes an inexplicable oath: "And Jephthah made a vow to the Lord, and said, 'If you will give the Ammonites into my hand, then whoever comes out of the doors of my house to meet me, when I return victorious from the Ammonites, shall be the Lord's, to be offered up by me as a burnt offering'" (Judges 11:30–31).

It has been suggested that Jephthah was assuming that he would be sacrificing an animal. This explanation, however, is not satisfactory. The language of the text indicates that it is not animal sacrifice that is promised by Jephthah.

If he indeed had human sacrifice in mind, it can be assumed that he expected a servant to greet him. And if this explanation is correct, it then leads to another mystery: Why is Jephthah later listed among the heroes of the faith in the Book of Hebrews? It can be assumed that he is included for his achievements as a judge, not for his rash oath.

Gruesome Tales of a Sewer in Ashkelon

While excavating a large sewer channel in the former Philistine city of Ashkelon, archaeologists came across a large number of skeletal remains that they at first took to be animal bones. Closer examination, however, revealed that they were the bones of nearly a hundred babies. Forensic examination determined that the babies had been killed and thrown into the sewer shortly after birth.

How could such a thing have happened? The Philistines apparently considered infanticide to be an acceptable form of birth control. Typically, an unwanted child would be callously left to

The archaeological remains of Ashkelon, one of the five ancient cities of the Philistines, are located about 12 miles from Gaza on the Mediterranean coast.

the elements or to ravaging animals—or in the case of the inhabitants of Ashkelon, dumped into the municipal sewer.

Both Jews and Christians were appalled at the idea of infanticide and steadfastly condemned the practice. In the fourth century, when the Emperor Constantine made Christianity the official religion of the Roman Empire, infanticide became illegal.

In Ashkelon, however, the new law could not prevent fathers and mothers from secretly discarding their unwanted newborns, a practice that continued for some 200 years after Constantine.

Jephthah succeeded in routing the Ammonites in battle and returned home, where his only daughter came out to greet him. In ancient Israel, oaths were considered absolutely binding. In the absence of a formal legal system, contracts and other legal affairs were often conducted verbally.

The binding power of oaths extended to vows made to the Lord: "When a man makes a vow to the Lord, or swears an

oath to bind himself by a pledge, he shall not break his word; he shall do according to all that proceeds out of his mouth" (Numbers 30:2).

Realizing this, Jephthah said: "Alas, my daughter! You have brought me very low; you have become the cause of great trouble for me, for I have opened my mouth to the Lord, and I cannot take back my vow" (Judges 11:35). His daughter courageously accepted her fate, asking only for two months to retreat to the hills to mourn with her companions.

The tragedy of Jephthah continued as he presided over a bloody civil war between Gilead and Ephraim. In the end, he would die childless.

Flemish painter Erasmus Quellinus depicted this fateful scene of Jephthah being greeted by his daughter. This tragic story emphasizes the importance placed upon oaths in ancient Israel.

Samson's Revenge

*T*he tragic account of Samson's life and death is a powerful story. After Samson had been betrayed by Delilah, the Philistines gouged out his eyes and took him to Gaza, where he was subsequently imprisoned and forced to work grinding grain for his enemies.

Archaeological evidence indicates that prisoners were routinely interred in "grinding houses," where they were forced to perform what was one of the most time-consuming and tedious tasks of antiquity, that of milling flour. In the home, this task was performed by women using a hand-held pestle and a mortar placed in the lap.

Grinding houses provided flour for the elite of Philistine society. The mills they used consisted of large stones with protruding wooden shanks on either side set upon a flat stone. The top stone would be rotated by human labor, thus grinding the grain against the bottom stone. Limestone was used, but the superior mills were made of basalt, an extremely hard volcanic rock found in northern Israel.

Samson, his strength renewed by the growth of his hair, topples the temple of the Philistines. Canaanite temples similar to the one depicted here have been excavated in the land of Israel.

According to the biblical text, one day Samson was brought forth to entertain the assembled Philistines. Once in their company, he asked to be guided to two pillars in the center of the building so he could lean against them. Then we read: "He strained with all his might; and the house fell on the lords and all the people who were in it. So those he killed at his death were more than those he had killed during his life" (Judges 16:30).

But is it possible that such a thing could actually have happened? Archaeological excavation of the Philistine cities provides us with some illuminating evidence related to the biblical story. Philistine temples have been uncovered at Tel Qasile in northern Tel Aviv and at Tel Miqne, the ancient Ekron. Interestingly, the roofs of both temples were supported by twin central pillars made of wood resting on stone support bases. The pillars were about six feet apart, making it theoretically possible for them to be dislodged, thus collapsing the roof.

It would take a person of superhuman strength to accomplish a feat such as this; certainly, the description fits Samson before he was compromised by Delilah. The Bible states that Samson's hair, which was the source of his great might before the Philistines cut it off, had indeed grown back in prison.

People of the Book: The Moabites

A land as rich in biblical history as it is desolate, Moab occupies a plateau east of the Dead Sea.

The ancient trade route known as the King's Highway passed through Moab on its way south to Arabia or north to Syria. It was this route that the Israelites took on their way to Canaan. After defeating the Amorites and King Og of Bashan, the Israelites camped in the plains of Moab before entering the Promised Land.

The constant temptation of the people of Israel to adopt the idolatrous practices of their neighbors once again surfaced in the plains of Moab. We read that "while Israel was staying at Shittim, the people began to have sexual relations with the women of Moab. These invited the people to the sacrifices of their gods, and the people ate and bowed down to their gods. Thus Israel yoked itself to the Baal of Peor, and the Lord's anger was kindled against Israel" (Numbers 25:1–3).

Also, while the Israelites were encamped on the plains of Moab there was a curious encounter between King Balak of Moab and the prophet Balaam. Balak attempted to induce Balaam to curse Israel, but the prophet finds that he is only able to bless the dreaded enemies of the king.

During the period of the judges, a left-handed Benjaminite named Ehud is sent to assassinate the obese King Eglon of Moab. However, relations between Moab and Israel were often good, as is evident from the story of Ruth.

Ruth's father-in-law Elimelech had migrated to Moab during time of famine. Though blessed with few springs, the rich soil of Moab is well-watered by winter rains, making it suitable for growing wheat and barley and for pasturing sheep and goats. We read that "King Mesha of Moab was a sheep breeder, who used to deliver to the king of Israel one hun-

James Tissot's depiction of the Moabites being taken prisoner by the victorious Israelites. Moab was an ancient enemy of Israel.

dred thousand lambs, and the wool of one hundred thousand rams" (2 Kings 3:4).

After Elimelech died, Ruth returned with Naomi to Bethlehem, where she married Boaz and became part of King David's lineage.

Relations between Israel and Moab continued to fluctuate. David sent his parents to Moab for protection while he was being pursued by Saul. Yet later he defeated Moab in battle and executed two-thirds of the Moabite prisoners.

The worship of the Moabite god Chemosh eventually made its way into Israel. Solomon married Moabite women and permitted the worship of Chemosh in Jerusalem. Moab was able to secure its independence from Israel as recorded in the Moabite Stone, a ninth-century B.C. inscription written by King Mesha of Moab.

However, Moab eventually fell to Assyria, as did Israel and other surrounding nations. Aside from a few scattered references, we hear nothing more about the land of Moab, which faded from the stage of history.

ISRAEL'S UNITED MONARCHY

Saul's Bizarre Final Night

*T*he last battle of King Saul was fought against the Philistines in the Jezreel Valley. Saul's army was at the foot of Mount Gilboa, while the Philistines were encamped across the valley at the town of Shunem on the hill of Moreh.

Saul, overwrought with fear about the impending battle, sought divine guidance. However, because of his disobedience, "the Lord did not answer him, not by dreams, or by Urim, or by prophets" (1 Samuel 28:6).

Determined to obtain supernatural knowledge about what would happen the next day, Saul disguises himself and travels to the village of Endor, located on the other side of the Philistine camp, to visit a spiritual medium known to reside there. It is a dangerous journey, requiring a considerable detour around enemy forces.

That Saul would consult a medium is a reversal of a policy established earlier in his reign, when he "expelled the mediums and the wizards from the land" (1 Samuel 28:3). He asks the medium to conjure up the ghost of the prophet Samuel, and the woman does as he asks, but something goes wrong. When Samuel appears, the medium becomes terrified.

It seems that the medium did not expect to see what she saw. Does this imply that she was a fraud who intended to perform her usual tricks but was shocked to actually see the venerated prophet? Perhaps. Another reason for her terror could

have been Samuel's well-known opposition to the practice of witchcraft.

Saul, who apparently cannot see the apparition, tries to calm her fears and asks her to tell him what she sees. The woman replies that she sees a "divine being" coming out of the ground, whom she describes as "an old man" who is "wrapped in a robe" (1 Samuel 28:14).

The reference to being wrapped in a robe may be a reference to Samuel's burial clothes. Saul realizes it is the prophet, and he bows with his face to the ground, describing his plight to the apparition. The news could not be worse. In his final prophecy, Samuel informs Saul that he has been rejected by the Lord and that Israel would be defeated. Saul and his sons would die on the battlefield.

Upon hearing this dreaded prophecy, Saul became "filled with fear because of the words of Samuel; and there was no strength in him, for he had eaten nothing all day and all night" (1 Samuel 28:20).

In a final irony, the medium insists on preparing him a meal for which he could have had little appetite. It would be his last.

Samuel rises from the netherworld in James Tissot's depiction of Saul's anguished final night, as he sought to learn his fate from the witch of Endor.

The Daring Capture of Jerusalem

*T*he Book of 2 Samuel tells the story of how David's men captured the city of Jerusalem and made it the capital of the Jewish kingdom. The city was inhabited by the Jebusites, who were so confident of their secure position that they taunted the Israelites: "You will not come in here, even the blind and the lame will turn you back" (2 Samuel 5:6).

Scholars are divided as to the meaning of the Hebrew word *tsinnor* which is translated "water shaft" in the following passage: "Nevertheless, David took the stronghold of Zion, which is now the city of David. David had said on that day, 'Whoever would strike down the Jebusites, let him get up the water shaft (*tsinnor*) to attack the lame and the blind, those whom David hates'" (2 Samuel 5:8). Since the word *tsinnor* only occurs one other time in the Bible, a number of possibilities for its meaning have been suggested, including various weapons or parts of the defenses of the city.

Most translations of the Bible, however, translate *tsinnor* as a shaft, conduit, or channel used for carrying water. This interpretation has been supported by the discovery of an ancient water shaft that served the Jebusite city and would have been an ideal means for entering the city by stealth. The shaft, named after the British explorer Charles Warren who discovered it in the nineteenth century, brought water from the Gihon Spring inside the city walls.

In ancient times, a city deprived of its water supply could not withstand a siege for long. The Jebusites protected their water supply by sealing off the original entrance to the

The descent into Warren's Shaft, named after nineteenth-century English explorer Charles Warren. The water system enabled the Jebusites to obtain the precious liquid when the city was under siege.

Gihon Spring and diverting the water to a tunnel leading under the city walls. The tunnel then connected with a 40-foot vertical shaft from which water could be drawn and carried into the city.

The Jebusite city occupied a small yet highly defensible knoll of land extending south from the Turkish walls of Jerusalem so familiar to tourists. Surrounded by the steep hillsides of the Kidron and Tyropoeon valleys, the city would have presented a daunting challenge to any potential invaders.

Polydactylism

*I*n a story reminiscent of David and Goliath, we read in the Book of 2 Samuel about David's nephew Jonathan slaying a "giant." In this passage we find the curious but not uncommon phenomenon of polydactylism—or being born with more than the usual number of fingers or toes:

"In still another battle, which took place at Gath, there was a huge man with six fingers on each hand and six toes on each foot—twenty-four in all. He also was descended from Rapha (pl. Rephaim). When he taunted Israel, Jonathan son of Shimeah, David's brother, killed him" (2 Samuel 21:20–21).

In the Near East, polydactylism was connected with a race of giants known as the Rephaim. They are mentioned in Genesis as one of the peoples inhabiting Canaan during the time of the patriarchs. Og, the last king of the Rephaim, was a huge man who slept in an iron bed "nine cubits long" —or more than 13 feet.

References to polydactylism are to be found in other ancient Near Eastern literature. A seventh-century Assyrian poem indicates that having six fingers or toes was an omen for either good or evil, depending on which hand or foot the six fingers or toes were found. Thus we read: "If a woman gives birth, and the child has six fingers on the right hand, poverty will seize the house of the man."

However, if "the child has six fingers on the left hand, the mother is endowed with prosperity; the man's adversary will die." The rule seems to be that six fingers on the left hand is a good portent, while six fingers on the right hand is an evil omen.

But elsewhere in the ancient Near East that rule does not hold. Rather, there seems to be a variety of meanings conveyed by polydactylism. On one of the clay sarcophagi found at Dier el-Balah near Gaza, for example, is the portrayal of a man with six fingers on his left hand. A three-foot-tall ancient statue uncovered in Jordan has six toes, apparently meant to convey spiritual power.

When the Greeks, with their ideal of physical perfection, conquered the ancient world, the fascination with polydactylism disappeared from the Near East. However, during the late Middle Ages we find this phenomenon portrayed in works of art. Once again, the meaning is unclear.

John the Baptist, for example, has been pictured with six fingers on his right hand, and St. Paul has been depicted with six toes. Ann Boleyn, second wife of England's Henry VIII, was said to have had six fingers on her right hand, which, to many people of her day, indicated she was a witch.

Hence the bold confidence of the Jebusites, who seemingly did not consider the possibility that the secret of their concealed water system had been detected by the Israelites. Apparently, the Israelite commander Joab uncovered the original entrance to the spring during the night. He and his men then crept through the channel and ascended Warren's Shaft. Once inside the city, they could have opened the city gates thus allowing the rest of the army to swarm in and capture it.

To remove any doubt as to the feasibility of entering the city this way, a group of archaeologists traced the likely steps of Joab and his men. Without the benefit of special climbing equipment, they were able to scale Warren's Shaft unaided, just as Joab and his men probably did three thousand years ago.

The Temple of King Solomon

*T*he biblical depiction of the vast quantities of gold used in King Solomon's Temple staggers the Western mind, causing some scholars to label it a gross exaggeration.

We read that "Solomon overlaid the inside of the [Temple] with pure gold, then he drew chains of gold across, in front of the inner sanctuary, and overlaid it with gold. Next he overlaid the whole [Temple] with gold, in order that the whole house might be perfect" (1 Kings 6:21–22).

Some biblical commentaries allow that perhaps selected parts of the temple, such as the altar, could have been gold-plated. Others suggest that it was actually gold paint that was applied to the walls. Clearly, they say, the so-called Golden Temple was a tale that grew with the telling.

The list of sacred objects and utensils crafted with gold seems endless: "King Solomon made two hundred large shields of beaten gold; six hundred shekels of gold went into each large shield. He made three hundred shields of beaten gold, three minas of gold went into each shield . . . The king also made a great ivory throne, and overlaid it with the finest gold . . . All King Solomon's drinking vessels were of gold, and all the vessels of the House of the Forest of Lebanon were of pure gold; none were of silver—it was not considered as anything in the days of Solomon" (1 Kings 10:16–18, 21).

To the modern mind, such lavish use of gold may seem garish. By comparing the biblical depiction of King Solomon's wealth with that of the kings of neighboring cultures, we find his use of gold to be remarkably similar to that of his contemporaries.

Perhaps the least unusual of the biblical claims is that all of King Solomon's tableware was pure gold. Exquisite examples of golden tableware have been found throughout the ancient Near East. Between 1927 and 1931, Sir Leonard Woolley, the excavator of Ur, found numerous elegant specimens of pure gold in his excavation of the Royal Cemetery.

Neither is the description of Solomon's golden throne to be considered implausible. Furniture made of precious metal was prized by ancient potentates, as demonstrated by the splendidly carved wooden chairs plated with gold found in the tomb of Pharaoh Tutankhamen in Upper Egypt. Baby-

Archaeologists have yet to find remains of the magnificent temple built by Solomon, here depicted at its dedication in a painting by James Tissot.

lonian cuneiform documents record gifts of golden furniture to the gods and goddesses or from one king to another.

The Bible describes Solomon's throne as being composed of both ivory and gold: "The King also made a great ivory throne and overlaid it with the finest gold" (1 Kings 10:18). The similar use of gold-overlaid ivory in furniture has been discovered at the ancient Assyrian palaces at Nineveh. Thousands of ivory fragments were found, some with bits of gold foil still sticking to them. When the Babylonians and the Medes sacked the city, they smashed the ivory furniture, ripping off the gold.

Since gold is not strong enough to withstand an arrow or a blow from an ax, the five hundred shields of hammered gold mentioned in the biblical text would have been of little practical use. Sir Leonard Woolley uncovered similar artifacts at Ur, including a golden helmet that, although of superb workmanship, would have been a hazard to wear.

Finally, the sheer quantity of gold mentioned in the text is almost inconceivable to the modern mind. Solomon's golden shields weighed nearly two tons; the Queen of Sheba presented Solomon with a gift of 120 talents of gold (9,000 pounds, or four and one-half tons of gold); and Hiram, king of Tyre, presented Solomon with a similar amount.

As astounding as these figures may be, they are not unusual for the ancient Near East, where we find records of gifts of gold that exceed those mentioned in the biblical account. When the Assyrian king Tiglath-pileser III subjugated Tyre in 730 B.C., he received a tribute of 150 talents of gold. In Egypt, Thutmos III presented a gift of 13.5 tons of gold to the temple of Amun at Karnak.

All this underscores the vast quantities of gold that must have been circulating in the ancient world. Most of it has disappeared from history. Greek sources confirm that when Alexander the Great conquered Persia, he found almost 7,000 tons of gold.

Where did all this gold come from? There are no significant sources of gold in Israel. The Egyptians mined gold at the headwaters of the Nile, and the Queen of Sheba likely used gold mines in western Arabia. The mention in the biblical text of "gold of Ophir" (1 Kings 10:11) remains a puzzle to scholars. Some think it refers to the mines of western Arabia, while others suggest India or the Horn of Africa.

The Infamous Parker Expedition

*B*y the nineteenth century, explorers had already ventured into various underground sites below Jerusalem's Temple Mount, the ancient ritual center of the Jewish people.

Captain Charles Wilson, one of the most famous of these early adventurers, led the British Ordnance Survey Expe-dition of 1864–5. The expedition found 20 underground cisterns underneath the Temple Mount with a total capacity of more than 10 million gallons.

In contrast to the serious scientific research conducted by men like Wilson stands the Parker Expedition, one of the most bizarre episodes in the history of archaeology. Sponsored by an eccentric Swedish self-described "biblical scholar" and "master philosopher" named Valter H. Juvelius, a young Englishman by the name of Montague Brownslow Parker, who had no archaeological training or experience whatsoever, was sent to the Holy Land to locate and unearth the fantastic treasure of Solomon, said to be buried beneath the Temple Mount.

Arriving in Palestine in the early 1900s, Parker settled himself and his aristocratic accomplices into the spacious Augusta Victoria Hospice on the Mount of Olives. He then proceeded to bribe two high-ranking Turkish officials in Jerusalem to allow him to begin digging.

Permission granted, he ordered his digging crew to begin excavating the City of David, located south of the present Turkish walls of Jerusalem. They reopened a shaft that had been dug in 1867 by another Englishman, Charles Warren, hoping to find a secret passage leading to the treasure.

After several months of effort, no passage—or treasure—had been discovered. Parker's supporters back in England and America were getting edgy. To complicate matters, his bribed Turkish officials left town when they realized they were not likely to share in any fabulous reward. Parker was informed by the authorities that he had only until the summer of 1911 to complete his excavations. By late spring of that

"X" Marks the Spot

There are numerous theories about whether the Ark of the Covenant still exists and where it might be located. However, scholars believe they have solved another fascinating question, that of where it was positioned in Solomon's Temple.

The Temple Mount is considered a Muslim holy site, and archaeological investigation by non-Muslims is not permitted. Thus it is difficult to find proof to support any theory about the location of the Ark. However, by utilizing historical records, aerial photographs, and personal examinations, some scholars believe they have found where the Ark stood.

Attention is focused on the most prominent structure on the Temple Mount, the golden Dome of the Rock. Completed in 691 A.D., the Dome of the Rock is the first major sanctuary built by Islam. The magnificent edifice stands at the center of the Temple Mount built by Herod the Great. Most scholars believe that the Temple of Solomon must have stood somewhere in the vicinity of a large section of bedrock known as es-Sakhra, which lies in the center of the Muslim shrine.

The Dome of the Rock was built upon the Temple Mount around A.D. 688–691. The rock over which the shrine is built is thought by some scholars to be the Holy of Holies of the Jewish Temple.

In the exact center of the bedrock es-Sakhra is a rectangular cutout measuring four feet four inches by two feet seven inches. This corresponds to the measurement of the Ark as given in the Bible. It is believed that the Ark of the Covenant once fit into this depression.

Since the depression is in bedrock and appears to be ancient, it is possible that it goes back to the time of Solomon. If so, then the Dome of the Rock, one of the most revered sanctuaries of Islam, is built over the most sacred site of Judaism, the Holy of Holies of the First Temple. A popular belief among Christians is that the Bible predicts that the Jewish temple will one day be rebuilt.

Previous theories had put the temple slightly to the north or to the east of the Dome of the Rock, making it theoretically possible for a temple to be built next to the Moslem shrine. However, if the Holy of Holies indeed sits directly underneath the Dome of the Rock, this complicates matters considerably.

Some suggest that the Dome of the Rock could be destroyed by an earthquake, thus paving the way for the rebuilding of the Temple. However, it is frankly inconceivable that any Moslem authorities will agree to the construction of a Jewish temple on the site of one of Islam's most holy shrines.

The Acropolis of Sion, one of the excavated areas on the slopes of the ancient City of David. The stepped slope is thought to be part of the base for King David's palace.

year, Parker was getting desperate, and he decided on a risky venture.

Parker bribed the local Turkish governor with a huge sum of money for permission to secretly do what no Westerner had ever been permitted to do: excavate on the Temple Mount itself. For centuries, no non-Muslims were allowed entrance to the Temple Mount, let alone to dig there. It was vital that his work be accomplished with the greatest

stealth; as a precaution, some of the Muslim guards were also bribed.

Late one evening, Parker and a small group of workmen were secretly admitted to the Temple Mount. Their first target was the underground vaults known as Solomon's Stables, but after a week of nocturnal digging, nothing had been found, despite the assurances of the Danish clairvoyant guiding them.

The time of year was especially dangerous; it was the Moslem feast of Nebi Mussa, and the city was mobbed with pilgrims from around the world, but Parker was determined to press on with his search for Solomon's treasure.

On the night of April 17, 1911, Parker and his men decided to enter the Dome of the Rock, a sanctuary that had barred its doors to non-Muslims since the Crusades. In the late-night darkness, they quietly entered the Dome of the Rock and went to a natural cavern beneath the surface of the sacred rock. Parker and his men lowered themselves by ropes into the cavern and began to break apart a stone that covered the ancient shaft below.

But as fate would have it, a guard who was not a part of the bribery scheme heard the strange noises and decided to investigate. Entering the Dome of the Rock and seeing the strangely dressed Englishmen (they were wearing Arab clothing), he bolted from the shrine and spread the alarm throughout the city.

Parker and his men wasted no time in fleeing the same evening to Jaffa, where they were arrested as they attempted to reach their private yacht. Realizing the uproar that his venture had caused, Parker knew he had to escape at once. He invited the officials to discuss the matter of his arrest in the more comfortable surroundings of his ship. The officials grudgingly agreed and permitted Parker and his men to row out to the vessel to prepare to receive their guests. Long before the officials arrived, however, Parker steamed out to the open sea.

Riots and other disturbances in Jerusalem continued for days. Soon, newspapers around the world were telling the strange story of the Parker Expedition.

The Story of Royal Blue

*I*n the ancient world, the color purple was symbolic of elegance and wealth. Purple is mentioned as the color of the tabernacle furnishings in Israelite temples, and priests were commanded to have purple in their garments.

In Proverbs, a good wife was worthy of being clothed in purple (31:22). In the New Testament parable of the rich man and Lazarus, the rich man "was dressed in purple and fine linen" (Luke 16:19). Jesus was mockingly honored as a king and clothed in a purple robe at his trial (Mark 15:17), and

in the Book of Acts, Lydia is called a "dealer in purple" (Acts 16:14).

The colorfast purple dye was associated with wealth because it was extremely costly to obtain. In ancient times, the dye had only one known source: the murex, a marine mollusk that is native to the eastern Mediterranean.

Each murex contains only a pinprick amount of the dye, which must be laboriously removed by hand. In Capernaum, on the shores of the Sea of Galilee, a murex production facility was excavated, and a thin needle used to extract the dye was found. Thousands of murex mollusks are required to produce even a small amount of dye, and heaps of discarded shells can be seen at various sites along the coastline.

The Phoenicians maintained a monopoly on murex throughout ancient times. The names "Canaan" and "Phoenician" are both related to the color purple. Some scholars think "Canaan" is derived from the Akkadian word for "red-purple." Similarly, the Greeks named Phoenicia after their word for the color purple.

King Solomon, realizing the skill of the Phoenicians in working with murex dye, asked King Hiram of Tyre to send artisans skilled in working with "purple, crimson, and blue fabrics" (2 Chronicles 2:7). In response, Hiram sent one Huram-abi, who did the work Solomon requested (2 Chronicles 2:13–14).

In the 1970s, the ancient Phoenician site of Zarephath (modern Sarafand in Lebanon) was excavated. Zarephath was an important site for the production of murex dye. A vat containing purple sediment was uncovered, as well as large numbers of discarded murex mollusks. A similar vat was found at the archaeological site of Dor on the Mediterranean coast in Israel. These vats were used to immerse cloth for dying. Waterproof and permanent, the dye was superior to vegetable-based colors.

Murex dye continued to be prized until less costly substitutes were developed. However, its value is still reflected in the use of colors such as royal blue to signify authority.

Peoples of the Bible: The Phoenicians

*T*hough not mentioned by name until the travels of the apostles in the Book of Acts, Phoenicia was a powerful maritime kingdom with extensive influence throughout the western Mediterranean and the the known world.

Phoenicia occupied a narrow strip of coastal land in what is now northern Israel and southern Lebanon. Its territory included an abundance of natural harbors, and the vast forests of the Lebanese mountains provided excellent lumber for its sailing fleets. It is the "cedars of Lebanon" which are said to rejoice over the fall of Babylon: "The cypresses exult over you, the cedars of Lebanon, saying, Since you were laid low, no one comes to cut us down" (Isaiah 14:8).

Tyre and its neighbor Sidon were the two most important cities of Phoenicia. They are mentioned outside the Bible as early as 2000 B.C. and were renowned for their ship-building and maritime exploits.

An ancient sculpture depicting the unique headdress of the Phoenicians, a seafaring people who traded and established colonies throughout the Mediterranean and beyond.

We first read about the land of Phoenicia in the Bible when Hiram, king of Tyre, sent messengers to David to congratulate him on his ascension to the throne. Hiram also sent "cedar trees, and carpenters and masons who built David's house" (2 Samuel 5:11).

Hiram continued his good relations with the Israelites when Solomon succeeded David to the throne: "There was peace between Hiram and Solomon; and the two of them made a treaty" (1 Kings 5:12). In addition, the Phoenicians provided much of the lumber and skilled labor for the construction of Solomon's temple.

The good relations between Hiram and Solomon were marred by an apparent lack of generosity on Solomon's part. After assisting Solomon for some twenty years in the building of the temple and his palace, Hiram was repaid with a gift of twenty cities in the land of Galilee: "But when Hiram came from Tyre to see the cities that Solomon had given him, they did not please him. Therefore he said, 'What kind of cities are these that you have given me, my brother?'" (1 Kings 9:12–13).

The rift over Hiram's reward for his services seems not to have jeopardized their good relations. We read later that Hiram sent his sailors to assist Solomon in establishing his fleet at Ezion-geber, which is thought to have been located at the northernmost tip of the Gulf of Aqaba.

Phoenicia was destined to have a corrupting influence upon the religion of the Israelites in the person of the Sidonian princess Jezebel, who attempted to replace the prophets of Israel with the prophets of the Canaanite-Phoenician gods of Baal and Asherah. After the decisive confrontation between Elijah and the prophets of Baal on Mount Carmel, the threat of these foreign gods was diminished but not completely eradicated. Manasseh, king of Judah, reversed the reforms of Hezekiah and reintroduced Baal worship: "He did what was evil in the sight of the Lord, following

Masters of the Sea

The Phoenicians were renowned shipbuilders and seafarers. In the fifth century B.C., Greek historian Herodotus complimented the quality of their vessels and their skill in sailing around Africa.

The extent of their prowess on the open seas is also indicated by an Assyrian inscription, which records an expedition to Phoenicia around 876 B.C. The inscription provides a glimpse at the sophistication of Phoenician culture and the extent of their trading empire.

According to the inscription, the expedition yielded a tribute that included objects of silver, gold, lead, copper, bronze, brightly colored wool, linen, and ivory. The Phoenicians excelled in trading such luxury items, which came from such far-flung locations as Spain, Arabia, Africa, and India.

We know from the Bible that King Hiram of Tyre, a principal Phoenician city, maintained economic ties with both King David and King Solomon of Israel. The relationship between the two nations was mutually beneficial. Israel, situated on the land bridge between Africa, Europe, and Asia, controlled the important land routes linking these three continents. Phoenicia, on the other hand, as a major sea power, was able to assist Israel in establishing trading links with other lands.

the nations that the Lord drove out before the people of Israel" (2 Kings 21:2).

Many hundreds of years later, the tide of religious influence would be reversed when Jesus visited the Phoenician cities of Tyre and Sidon. While there, he commended a Canaanite woman who begged him to heal her daughter: "'Woman, great is your faith! Let it be done to you as you wish.' And her daughter was healed instantly" (Matthew 15:28).

The Book of Acts records the spread of the gospel in the region after the time of Jesus. We read that, as the apostles Paul and Barnabas "passed through both Phoenicia and Samaria, they reported the conversion of the Gentiles, and brought great joy to all the believers" (Acts 15:3). The ascendancy of the new faith of the prophet from Galilee would eventually bring to an end the influence of the Canaanite-Phoenician god Baal.

Ancient Water Systems

Although the ancient Israelites were remarkably innovative in their efforts at supplying water, the threat of drought was never far from their minds.

Rainfall occurs in Israel during what the Bible calls the "former rains," which begin in late autumn, and the "latter rains," which come in the spring. Throughout the long, hot summer, scarcely a rain-bearing cloud can be seen in the sky, and watchful eyes wait in vain for precipitation.

The agriculture of the Israelites was adapted as much as possible to the annual cycle of rain. Wheat and other grain crops were grown in the winter, when the soil was damp and rain could be expected. Vines, on the other hand, produced their fruits in the summer, requiring painstaking watering by hand. Fortunately, it was not necessary to water the olive trees, as their deep roots are adept at drawing nourishment from the ground.

In ancient Israel, it was important to live near a water source. This was often a perennial spring, but some communities depended upon wells. These would be dug to great depths to ensure a reliable supply. Wells excavated at Beersheba, Lachish, and Ein Rogel in Jerusalem's Kidron Valley are as deep as 150 feet or more.

Since water was the lifeblood of towns and cities, protecting the source was a serious matter. It is possible to survive for extended periods of time without food, but only a few days without water. Knowing this, invading armies would move quickly to attempt to deprive the inhabitants of a besieged city of their water supply. By the same token, careful measures were taken to prevent a source of water from falling into enemy hands.

Archaeologists have uncovered some rather impressive efforts to safeguard ancient springs. At Megiddo in the plain of Jezreel, the opening to the spring was concealed, and a 225-foot-long tunnel was carved 100 feet under the surface, diverting the water to within the city walls. Similarly, in Jerusalem during the eighth century B.C., King Hezekiah had a 1,700-foot-long tunnel carved deep underground to bring water into the city. Visitors to these sites can walk through the excavated tunnels today.

After the Roman Empire extended its power to Israel, aqueducts were used to supply water to cities and important fortresses. Along the Mediterranean, an impressive system of aqueducts supplied the city of Caesarea for many centuries. The aqueducts extend ten miles to the foot of Mount Carmel, where a channel tunnels through the bedrock for another six miles to reach the springs. These aqueducts, designed to govern the rate of decline at one meter per 1,000, were truly a remarkable feat of engineering.

Jerusalem has always had a water problem, there being no springs within the ancient city walls. The one spring outside its walls—the Gihon Spring—was not sufficient to provide for the expanding population. The shortage became acute when King Herod, who ruled Palestine from 37 B.C. to 4 B.C., embarked upon an ambitious building program in Jerusalem intended to placate his Jewish subjects and serve as a lasting memorial to himself.

The central structure of Herod's Jerusalem was the massive Temple—called "Herod's Temple" or the "Second Temple," constructed as a grand replacement to the original temple built some 1,000 years earlier by Solomon. The huge numbers of animal sacrifices performed there on a daily basis required vast amounts of water, used to carry off blood and other remains to the adjoining Kidron Valley.

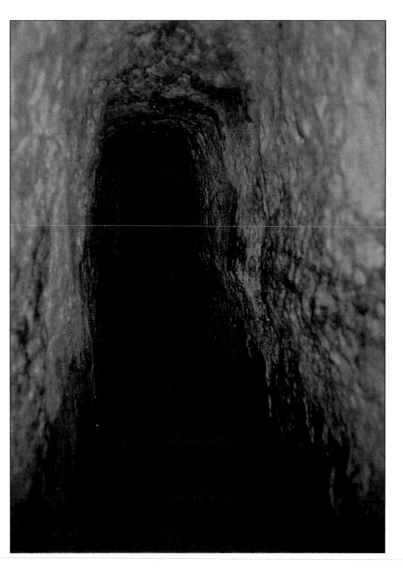

Herod's architects faced a difficulty. Where was all this water going to come from? The difficulty was solved with typical Roman ingenuity. Through a complex system of dams, reservoirs, aqueducts, and underground channels, water was ≈

Water still flows through one of the most famous ancient water systems found in Israel, the 1,750-foot-long Hezekiah's Tunnel carved underneath the City of David.

brought from springs in the hill country near Hebron, 20 miles to the south.

This impressive water system—parts of which continued functioning until as recently as the nineteenth century—had many ingenious features. A network of dams and underground channels funneled the water from miles around to three enormous interconnected reservoirs, known today (erroneously) as "Solomon's Pools." These reservoirs collected the water and fed it to the aqueduct.

At Bethlehem, the aqueduct entered a channel cut underneath the hill on which the town was built. Constructed of hollowed blocks of limestone, it worked like a huge siphon to bring water across a valley. After tunneling through yet another hill, the aqueduct reached Jerusalem, where it was diverted to the Temple and other principal buildings.

Obviously, such an aqueduct could not extend to every building in the city. Ordinary homes in Jerusalem depended on private underground reservoirs, or cisterns, for much of

their water supply. As late as the nineteenth century, municipal ordinances in Jerusalem required that every house have one. This was to ensure that all citizens did their part to contribute to the overall water supply of the city.

During the rainy season, water from the roofs of homes, and often from the streets as well, was diverted into the cisterns, where it was drawn upon throughout the year. Unfortunately, health hazards arose because refuse from the streets would wash into the cisterns along with the rainwater. It was in one such unused cistern in ancient Jerusalem that the prophet Jeremiah was imprisoned by Malchijah, King Zedekiah's son.

In the Old Testament Book of Jeremiah, pagan gods are likened to broken cisterns that cannot hold water. Given the importance of cisterns for providing life-sustaining water in the desert lands of the ancient world, the symbolism is clear: In the same way that depending upon a leaky cistern could prove to be a fateful mistake, it is folly to put one's trust in anyone but the true God.

THE KINGDOM IS DIVIDED

The Moabite Version of a Biblical Story

An extraordinary inscription on the so-called Moabite Stone sheds light on a little known corner of biblical history.

The inscription is the longest monumental record found in Palestine. It begins with the introduction: "I am Mesha, son of Chemosh[it], king of Moab, the Dibonite."

Mesha was a contemporary of Jehoshaphat (872–848 B.C.), king of the southern kingdom of Judah, and Jehoram (852–841 B.C.), king of the northern kingdom of Israel.

Mesha ruled the kingdom of Moab, east of the Dead Sea. He is mentioned in only one biblical text, 2 Kings 3, where after the death of Ahab he revolts against his successor Jehoram.

Attacking Mesha's forces from the south, Jehoram joined Jehoshaphat and the king of Edom in putting down the revolt. The Moabite forces were routed, and many towns were destroyed as the grip closed around Mesha's remaining forces. When he saw that he was surrounded, Mesha sacrificed his firstborn son to the Moabite god Chemosh, causing the Israelites to withdraw.

The revolt must have taken place between 852 and 848 B.C., when both Jehoram and Jehoshaphat were ruling. Mesha recorded his version of the same event on a stone slab measuring three feet high and two feet wide. Unfortunately, this stela was smashed by Bedouins when they realized its value to Western archaeologists; they reasoned that they could sell the pieces for a greater price than they could get for the whole. Fortunately, an imprint of the inscription had been made, and most of the pieces were eventually recovered.

The message it bears is written in the Moabite language, which is almost identical to Hebrew, and consists of 34 lines. The inscription gives Mesha's version of events, being careful to sidestep the matter of his defeat at the hands of Jehoram, Jehoshaphat, and the king of Edom. Mesha's version describes a successful revolt and the recapturing of Moabite territory, being careful to give credit to Chemosh, the national god of Moab.

The inscription also avoids mention of Jehoram's successful attack from the south. Instead, it tells of the conquest of

The famous Moabite Stone, dated to the ninth century B.C., was restored by archaeologists after having been smashed by Bedouins who intended to sell it in pieces.

The restored Ishtar Gate of the ancient city of Babylon, originally built by Nebuchadnezzar II, who ruled from 604 to 562 B.C.

the town of Nebo and the spoils of war Mesha acquired, including the "altar-hearths of Yahweh." Here is the earliest mention of Yahweh, the god of the Israelites, outside the Bible. The name of the Moabite god Chemosh appears on the inscription eleven times.

The Moabite Stone also states: "And I built...the temple of Baal Meon, and I established there...the sheep of the land." The mention of sheep refers to the primary occupation of the Moabites, which is also mentioned in the biblical text: "Now King Mesha of Moab was a sheep breeder, who used to deliver to the king of Israel one hundred thousand rams" (2 Kings 3:4).

Mad About Idols

*I*n the Book of Jeremiah (50:35–36, 38), we read a harsh denunciation of Babylon and a prediction of its doom because of its obsession with the worship of false gods:

> *"A sword against the Chaldeans, says the Lord,*
> *and against the inhabitants of Babylon,*
> *and against her officials and her sages!*
> *A sword against the diviners,*
> *so that they may become fools!*
> *A sword against her warriors,*
> *so they may be destroyed!...*
> *A drought against her waters,*
> *that they may be dried up!*
> *For it is a land of images,*
> *and they go mad over idols."*

Archaeology confirms the worship of idols in Babylon. In 605 B.C., Nebuchadnezzar became king of the city, reigning for 43 years. Rather than boast about his prowess on the battlefield, as did the militant Assyrians before him, Nebuchadnezzar preferred instead to record the numerous temples that he had built during his lengthy rule.

The city's patron god, Marduk, who is identified as Bel in the Bible, is condemned by God speaking through the prophet Jeremiah: "I will punish Bel in Babylon, and make him disgorge what he has swallowed. The nations shall no longer stream to him; the wall of Babylon has fallen" (Jeremiah 51:44).

Babylon was the largest and one of the most important cities of ancient Mesopotamia. In classical times, the massive walls of the city and its renowned Hanging Gardens were listed among the Seven Wonders of the Ancient World. The Greek historian Herodotus reportedly visited the city in 460 B.C., claiming that it "surpasses in splendor any city of the known world."

Inside the massive walls were more than a thousand temples and religious structures that served a population of nearly 100,000. One ancient inscription provides the details: "Altogether there are in Babylon 53 temples of the chief gods, 55 chapels of Marduk, 300 chapels of earthly deities, 600 for the heavenly deities, 180 altars for the goddess Ishtar, 180 for the gods Nergal and Adad, and 12 other altars for different gods."

The most prominent temple in Babylon was Esagila ("the temple that raises its head"), in which dwelled Marduk himself, according to popular belief. The huge temple enclosure contained at least 50 shrines. Excavators found more than 6,000 figures and figurines at the site, attesting to Jeremiah's comment that the city was "mad over idols."

Next to Esagila was the great ziggurat named Etemenanki ("the foundation house of heaven and earth"). Thought to be similar to the biblical Tower of Babel, the stepped, pyramid-shaped temple was nearly 300 feet square at its base and rose to a height of nearly 300 feet.

So confident were the Babylonians of their fortifications that they named the city's famous processional way Aibur-shabu, which means "the enemy shall never pass here." The city was surrounded by three massive concentric walls as much as 11 miles in circumference. The space between them was wide enough for Herodotus' four-horse chariot to turn around without difficulty. As an added security precaution, the outermost wall formed the scarp of a moat that was up to 330 feet wide.

However, the mighty kingdom of Babylon gradually entered a period of internal decline. Despite its elaborate defensive fortifications, the city was captured without a struggle in 539 B.C. by the Persians under Cyrus the Great. This defeat finally ended Babylon's dominant role in the ancient Near East.

The city was still impressive in the days of Herodotus, and more than a century later, in 323 B.C., Alexander the Great was sufficiently enchanted with Babylon to embark upon an ambitious scheme to restore the city to its former glory. Those plans were cut short, however, when Alexander succumbed to fever in the city that same year, thus sealing its fate with his demise. By 200 B.C., Babylon lay deserted.

Sacrifice on the City Wall

The Book of 2 Kings relates a baffling incident in the story of the revolt of King Mesha of Moab against an alliance led by King Jehoram of Israel.

When the battle went against Mesha, we read: "Then he took his firstborn son who was to succeed him, and offered him as a burnt offering on the wall. And great wrath came upon Israel, so they withdrew from him and returned to their own land" (2 Kings 3:27).

The act of sacrificing his own son, the crown prince, on the walls of the city apparently achieved what Mesha intended. The Israelite forces withdrew, and for the next two centuries Moab remained independent.

Scholars have been at a loss to explain what to the modern mind is a shocking action the part of King Mesha. Recent discoveries, however, have shed light on the religious and cultural atmosphere in which the sacrifice of Mesha's son took place.

A cuneiform tablet from the city of Ugarit in Syria reveals that Mesha's sacrifice of his son was not unique. Such actions were considered religious acts, intended to obtain the protection of the Canaanite god Baal.

The Ugaritic text states that, when an enemy force attacks the walls of the city, the following promise is to be made to Baal: "We shall sacrifice a bull to thee, O Baal, A votive-pledge we shall fulfill: A firstborn, Baal, we shall sacrifice,

A child we shall fulfill . . ." The text then promises that Baal will subsequently answer the prayers of the inhabitants of the city and drive the enemy forces away.

The Phoenicians, who also worshipped Baal, founded Carthage in North Africa. Writing around 50 B.C., Roman historian Diodorus describes a military campaign that went against the Carthaginians. He relates that, when they saw the enemy besieging the walls of their city, "they selected two hundred of the noblest children and sacrificed them publicly."

Another Roman historian, Rufus, reports that a similar incident occurred when Alexander the Great was besieging the Phoenician city of Tyre. It was suggested that a freeborn boy be sacrificed, but the elders of the city opposed the idea. Despite such exceptions, Phoenician historian Sanchuniaton attests to the practice of sacrificing children to appease their god in times of danger or distress.

The biblical story simply relates that, upon seeing Mesha's sacrificed son, "great wrath came upon Israel, so they withdrew from him and returned to their own country" (2 Kings 3:27). The "great wrath" can be understood to mean a traumatic response, in this case as a result of witnessing the act of human sacrifice. In all likelihood, the Israelites were so sickened by the sight that they no longer had the will to fight.

The Israelite alliance that came against Moab was likely not the first army to be turned away by the sight of persons—often children—being sacrificed. The Ugaritic text, in offering assurances that the ploy would work, apparently was based on experience.

The biblical story of King Mesha sacrificing his son illuminates the sharply contrasted ethical standards of Israelite and Canaanite religions.

OLD TESTAMENT: POETIC BOOKS

Serving to enrich the spirit and inspire the search for divine wisdom, the Poetic Books—Job, Psalms, Proverbs, Ecclesiastes, and the Song of Solomon—are a fascinating collection of lyrics, hymns, stories, and sayings. Beautifully written and filled with meaning, they provide religious and moral instruction as they raise issues about good and evil, address human weakness and suffering, and discuss the nature of love in both its divine and earthly forms.

The legendary King Solomon in all his splendor as depicted in Southwark Cathedral in London.

ANCIENT WISDOM, TIMELESS VERSE

The Mystery of Evil

*I*n the first chapter of the Book of Job, a confrontation takes place in the realm of Heaven between God and Satan.

We read that "one day the heavenly beings came to present themselves before the Lord, and Satan also came among them" (Job 1:6). A dispute arises regarding the character of righteous Job, which leads to his profound trial by fire as described in the book.

"Satan" is the English transliteration of a Hebrew word meaning "adversary." In the New Testament, Satan is called "the accuser of our comrades" (Revelation 12:10).

In the Old Testament, the name Satan occurs in 14 passages, most of them in Job. It may seem inexplicable that Satan would be present at the very throne of God. However, he is also found there in Zechariah's heavenly vision, where he observes "the high priest Joshua standing before the angel of the Lord, and Satan standing at his right hand to accuse him" (Zechariah 3:1).

Even in the Bible, the origins of Satan are shrouded in mystery. We know nothing directly of his beginnings. However, two Old Testament passages, Isaiah 14 and Ezekiel 28, are thought by some to speak cryptically of the Prince of Darkness.

The primary subject of Ezekiel 28 is a prophecy against the king of Tyre. However, a portion of the prophecy appears to transcend any earthly ruler to describe a magnificent being who sinned and was cast from heaven:

"Thus says the Lord God: You were the signet of perfection, full of wisdom and perfect in beauty.

"You were in Eden, the garden of God; every precious stone was your covering.... On the day that you were created they were prepared.

"With an anointed cherub as guardian I placed you; you were on the holy mountain of God; you walked among the stones of fire.

"You were blameless in your ways from the day that you were created, until iniquity was found in you...so I cast you as a profane thing from the mountain of God, and the guardian cherub drove you out from among the stones of fire"

(Ezekiel 28:12–16).

If this passage is taken to refer to Satan, we learn that he was an extraordinary creation of God who occupied an exalted place on the "holy mountain of God." But at some point—the Bible gives no indication when—Satan became corrupted by the desire for greater glory, as the prophecy explains: "Your heart was proud because of your beauty; you corrupted your wisdom for the sake of your splendor. [Therefore] I cast you to the ground..." (Ezekiel 28:17).

We find another description of a cosmic fall from Heaven in chapter 14 of the Book of Isaiah, which begins as a prophecy against a human ruler, the king of Babylon. But as the prophecy progresses, the prophet's condemnation takes a different tone:

> *"How you are fallen from heaven, O Day Star, son of Dawn! How you are cut down to the ground, you who laid the nations low!*
>
> *"You said in your heart, 'I will ascend to heaven; I will raise my throne above the stars of God; I will sit on the mount of assembly on the heights of Zaphon; I will ascend to the tops of the clouds, I will make myself like the Most High.'*
>
> *"But you are brought down to Sheol, to the depths of the Pit"*
>
> (Isaiah 14:12–15).

The name "O Day Star" was translated into Latin as "Lucifer," which became a synonym for Satan.

When Satan was cast down from Heaven he did not go alone. The Bible speaks of Satan's minions, known as fallen angels and demonic spir-

This unattributed Flemish work attempts to capture the sinister, predatory nature of evil, depicting the Devil as a half-human and half-beast demon.

its, who evidently allied themselves with Satan and fell with him. A passage in the Book of Revelation (12:3) describes a "great red dragon," which from the context is Satan. We read: "His tail swept down a third of the stars of heaven and threw them to the earth..." (Revelation 12:4).

Some take this reference to "a third of the stars" being cast down to mean the number of angels who joined Satan's unsuccessful rebellion. Their fate is described in the Book of Jude: "And the angels who did not keep their own position, but left their proper dwelling, he has kept in eternal chains in deepest darkness for the judgment of the great Day" (Jude 6).

According to the Book of Revelation, the leader of the rebel angels is destined to join them in suffering: "And the devil who had deceived them was thrown into the lake of fire and sulfur, where the beast and the false prophet were, and they will be tormented day and night forever and ever" (Revelation 20:10).

The Preacher

The Book of Ecclesiastes, which derives its name from the Hebrew word meaning the "preacher" or "teacher," exhibits a certain pessimism and cynicism.

The writer identifies himself as ruling in Jerusalem and having "acquired great wisdom, surpassing all who were over Jerusalem before me" (Ecclesiastes 1:16), and has thus been traditionally identified as Solomon.

At the beginning of his book, the preacher states his stark view of reality: "Vanity of vanities, says the Teacher, vanity of vanities! All is vanity. What do people gain from all the toil at which they toil under the sun? A generation goes, and a generation comes, but the earth remains forever" (Ecclesiastes 1:2–4).

We follow the preacher as he seeks fulfillment through ever-greater possessions, through wisdom and knowledge, and through various pleasures. In the end, he realizes none can bring the happiness he seeks, and
he rejects them for the virtue of simplicity: "There is nothing better for mortals than to eat and drink, and find enjoyment in their toil. This also, I saw, is from the hand of God" (Ecclesiastes 2:24).

The preacher also laments the injustices he sees in the world around him: "Again I saw all the oppressions that are practiced under the sun. Look, the tears of the oppressed—with no one to comfort them!... And I thought the dead, who have already died, more fortunate than the living, who are still alive; but better than both is the one who has not yet been, and has not seen the evil deeds that are done under the sun" (Ecclesiastes 4:3).

This deep pessimism toward life has led some to question whether Ecclesiastes belonged in the canon of Sacred Scripture. However, the purpose of the writer may be to present the futility of life when lived without reference to God. In this he is entirely orthodox. He also wrestles candidly with the injustices of life, but without losing sight of the inevitable justice of God.

Satan and his demons are never presented in the Bible as the equals of God. They are created beings with considerable powers who were given the opportunity to rebel. In the end, there will be a complete and final defeat of the forces of evil, as promised by the Apostle Paul: "The God of peace will shortly crush Satan under your feet" (Romans 16:20).

Mythical Monsters?

*T*wo fearsome creatures that live in or near water are mentioned in the Bible and are used as object lessons to demonstrate the power and majesty of God.

The first of these is described by the Lord in the Book of Job: "Look at Behemoth, which I made just as I made you; it eats grass like an ox. Its strength is in its loins, and its power in the muscles of its belly. It makes its tail stiff like a cedar; the sinews of its thighs are knit together. Its bones are tubes of bronze, its limbs like bars of iron" (Job 40:15–18).

The reference to its "tail stiff as a cedar" has caused some to suggest that a crocodile is being described here, a view supported by the fact that Behemoth is a water animal: "Even if the river is turbulent, it is not frightened; it is confident though Jordan rushes against its mouth" (Job 40:23).

The crocodile, however, does not eat grass like an ox, leading to the suggestion that the biblical description is that of

Medieval depiction of a multiheaded beast. Many of the monsters and other mythical creatures described in the Bible are used to demonstrate God's power and his authority over the earth.

a hippopotamus. Although a hippo can give the impression of serenity—"under the lotus plants it lies"—it is an immensely powerful and dangerous animal.

We are told that Behemoth is "the first of the great acts of God—only its Maker can approach it with the sword" (Job 40:19). To this day, the hippopotamus kills more humans in Africa each year than any other animal.

More mysterious is the creature described in the Book of Isaiah, where we read that the Lord will punish "Leviathan the fleeing serpent, Leviathan the twisting serpent, and he will kill the dragon that is in the sea" (Isaiah 27:1).

In the ancient Near East, Leviathan appears as a great sea monster who battles the Canaanites' most significant god, Baal. Symbolizing chaos, Leviathan was the enemy of all order in the universe.

The grave threat this would have posed to the ancients cannot be overestimated. As farmers, they depended for their survival upon the regularity of the seasons, and any disruption in the weather could be life-threatening. Droughts, floods, and other natural disasters were attributed to the forces of chaos.

The Book of Psalms (74:13–14) expresses confidence in the all-surpassing power of the Lord: "You divided the sea by your might; you broke the heads of the dragons in the waters. You crushed the heads of Leviathan; you gave him as food for the creatures of the wilderness."

Some scholars have identified Leviathan, like Behemoth, as being a giant crocodile, a creature known not only in Egypt, but also, in former times, found along the marshy coast of Palestine. Others suggest that Leviathan may be some unknown aquatic animal that is extinct or, as Scotland's Loch Ness Monster is alleged to be, still dwelling somewhere in the deep.

Mistaking the Obvious

Perhaps embarrassed by the unrestrained eroticism in the text, scholars throughout the centuries have sought to discern the true meaning of the Song of Songs, known in some translations as the Song of Solomon.

In a world in which women were expected to be quiet and subject to men, and in Scripture, where women normally do not speak except through the mediated voice of a male narrator or author, the words of the female lover are notable. This said, she speaks in a manner that is nothing less than stunning: "Let him kiss me with the kisses of his mouth!" (SS1:2).

By chapter 7, it is clear that this is not like other books of Scripture: "Your navel is a rounded bowl that never lacks mixed wine. Your belly is a heap of wheat, encircled with lilies. Your two breasts are like two fawns, twins of a gazelle" (SS 7:2–3).

One immediately notices that the metaphors and similes used do not necessarily translate all that well into a different culture. In fact, much of the eroticism simply is lost in the English translation.

King Solomon had "seven hundred wives, princesses, and three hundred concubines" (1 Kings 11:1), making him uniquely qualified to speak on the subject of erotic love as found in the Song of Solomon.

Inept Editor or Profound Truth?

The Book of Ecclesiastes has been questioned because of its alleged contradictions. On the one hand, the author states: "And I thought the dead, who have already died, more fortunate than the living, who are still alive" (Ecclesiastes 4:2) only to seemingly reverse himself by admitting that "whoever is joined with all the living has hope, for a living dog is better than a dead lion" (Ecclesiastes 9:4).

Such apposition—the setting forth of two extremes to bring out the truths of each—is a recognized feature of Hebrew verse. In the Book of Proverbs, for example, we read: "Do not answer fools according to their folly, or you will be a fool yourself" (Proverbs 26:4), only to be followed in the next verse by: "Answer fools according to their folly, or they will be wise in their own eyes" (Proverbs 26:5).

This is not, as some have suggested, evidence of ineptness on the part of a biblical editor who, it is presumed, should have known better than to put contradictory statements side by side. Far from it. The Hebrew mind was quite familiar with this literary device, in which the writer expresses a deeper truth that acknowledges both statements but transcends each of them.

In the illustration from Proverbs, then, the meaning could be expressed as: *There are times when it is better not to* answer fools according to their folly. *However, there are also times when one should* answer fools according to their folly, or they will be wise in their eyes.

Similarly then, we might rephrase the statements of the preacher as: I have thought that *there are times when it appears that* the dead are more fortunate than the living. *However* [after further discussion], *in the final analysis,* whoever is joined to the living still has hope.

The writer is not named in the text, but has been traditionally identified as Solomon. The book, which is a collection of love poems, has been a source of inspiration for untold melodies and songs throughout the centuries.

If it weren't troubling enough that the Song of Solomon was controversial because of its sexual nature, it should also be noted that this writing does not mention God, has no theology or moral lesson, and does not even have a nationalistic emphasis.

From the beginning, Bible scholars approached this book with mixed emotions. Some saw it as a love story between a young woman and a young man, some as a story about a woman in King Solomon's harem who pines for her lost love, a shepherd. Some even suggested that it was ancient drama. In fact, the Song of Solomon was among the last of the biblical writings to be accepted as Scripture.

The rabbis saw the book as an expression of the love of God for his people, the Israelites. Indeed, prophets often depicted the relationship between the Lord and his chosen people in terms of a marriage. Speaking through the prophet Hosea, the Lord says: "And I will take you for my wife forever; I will take you for my wife in righteousness and in justice, in steadfast love, and in mercy" (Hosea 2:19).

Replying to those who argued against including the book in the Hebrew canon, a prominent rabbi affirmed: "The whole world is not worth the day on which the Song of Songs was given to Israel; all the Writings are holy, but the Song of Songs is the holy of holies."

The Fathers of the Church focused on the "spiritual" sense of the text to the exclusion of the literal. One expressed view, that the book celebrated Solomon's marriage to an Egyptian princess, was condemned by the Second Council of Constantinople in A.D. 553. For well over a thousand years, the spiritual interpretation of the "Song of Songs" prevailed.

The modern period has brought a variety of interpretations to the text. One theory is that the Song of Songs is a Hebrew adaptation of the liturgy of ancient pagan fertility rites, as well as Mesopotamian and Egyptian wedding songs.

Others admit a literal meaning, but deny that Solomon is the lover in the poems. They view it as a drama between the Shulammite maid and her shepherd lover as they resist Solomon's attempt to make the girl yet another addition to his harem.

Still others believe it simpler and more enlightening to view the Song of Solomon as love poems between two people. The emphasis on the erotic, they believe, is the rightful celebration of God's gift of bodily love between man and woman.

In any case, the literal interpretation of the book Song of Songs, which most scholars adopt today, still does not prevent a deeper level of meaning, such as the intense and loving relationship between God and his people.

OLD TESTAMENT: PROPHETIC BOOKS

The books of the prophets—Isaiah, Jeremiah, Lamentations, Ezekiel, Daniel, Hosea, Joel, Amos, Obadiah, Jonah, Micah, Nahum, Habakkuk, Zephaniah, Haggai, Zechariah, and Malachi—admonish those who have lost or abandoned their faith, presenting sobering visions of the inevitable consequences of sin. For those who remain true to God and live by his teachings, they provide hope for the future with the promise of redemption and a permanent place in the province of the divine.

A stained-glass rendition of the prophet Daniel in the lions' den, from St. Helena's Church in Minneapolis, Minnesota.

A PROPHETIC VOICE IN ISRAEL

Confrontation on Mount Carmel

Trouble visited the kingdom of Israel when King Ahab married a Sidonian princess by the name of Jezebel. The meaning of her name, "Baal is the prince," foreshadows the fierce struggle that her reign would initiate between the god Baal and Yahweh, the God of the Israelites.

Jezebel sought to replace the prophets in Israel with prophets of Baal and his consort Asherah. Baal, whose name means "lord" or "owner," was the supreme deity of Canaan and was worshiped by the Phoenicians, the Philistines, and other peoples of the region. Hence the various derivatives of Baal mentioned in the Bible, including the Philistine Baal-Zebub, or "lord of the flies" (or "lord of the prince"); the Moabite Baal-Meon, or "lord of the residence"; and Baal-Gad, "the lord of Gad" of Lebanon.

Baal was a storm-god who was believed to send the rains in their seasons. His entourage included rain clouds, and lightning was his weapon.

A miniature statue of the Canaanite/ Phoenician deity Baal, the god of storms and thunder. He was also a god of fertility.

Baal worship proved to be a great temptation in the water-poor land of Israel. Unlike the great river cultures of Egypt to the south and Mesopotamia to the east, Israel had no constant supply of water and was thus dependent upon the winter rains to sustain its crops.

In return for supplying rain, Baal was thought to demand submission in the form of human sacrifice. In the Bible, this form of sacrifice is termed "to pass through the fire." As the phrase suggests, the victims were burned alive, and such sacrifice was given as a primary cause for the fall of the kingdom of Israel: "They made their sons and their daughters pass through fire; they used divination and augury; and they sold themselves to do evil in the sight of the Lord" (2 Kings 17:17).

The degradation that Baal worship threatened to bring upon Israel prompted the prophet Elijah to force a confrontation with the prophets of Baal. Elijah challenged King Ahab, Jezebel's husband, to assemble on Mount Carmel "the four hundred fifty prophets of Baal and the four hundred prophets of Asherah, who eat at Jezebel's table" (1 Kings 18:19).

Despite the odds, Elijah confidently proclaimed to all those present: "How long will you go limping with two different opinions? If the Lord is God, follow him; but if Baal, then follow him" (1 Kings 18:21). The people, however, "did not answer him a word."

Undeterred, Elijah ordered that an altar be built, after which the prophets of Baal would call upon their god to send down fire to consume the bull that had been sacrificed upon it. This would seem to be a reasonable request to make of a god who was depicted with a lightning bolt in his clenched fist. We read that the prophets of Baal danced around the altar crying, "O Baal, answer us!" to no avail. At noon, Elijah could not resist mocking them: "Cry aloud! Surely he is a god; either he is meditating, or he has wandered away, or he is on a journey, or perhaps he is asleep and must be awakened" (1 Kings 18:27).

The earthiness of Elijah's mockery is lost in the English translation. The

This painting, "Elijah Dwelleth in a Cave" by James J. Tissot, portrays the prophet who played a pivotal role in the confrontation on Mount Carmel.

Window to the Future

Perhaps no passages in Scripture are more mysterious than those that speak about the future. The Book of Amos tells us that "surely the Lord God does nothing, without revealing his secret to his servants the prophets" (Amos 3:7).

A biblical prophet was one who represented God among men, just as his counterpart, the priest, represented man before God. The Book of 1 Peter gives the source of prophetic inspiration: "No prophecy ever came by human will, but men and women moved by the Holy Spirit spoke from God" (2 Peter 1:21).

So why are there so many conflicting interpretations of the prophetic passages in the Bible? One reason is the nature of prophecy, called "apocalyptic literature" by scholars. Although speaking about the future, apocalyptic literature uses symbolism that is rooted in the history and culture of the time in which it was written.

The Book of Daniel and Book of Revelation are the only books in the Bible that are entirely apocalyptic.

Portions of Joel, Amos, Zechariah, and Isaiah are also apocalyptic. In these books, we read startling descriptions of many-headed beasts, mythical monsters, and strange visions.

Typically, the prophecies speak about a time of great trouble, which will come before the ultimate victory of God over the forces of evil. They encourage a suffering people to remain faithful to God and to continue to hope for his promised coming.

This may be the key to understanding why, despite countless attempts at interpretation, the prophetic symbolism defies easy explanation. At the end of the Book of Daniel, the prophet is told by the Lord: "Go your way, Daniel, for the words are to remain secret and sealed until the time of the end" (Daniel 12:9).

That may explain why there have been so many conflicting interpretations of prophetic symbolism through the years, as those who are not meant to know the true meaning seek in vain to discover it.

---

phrase "(perhaps) he has wandered away" is in Hebrew a euphemism for stepping aside to a private place to relieve oneself. This enraged the prophets of Baal, and they "raved on until the time of the offering of the oblation, but there was no voice, no answer, and no response" (1 Kings 18:29).

Elijah then offers a brief yet eloquent prayer to the Lord, after which we read that "the fire of the Lord fell and con-

sumed the burnt offering, the wood, the stones, and the dust, and even licked up the water that was in the trench" (1 Kings 18:38). The irony of the storm god Baal's failure to provide fire was made even more acute by his apparently being unable to prevent a three-year drought from coming to an end after Elijah's triumph: Elijah had predicted the drought (1 Kings 17:1–4), and he also predicted its end (1 Kings 18:41–45).

The Bible's Mysterious Hidden Codes

"Do not think that I have come to abolish the law or the prophets; I have come not to abolish but to fulfill. For truly I tell you, until heaven and earth pass away, not one letter, not one stroke of a letter, will pass from the law until all is accomplished" (Matthew 5:17–18). With these words Jesus established the enduring authority of the Old Testament—an authority extending to the very words and letters of the Bible's text.

Some scholars hold that the text of the Bible is "inspired" like any great piece of literature—that is, it is found to have an unusual meaning or significance to those who read it.

Others believe that the Bible was composed by men who wrote under divine supervision so that their very words conveyed exactly the meaning that God intended. In this view, the Bible is by nature a spiritual book.

Orthodox rabbis have been among those who have held this view of divine inspiration. For them, not merely every word but every letter of the Torah (the first five books of the Bible) was directly inspired by God.

Recent analysis by Israeli scholars using computers has resulted in some surprising conclusions that lend support to the orthodox rabbinic view of Scripture.

The researchers took the Hebrew text of the Book of Genesis and systematically studied sequences of letters looking for meaningful word combinations.

Incredibly, each of 300 selected word pairs were found to be in close proximity in the biblical text.

Related biblical names were also discovered in close proximity. To ensure that these results were not due to chance, the same search was performed on numerous random scramblings of the text of Genesis without success. The chances that the word pairs occurred purely by chance were calculated to be less than 1 in 50 quadrillion.

Was the information merely related to ancient times, or did the Book of Genesis have hidden knowledge related to other ages? To answer this fascinating question, the researchers took from standard reference works the names of 34 influential men from the ninth to the nineteenth century. Every one of the names was discovered, along with each one's date of birth or death.

With some still not persuaded, the researchers then applied the same search for equidistant letters to a Hebrew translation of Tolstoy's *War and Peace*. However, the word and date combinations did not appear in Tolstoy's text.

Critics and believers agree that there is no known explanation for this phenomenon. In addition, the hidden word combinations cannot be attributed to human ingenuity, for advanced computers are required to detect the information hidden in the letter sequences.

But what was the purpose of the mysterious encoding of information into the text? Could it have been proof of divine inspiration, intended especially for an age both of technology and of radical skepticism?

Coincidence or
Fulfilled Prophecy?

The Phoenicians were a seafaring people, and they controlled the lucrative trade routes in the Mediterranean and beyond. Psalm 45:12 describes the citizens of Tyre as "the richest of the people with all kinds of wealth."

However, along with the other peoples of the ancient Near East, the Phoenicians were idolaters who worshiped many gods. For hundreds of years, they also practiced infant sacrifice as a means of appeasing their gods and gaining their favor. Archaeologists have brought this dark side of Phoenician religion to light at their colonies at Carthage and other sites around the Mediterranean.

The practice was an abomination to the Lord, who foretold the destruction of the Phoenician city of Tyre through Ezekiel: "Therefore, thus says the Lord God: See, I am against you, O Tyre! I will hurl many nations against you, as the sea hurls its waves. They shall destroy the walls of Tyre and break down its towers. I will scrape its soil from it and make it a bare rock" (Ezekiel 26:3–4).

The reference to scraping the soil of Tyre is puzzling and occurs nowhere else in the Bible. A few verses later, another detail is added: "They will plunder your riches and loot your merchandise; they shall break down your walls and destroy your fine houses. Your stones and timber and soil they shall cast into the water" (Ezekiel 26:12).

The prophecy of Ezekiel indicates that Tyre would be utterly destroyed and that her ruins would be cast into the water. But why? While cities were routinely destroyed by invading armies in ancient times, the rubble was not thrown into the sea.

This prophecy appeared to make little sense—until the time of Alexander the Great. In 333 B.C., fresh from a decisive battle over the Persians in northern Syria, the 24-year-old Alexander was on his way south to Egypt. He met his first opposition at Tyre. The city had been moved to a heavily defended island in the Mediterranean, some two thousand feet offshore.

There, as the prophet Zechariah writes, the inhabitants thought they occupied an impregnable position: "Tyre has built itself a rampart, and heaped up silver like dust, and gold like the dirt of the streets. But now, the Lord will strip it of its possessions and hurl its wealth into the sea, and it shall be devoured by fire" (Zechariah 9:3–4).

Alexander fulfilled this prophecy when he built a causeway from the mainland to the island. He obtained the material for this massive causeway by literally scraping away the ruins of the original city on the shore.

Observing the high walls of the island fortress, Alexander devised yet another innovation. His engineers designed massive movable towers that held bowmen and light artillery. These towers soared as high as 160 feet over the tallest defensive walls of Tyre and were the largest siege machines ever used in ancient warfare.

After seven months, the towers were completed and pushed across the causeway towards the terrified inhabitants of the city. Bowmen inside were able to quickly gain the advantage

Alexander the Great (356–323 B.C.) was one of the greatest military leaders of all time. He began his conquests with the defeat of Persia, followed by Anatolia, the eastern Mediterranean, Egypt, and Mesopotamia.

by firing down upon the hapless defenders. A drawbridge on the front enabled detachments of soldiers to climb out atop the city walls.

It was in anticipation of just such an unusual fulfillment of his prophecy that Ezekiel wrote: "In their wailing they raise a lamentation for you, and lament over you: 'Who was ever destroyed like Tyre in the midst of the sea?'" (Ezekiel 27:32).

The Great and Terrible Day

The religions of the nations surrounding the Israelites viewed time as cyclical. In their view, the events of life eternally repeated themselves.

The Hebrews, on the other hand, viewed time as linear. It began with Creation and moves toward its consummation, a time when God will execute judgment upon the unrighteous.

The prophet Joel announced the coming of a terrifying day: "Blow the trumpet in Zion; sound the alarm on my holy mountain! Let all the inhabitants of the land tremble, for the day of the Lord is coming, it is near—a day of darkness and gloom, a day of clouds and thick darkness! Like blackness spread upon the mountains a great and powerful army comes; their like has never been from of old, nor will be again after them in ages to come" (Joel 2:1–2).

The "day of the Lord" that Joel speaks of here transpired with the destruction of Jerusalem in 586 B.C. The army

mentioned belongs to Babylonia, which soon after the prophecy of Joel captured Jerusalem and sent its inhabitants into exile.

However, as the description of the day of the Lord continues, it is apparent that an even more ominous event is also in mind: "The Lord utters his voice at the head of his army; how vast is his host! Numberless are those who obey his command. Truly the day of the Lord is great; terrible indeed—who can endure it?" (Joel 2:11).

What is Joel talking about in this dramatic passage? Obviously, the Lord did not intervene in the destruction of Jerusalem. We also read that "the sun shall be turned to darkness, and the moon to blood, before the great and terrible day of the Lord comes" (Joel 2:31). There is no record of such signs in the heaven at the destruction of Jerusalem.

This detail by Hans Memling depicts the Last Judgment, which, according to the Bible, is to take place after unprecedented trouble and dramatic signs in the heavens.

The answer to this puzzle is that Joel's use of the term "day of the Lord" has what is called a "dual reference." It is a prophecy that refers both to an event that will soon take place in history and to an event still far away in the future.

This becomes clear in the Book of Zephaniah, where the day of the Lord takes on cataclysmic proportions: "Neither their silver nor their gold will be able to save them on the day of the Lord's wrath; in the fire of his passion the whole earth shall be consumed; for a full, a terrible end he will make of all the inhabitants of the earth" (Zephaniah 1:18).

In Zephaniah, the day of the Lord extends beyond Judah to "all the inhabitants of the earth" and involves the burning of the earth itself.

The New Testament Book of 2 Peter also describes this worldwide destruction: "But the day of the Lord will come like a thief, and then the heavens will pass away with a loud noise, and the elements will be dissolved with fire, and the earth and everything that is done on it will be disclosed" (2 Peter 3:10).

The New Testament doctrine of the resurrection of the body prior to the final judgment is not clearly seen in the Old Testament. There is, however, a mention of resurrection at the final judgment at the end of the Book of Daniel: "There shall be a time of anguish, such as has never occurred since nations first came into existence. But at that time your people shall be delivered, every-

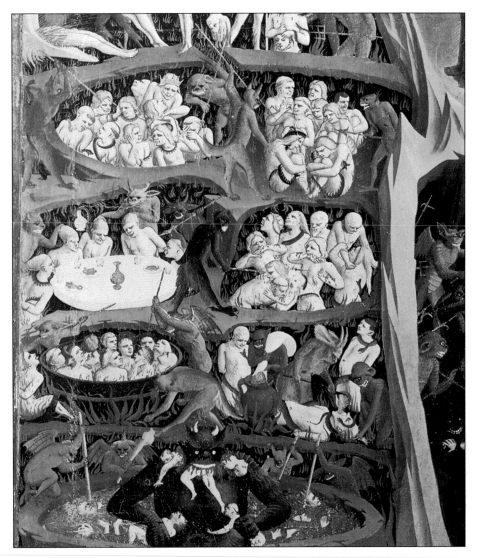

Medieval Italian artist Guido Di Pietro Angelico's rendition of the Last Judgment envisions descending levels of hellfire with the Devil occupying the lowest plane.

one who is found written in the book. Many of those who sleep in the dust of the earth shall awake, some to everlasting life, and some to shame and everlasting contempt" (Daniel 12:1–2).

Thus, according to the Bible, the day of the Lord will be preceded by a time of unprecedented trouble and will include dramatic signs in the heavens. There will be a general resurrection followed by judgment and the eternal Kingdom of God.

Certainly there can be no mistaking the admonition that is present in the biblical message: "Since all these things are to be dissolved in this way, what sort of persons ought you to be in leading lives of holiness and godliness…?" (2 Peter 3:11).

THE ASSYRIAN INVASION OF ISRAEL

The Assyrian Menace

The Assyrians were a fiercely militaristic people known for the cruelty of their predatory campaigns. Those who opposed the Assyrians suffered greatly, as was the tragic experience of Israel.

The earliest references to Assyria date to 2000 B.C., but it was not until the fourteenth century B.C. that Assyria emerged as a nation-state in what is now northern Iraq. The name of its capital and its national god was Ashur, from which is derived the name Assyria.

In the ninth century B.C., Assyria sent its armies beyond its borders in search of new conquests. Soon it threatened Israel and Judah. In 853, Assyrian king Shalmaneser marched against a coalition of 12 kings including Ahab of Israel. The battle was inconclusive, but in 841 Assyria was finally victorious. The Black Obelisk of Shalmaneser, found at Calah, shows King Jehu of Israel bowing before the Assyrian king.

Assyria entered a period of decline after Shalmaneser. For the next century, Israel, while required to pay tribute, found relative relief from the Assyrian menace. This hiatus came to an end with the ascension of Tiglath-pileser III to the throne in 744 B.C.

Tiglath-pileser III sought to tighten Assyria's grip on its conquered territories. In response, Israel and Aram-Damascus revolted, but were unsuccessful. Northern Israel was devastated, and a large part of its population was deported.

Around 725 B.C., Israel revolted again. The Assyrians smashed their rebellious subjects, bringing the end of the northern kingdom of Israel in 722 B.C. Assyrian records show that 27,290 of the surviving Israelites were deported, never to see their homeland again.

This bas-relief from Mesopotamia shows the horse in its common military role. Introduced into the Middle East during the second millennium B.C., the warhorse quickly proved its value on the battlefield.

kingdom of Judah, whose land would soon tremble underneath the marching armies of Assyria. Sennacherib's records claim that, before it was over, he destroyed 46 walled Judean cities and took some 200,000 prisoners.

Sennacherib would later glorify his capture of one of these cities, Lachish, in the walls of his palace at Nineveh, but Judah's capital, Jerusalem, would elude him. The Book of 2 Kings relates the story of how Sennacherib's armies were prevented by divine intervention from capturing Jerusalem. Hezekiah was the only ruler to survive Sennacherib's campaign and preserve both his throne and his kingdom.

However, Sennacherib was destined to die by the sword, murdered by his own sons in 681 B.C. After a brief period of expansion in the decades after Sennacherib, Assyria swiftly declined, falling to the Babylonians in 610 B.C.

For the next 20 years, Assyria was beset by widespread revolt elsewhere in the empire, but in 701 a new ruler, Sennacherib, secured the empire and turned his attention westward. Facing the threat was King Hezekiah of the southern

The Assyrian kings left unusually well-documented records of their military exploits, which were often supplemented by vivid pictorial reliefs sculpted into the walls of their palaces. These reliefs reveal an almost unimaginable savagery against conquered foes. One horrible but common punishment depicted by the reliefs was the flaying, or skinning alive, of captives. Impalings on stakes, the cutting off of hands and feet, and the ripping out of tongues were common punishments as well.

The depths of the Assyrian cruelty have caused some to question the historical accuracy of the depictions. After all, such records—whether in Assyrian or other ancient Near Eastern lands—were not intended as an accurate version of events, but rather to present the king in a favorable light. We never, for example, find representations of a defeated Assyrian army or king.

Still, the unabashed depiction of barbarism that is found throughout Assyrian history likely served a practical purpose, dissuading many a potential revolt in its conquered lands.

What Decimated Sennacherib's Army?

*B*oth Assyrian records and the Bible attest to a terrible catastrophe that devastated Sennacherib's army as it besieged Jerusalem in 701 B.C. A hexagonal prism found at Nineveh gives the Assyrian account of the battle, which, curiously, makes no claim that the Judeans were defeated.

After stating that King Hezekiah was shut up in his royal city "like a bird in a cage," the account mentions only the tribute of 30 gold talents that Hezekiah was forced to pay. The same figure is given in the biblical account: "The king of Assyria demanded of King Hezekiah of Judah three hundred talents of silver and thirty talents of gold" (2 Kings 18:14).

What caused Sennacherib to withdraw just as he was poised to complete his conquest of Judea by taking Jerusalem? The

Bible records what happened when the invading army camped around the city: "That very night the angel of the Lord set out and struck down one hundred eighty-five thousand in the camp of the Assyrians; when morning dawned, they were all dead bodies. Then King Sennacherib of Assyria left, went home, and lived at Nineveh" (2 Kings 19:35–36).

The Assyrian army may have been struck with pestilence. This possibility finds some support in another biblical incident that occurred in Jerusalem in which a large number of people also died virtually overnight.

In the Book of 2 Samuel, we read about David's decision to undertake a census of all of Israel. This incurred the anger of the Lord, and David was ordered to choose one of three alternatives as punishment: three years of famine; three months of fleeing from his enemies; or three days of pestilence.

After years of hiding from Saul, David could not stand the thought of fleeing for his life again. A pestilence was sent, and in a matter of a day or two, 70,000 people were dead.

But the three days are not yet over, and the ravaging pestilence causes the Lord to take pity: "But when the angel stretched out his hand toward Jerusalem to destroy it, the Lord relented concerning the evil, and said to the angel who was bringing destruction among the people, 'It is enough; now stay your hand'" (2 Samuel 24:16).

In this text, a destroying angel is responsible for inflicting pestilence. Could the "angel" that slew 180,000 men of the Assyrian army also have been pestilence?

Defeated by a Bird in a Cage

In the Book of 2 Kings, we read about a remarkable incident that took place when Jerusalem, the capital city of Judah, was in the grip of a siege, encircled by the army of King Sennacherib of Assyria.

It seems that all hope is lost until the prophet Isaiah delivers a divine message to Hezekiah, the king of Judah: "Therefore this is what the Lord says concerning the king of Assyria: 'He will not enter this city or shoot an arrow here. He will not come before it with shield or build a siege ramp against it. By the way that he came he will return'" (2 Kings 19:32–33).

What happens next has been a mystery to Bible students as well as scholars. In 2 Kings 19:35–36 we learn that 180,000 Assyrian troops died mysteriously overnight—struck down by "the angel of the Lord"—forcing Sennachrib to withdraw from Jerusalem.

Could such an event have really happened? The answer to that question lay undisturbed for thousands of years under the sands of Mesopotamia in the ruins of the city of Nineveh. In the mid-nineteenth century, British archaeologist A. H. Layard uncovered a fabulous palace built by Sennacherib after his return from his failed campaign against Judah.

This relief illustrates the military prowess of the Assyrian army, and are similar to the "Lachish Reliefs."

In his annals, Sennacherib called this complex the "palace without a rival." It contained more than 70 halls and rooms, including one covered with reliefs depicting the siege of the Judean city of Lachish. This room was the central focus of the palace, and it is apparent that Sennacherib intended to draw attention to Lachish as the crowning military achievement of his career.

But why Lachish? Jerusalem was the capital; Lachish was only a frontier outpost. A further clue is found inscribed on an ancient hexagonal-shaped prism, on which Sennacherib boasts about conquering 46 walled cities of Judah. The capital city of Judah, however, is absent from this list. Sennacherib can only make the ambiguous claim to have "shut up Hezekiah in Jerusalem like a bird in a cage."

Was Sennacherib attempting to cover up his inability to conquer Jerusalem and to focus attention away from the capital city? In a final act of desecration, the depiction of his face on the Lachish reliefs was mutilated. Sennacherib's pretentious efforts to obscure the record of his campaign in Judah in 701 B.C. had finally come to nothing.

Greek historian Herodotus mentions an intriguing parallel to the biblical account of the Assyrian siege of Jerusalem. During the same period, Sennacherib's army also invaded the Land of the Nile. To the disappointment of the Egyptian ruler Sethos, his dispirited Egyptians refused to take to the field. Sethos went into the shrine of his god and pleaded for assistance. In the midst of his prayers, Sethos fell asleep and dreamed that, with divine help, the enemy would be defeated.

With restored confidence, the Egyptian ruler mustered those of his troops as would fight and marched to meet the Assyrians. As they took up their positions and prepared for battle, a miracle took place. Herodotus records that, during the night, hordes of field mice swarmed over the Assyrian soldiers and devoured their quivers, bowstrings, and leather handles on their shields. Their weapons rendered useless, Sennacherib's army withdrew and, according to Herodotus, suffered great losses during their retreat.

It is unlikely that the Assyrian army could have been disabled by gnawing mice. What is Herodotus describing here?

The story, which was related to Herodotus by a temple priest in Egypt some 250 years afterward, may symbolically refer to the real cause of the Assyrian deaths. Like the rat in the Middle Ages, the mouse symbolized plague in the ancient Near East. Sennacherib's army may actually have been decimated by the plague, which Sethos' chroniclers conveniently altered to credit Sethos with a great slaughter of his enemies.

But is this what happened to the Assyrian army at the gates of Jerusalem? One piece of evidence suggests that it is. During the excavation of the Judean city of Lachish in 1948, archaeologists uncovered a mass grave containing the remains of 2,000 skeletons thrown together with great haste.

Lachish was the last stop of Sennacherib's army before it went up to Jerusalem. It may be that these skeletons were the first victims of a deadly plague that, as recorded in the Bible, would soon strike with devastating force.

A Ferocious Cast of Thousands

*I*n the mid-nineteenth century, British archaeologist A. H. Layard was excavating a fabulous palace at the ancient Assyrian capital of Nineveh. Containing more than 70 rooms and halls, the palace was built by Sennacherib, king of Assyria, and called by him the "palace without a rival."

When Layard dug his way into the center of the complex, he made an astonishing discovery: a room covered with exquisitely carved reliefs depicting the siege of the Judean city of Lachish. Layard cut the reliefs into 12 slabs, which he managed to spirit back to England where they still reside in the British Museum. The reliefs brilliantly evoke the fierce battle in which thousands of Assyrian soldiers assaulted and eventually breached the walls of the city.

Sennacherib's army can be seen employing the most sophisticated military tactics of its day. The Assyrians were deployed in ranks, each one wielding a different type of weapon, while their engineers constructed earthen slopes up to the walls of Lachish.

The Assyrian infantry attacked the mud-brick walls of the city with arrows, spears, and slingshots, as the defenders retaliated in kind. Behind the bowmen in the reliefs are the slingers, each holding a sphere in his hand as he swings another in his sling. Meanwhile, the spearmen approached the gate; one in the first row with arrows stuck in his shield.

Nearby are the battering rams; at least seven are depicted attacking Lachish. These siege machines were elaborate devices that were likely constructed at the site from prefabricated parts. They consisted of a turret with a window for the operator and spoked wheels underneath the body of the ram. A large sharpened beam protruded from the front of the machine, probably propelled forward by men inside the battering ram as the operator sought a weak point in the walls.

The reliefs continue as the battle reaches a critical stage. The attackers focused their assault upon the main gate tower. The defenders reached a point of desperation, casting down stones, arrows, torches, and chariot parts in a vain attempt to blunt the attack.

The reason for their frenzied efforts is soon made clear. The defenders of Lachish knew what their fate would be if the enemy was victorious. The Assyrians lived up to their reputation for savage brutality. According to the reliefs, three prisoners were stripped naked and impaled on poles in sight of the walls for the obvious purpose of driving fear into the hearts of the defenders.

Finally the city was taken. The relief shows soldiers carrying off booty as Judean prisoners-of-war make their way barefoot into captivity. Their salvaged belongings are strapped to carts pulled by emaciated oxen, a sober indication of the famine that the people of Lachish must have suffered during the siege.

The Assyrians showed very little, if any, mercy for those who opposed them. Grim scenes follow of defeated Judeans begging for mercy with outstretched hands. Nearby, one prisoner was being stabbed while others were lying on the ground, having just been flayed alive.

The Assyrian Palace of King Sennacherib at Nineveh as reconstructed by the Englishman Austen Henry Layard, one of the pioneer archaeologists of Mesopotamia.

In the final slab, Sennacherib is seated on his battle throne in front of his tent. The inscription reads: "Sennacherib, king of all, king of Assyria, sitting [on] his nimedu-throne while the spoils from the city of Lachish passed before him."

One final detail presents itself to the observer: The face of Sennacherib has been mutilated, probably after he was assassinated in 681 B.C., thus echoing the message of Psalm 7:16: "Their mischief returns upon their own heads, and on their own heads their violence descends."

Hezekiah's Tunnel

Many visitors to Jerusalem are awed by the majestic walls of the old city, but are surprised to learn that the walls date only to 1537, when the Turkish Sultan Suleyman the Magnificent ordered them restored. Even more surprising, no doubt, is learning that the original Jerusalem stood completely outside the present walls.

The Jebusites, one of the Canaanite peoples inhabiting the land before the Israelite conquest, built the first Jerusalem as their capital. The city stood on a low ridge of land extending southward from the present-day city walls.

Though occupying only 13 acres, the city was protected by deep valleys on all sides except the north, where strong defensive fortifications made the city virtually impregnable. Hence the boast of the Jebusites to David: "You will not come in here, even the blind and the lame will turn you back" (2 Samuel 5:6).

The Jebusites did not count on David's men sneaking into the city by night through the water system known as Warren's Shaft. The shaft led to the Gihon Spring, the Jebusites' water source and the reason for their settling at the site.

The Gihon is the major natural water source in the area. A copious spring, it flows even today. In ancient times, the Gihon could have supplied water for a population of several thousand people.

Warren's Shaft is only one of three water systems carved out of the rock underneath the Jebusite city, today called the City of David. The second was a channel carved by Solomon along the bottom of the hill where the city stood to provide water for irrigation. The water was channeled out to the fields in the Kidron Valley through a system of sluice gates. The third water system was created by King Hezekiah.

In Solomon's day, Israel lived securely, and Jerusalem was not threatened by besieging armies. Three hundred years later, however, the situation was very different. The northern kingdom of Israel had already been conquered by Sennacherib and the Assyrians, who were advancing towards Jerusalem.

We read of the king of Judah's response to this grave threat in the Book of Second Chronicles: "When Hezekiah saw that Sennacherib had come and intended to fight against Jerusalem, he planned with his officers and his warriors to stop the flow of the springs that were outside the city; and they helped him. A great many people were gathered, and they stopped all the springs and the wadi that flowed through the land, saying, 'Why should the Assyrian kings come and find water in abundance?'" (2 Chronicles 32:2–4).

The entrance to Hezekiah's tunnel at Gihon Spring. The only significant natural spring near Jerusalem, the Gihon has been in continuous use for several thousand years.

Solomon's system of sluice gates may have given the impression of several springs in the Kidron Valley—called here "wadi"—but in reality they were all connected to the Gihon. The Judahites camouflaged the opening of the spring so that the Assyrians would not discover it and have access to water. This would have posed a considerable hardship upon an army that numbered more than 185,000 men.

The people of Jerusalem could not content themselves with stopping up the spring. They also needed the water. We read in 2 Chronicles how the problem was solved: "This same Hezekiah closed the upper outlet of the waters of Gihon and directed them down to the west side of the city of David" (2 Chronicles 32:30).

By Hezekiah's time the limits of the city had expanded greatly to the north and west—areas that were also protected by strong walls. The Gihon is in the Kidron Valley, on the east side of the City of David. By directing the water from the east side over to the west side, Hezekiah was bringing it closer to where it was most needed, close to the quarter of his expanding population.

But how did he bring the water across? The answer was lost to history until the nineteenth century, when a passage was discovered deep underneath the City of David leading from the Gihon to the Pool of Siloam on the western flank of the city. Until the channel was discovered, it was thought that the Pool of Siloam was fed by a separate spring.

The 1,700-foot-long water channel—known as Hezekiah's Tunnel—is an admirable feat of engineering made all the more remarkable by the discovery of an ancient inscription written by its excavators.

The eighth-century B.C. inscription, now in the Istanbul museum, reads in part: "Behold the tunnel. This is the story of its cutting. While the miners swung their picks, one towards the other, and when there remained only 3 cubits to cut, the voice of one calling to his fellow was heard.... So the day they broke through the miners struck, one against the other, pick against pick, and the water flowed from the spring towards the pool, 1,200 cubits. The height of the rock above the head of the miners was 100 cubits."

However, one puzzle remained. The tunnel is not carved in a straight path to the Pool of Siloam. It takes a serpentine, roundabout route instead, which adds hundreds of feet to its length. Given the fact that the tunnel was dug in haste as the Assyrians advanced towards Jerusalem, it seems odd that the engineers would intentionally complicate what was already a daunting task.

Some have suggested that the excavators miscalculated, resulting in a crooked tunnel, but this is not likely. Engineers in ancient times were fully capable of excavating straight channels.

The inscription that is found in the tunnel shows that Hezekiah's engineers knew what they were doing. They correctly calculated both the distance and the depth of the tunnel underground.

Recent examination of the tunnel provides the likely reason for Hezekiah's crooked tunnel. The evidence indicates that it followed a natural fissure that wound its way underneath the City of David. Rather than carve a completely new channel through the hard limestone, the engineers decided to follow and enlarge an existing crevice.

THE FALL OF JERUSALEM

Secrets of the Balm of Gilead

Longing for the spiritual renewal of his fellow Judeans, the prophet Jeremiah laments: "Is there no balm in Gilead? Is there no physician there? Why then has the health of my poor people not been restored?" (Jeremiah 8:22).

In the ancient Near East, aromatic resins or gums, known as balms, were widely used for medicinal and cosmetic purposes. According to ancient tradition, the balm of Gilead was also used to anoint the kings of Israel.

Identification of the balm of Gilead is complicated by the fact that several different "balms" are referred to in the Bible. The Talmud, the exhaustive Jewish interpretation of the Hebrew Bible, identifies the balm of Gilead with

The Flemish painter Van Lint's lavish "The Queen of Sheba Before Solomon" depicts the meeting of these two illustrious historical figures.

balsam. Near-miraculous properties are ascribed to this oil, which is credited with everything from the healing of wounds to making men wild with lust.

The first-century Jewish historian Josephus states that balsam trees were first brought to Israel and presented as a gift to King Solomon by the Queen of Sheba. The Book of 1

Kings confirms that the Queen of Sheba presented to Solomon as a gift "a great quantity of spices, and precious stones; never again did spices come in such quantity as that which the queen of Sheba gave to King Solomon" (1 Kings 10:10).

According to ancient sources, in the Near East, balsam was grown only at Jericho, Zoar, and En-gedi. So renowned was the balm of Gilead from En-gedi that, after suppressing the First Judean Revolt, the Roman commander Titus displayed balsam branches on his victory march through Rome.

The Fiery Arms of Kronos

The Topheth is the name of a place in the valley of Hinnom where, as the kingdom of Judah fell into moral degradation, the Judahites sacrificed their children. With only a few references to Topheth in the Bible, little is known about the meaning of the word.

The worship of Baal, the preeminent Canaanite deity, is mentioned in relation to the Topheth, as is the Ammonite god Molech. The Bible describes the ominous-sounding practice of "building the high place of Topheth, which is in the valley of the son of Hinnom, to burn their sons and their daughters in the fire" (Jeremiah 7:31).

Exactly what "burning in the fire" meant eluded scholars until the discovery was made of similar sites at Phoenician Carthage, Sicily, Sardinia, and Tunisia. The Topheth at Carthage is the largest known cemetery of sacrificed humans in the ancient world. For more than 600 years, child sacrifice was performed at the site, which is believed to contain tens of thousands of urns filled with the remains of children.

In the third century B.C., Greek writer Kleitarchos described child sacrifice at Carthage. He stated that, whenever the Carthaginians desired to obtain something of special importance, they would vow one of their children to Kronos, the Greek equivalent to the Phoenician god Baal-Hammon.

But it is Kleitarchos' account of how the sacrifices were performed that may provide the key for understanding what the biblical phrase "passing through the fire" meant. In the middle of the Topheth at Carthage stood a bronze statue of Kronos, its open hands extended over a heated bronze brazier. The victim was placed into the fiery hands of the god Kronos and was consumed by the flames from the brazier.

Even the Romans, who themselves tolerated infanticide as a form of birth control, found the child sacrifices at Carthage to be despicable. The Roman theologian Tertullian describes how the emperor Tiberius hanged the priests who conducted the sacrifices from the very trees of the Topheth.

It may be that similar depravities performed in the Topheth in the valley of Hinnom only came to an end once and for all with the destruction of Jerusalem in 586 B.C.

Where the Worm Dies Not

To the southwest of the city of Jerusalem is the valley of Hinnom, marking the ancient border between the territories of the tribes of Benjamin and Judah.

Gehenna is the Greek form of two Hebrew words meaning "valley of Hinnom." In the Bible, the valley of Hinnom (or as it is sometimes called, Ben-hinnom, or "son of Hinnom") acquired an evil reputation because it was here that the cultic shrine of Topheth was located.

The prophet Jeremiah vehemently denounces the abominations committed at the shrine by his countrymen: "And they go on building the high place of Topheth, which is in the valley of the son of Hinnom, to burn their sons and their daughters in the fire—which I did not command, nor did it come into my mind" (Jeremiah 7:31).

Topheth is an Aramaic term meaning "hearth" or "fireplace." Thus the Topheth was a high place where human sacrifices were offered. The Bible indicates that the prophets engaged in a long and largely unsuccessful struggle against the Topheths.

The depravity of Kings Ahaz and Manasseh, who sacrificed their sons in the fires of the Topheth, was countered by King Josiah, who "defiled Topheth, which is in the valley of Ben-hinnom, so that no one would make a son or a daughter pass through the fire as an offering to Molech" (2 Kings 23:10). Later, however, during the time of Jeremiah, the Topheth became active once again.

Some scholars argue that terms such as "burning in fire" refer to an initiation rite instead of to human sacrifice. Others insist that the term "burning" should be interpreted as literal, especially in light of the known practice of human sacrifice by the Canaanites, Phoenicians, and others.

There is yet another ominous association with the valley of Hinnom. In the New Testament and in rabbinic literature, Gehenna is the place of judgment—and punishment—after death. Another term, Hades, refers to a temporary abode of the dead, while Gehenna is permanent.

Jesus spoke of Gehenna as the destiny of the wicked: "where their worm never dies, and the fire is never quenched" (Mark 9:48). This is a quote from the description of the valley of Hinnom in the last verse of the Book of Isaiah: "And they shall go out and look at the dead bodies of the people who have rebelled against me; for their worm shall not die, their fire shall not be quenched, and they shall be an abhorrence to all flesh" (Isaiah 66:24).

In New Testament times, the Hinnom Valley was the garbage dump of Jerusalem. The mention of worms and undying fire refers to the maggots and continual burning that characterized the valley, but at the same time symbolized corruption and suffering.

Excavations in Jerusalem have yielded clues to the city's past. For example, these pillars may have been reused during several different historical periods.

Excavation at the oasis of En-gedi reveals a long history of Jewish occupation, despite the extreme conditions and scant rainfall, which make farming difficult. How, then, did En-gedi survive? The answer is found in the profitable cultivation of the thorny, shrublike balsam tree. The economy of En-gedi was centered around it. Archaeologists have uncovered ovens used to process the tree's valuable oil, as well as the large barrel-shaped pottery jars used to store it.

It was at En-gedi that archaeologists uncovered a baffling curse in an inscription on a synagogue floor: "Whoever reveals the secret of the village to the gentiles, the one whose eyes roam over the entire earth and see what is concealed will uproot this person and his seed from under the sun."

Archaeologists puzzled over the curse for more than 25 years until subsequent excavations revealed a possible answer. In a large tower thought to be used to produce balsam, large vats were discovered. The design of the vats suggested that they contained not water but oil, leading archaeologists to conclude that the balsam was processed by boiling it in oil.

Could it have been this "secret recipe" for processing balsam that was a jealously guarded secret of the En-gedi community? The curse in the synagogue floor may have been intended to ensure that En-gedi continued to corner the market on the balm of Gilead.

The Search for the Lost Ark

Steven Spielberg's hugely successful motion picture *Raiders of the Lost Ark* popularized what has become for some a serious endeavor: the search for the biblical Ark of the Covenant.

Interestingly, the premise of the movie—that the Ark was taken by Pharaoh Shishak of Egypt in the tenth century B.C.—has been superseded by other views that have gained popular attention.

According to Jewish tradition as recorded in the Book of 2 Maccabees, at the time of the fall of Jerusalem in 586 B.C., the prophet Jeremiah "ordered that the tent and the ark should follow with him, and he went out to the mountain where Moses had gone up and he had seen the inheritance of God. Jeremiah came and found a cave-dwelling, and he brought there the tent and the ark and the altar of incense; and he sealed up the entrance" (2 Maccabees 2:4–5).

Moses died on Mount Nebo in Transjordan. When some of those who followed him attempted to mark the location on the mountain, Jeremiah rebuked them, saying: "The place shall remain unknown until God gathers his people together again and shows his mercy" (2 Maccabees 2:7).

Some investigators, convinced that they were living in the time when the location of the Ark would be revealed, have scoured Mount Nebo in hopes of finding it. However, with the exception of one discredited claim of the Ark having been found under an ancient church on nearby Mount Pis-gah, there is no evidence of the Ark's presence on the mountain.

Others believe the Ark was hidden near the ancient Essene settlement of Qumran by the Dead Sea. However, the excavation of a number of caves has proved fruitless in the search for the Ark. Still others have suggested a number of sites in Jerusalem, including a tunnel under the city and at Gordon's Calvary, the possible site of the crucifixion of Christ.

Many ultraorthodox Jews believe that the Ark is hidden in a secret chamber carved deep under the Temple Mount, waiting to be revealed when the Temple is rebuilt. It is thought that the builder of the First Temple, King Solomon, foresaw a time when the Ark would need to be hidden and carved out the underground chamber.

This subterranean chamber is not to be confused with the cave underneath the bedrock inside the Dome of the Rock, which any tourist can enter today. In the early 1980s, archaeologists were excavating underground along the western retaining wall of the so-called Second Temple, built by King Herod. The Second Temple was a much larger and grander edifice than Solomon's original Temple, built on the same location.

Orthodox rabbis were building a synagogue adjoining the wall when they accidentally broke through an ancient subterranean gate that led into the Temple through an underground passageway. Entering through a hole in the wall, they discovered a hall approximately 75 feet long leading in the direction of the area thought to be the Holy of Holies. The tunnel, however, was filled with mud and water, which the rabbis and their workers proceeded to drain and clean out.

Is the Ark in Ethiopia?

One of the oldest and most intriguing theories about the Ark of the Covenant is that it has resided in Ethiopia for the past 3,000 years. The story is preserved in the Ethiopian royal chronicles and is widely believed not only by Ethiopian Christians, but also by the Falashas—or Black Jews—of Ethiopia.

According to the chronicles, the Queen of Sheba mentioned in the Bible was from Ethiopia. As the story goes, she had a son named Menelik I by King Solomon. The Ark is said to have been secretly taken from Jerusalem by Menelik, with the assistance of the priests, after Solomon's death.

The Ark is reportedly kept in Saint Mary of Zion Church in Axum, Ethiopia, and can only be viewed once a year when it is brought out for a special ceremony. However, the covered object paraded during the ceremony is thought to be a replica of the true Ark.

The theory that the Ark of the Covenant is in Ethiopia has serious difficulties. For one, scholars

An Ethiopian Bar Mitzvah at the Western Wall. Large numbers of Ethiopian Jews have immigrated to the Holy Land.

believe that the kingdom of the Queen of Sheba was in the area of southwest Arabia known as Yemen, not in Africa. Also, it is doubtful whether anyone could have succeeded in removing the Ark from the Holy of Holies. It would be almost inconceivable even for priests to enter the Holy of Holies; only the High Priest was permitted to enter it, and only on one day each year.

It does not, in any case, appear that the Ark was moved at such an early date as the Ethiopian theory requires. There is a reference to the Ark during the time of Josiah, almost 300 years after the time when it was thought to have been taken to Ethiopia: "[Josiah] said to the Levites who taught all Israel and were holy to the Lord, 'Put the holy ark in the house that Solomon son of David, king of Israel, built; you need no longer carry it on your shoulders'" (2 Chronicles 35:3).

Thus it appears that the Ark was still in Jerusalem at a much later time than allowed by those who believe the Ethiopian theory.

They continued their clandestine excavation cautiously, fearing that the Muslims controlling the Temple Mount above them would discover the project and demand an end to it. After eighteen months of excavations, the passageway ended at a sealed wall. The rabbis were convinced that on the other side lay the Holy of Holies and the Ark of the Covenant.

At this point, Muslim authorities learned of the excavation. A riot was narrowly averted, and the rabbis were forced by the Israeli government to end their excavations and seal up the tunnel.

The rabbis remain as convinced as ever that the Ark of the Covenant lies somewhere deep beneath the Temple Mount and that it will be brought to light one day when, as 2 Maccabees states, "God gathers his people together again and shows his mercy."

The Queen of Heaven

*J*eremiah prophesied during the last days of the kingdom of Judah, when moral corruption was at its worst.

Speaking in the voice of the Lord, he denounced one particular form of idolatry: "The children gather wood, the fathers kindle fire, and the women knead dough, to make cakes for the queen of heaven; and they pour out drink offerings to other gods, to provoke me to anger" (Jeremiah 7:18).

The "queen of heaven" mentioned in Jeremiah may be related to the goddess Ashtoreth mentioned elsewhere in the

Bible. The various cultures of the ancient Near East adapted many of the same gods and goddesses, giving them equivalent names in their own language.

Thus the goddess that the wayward Judeans worshiped was likely related to the Syrian goddess Atargatis. Similarly, the Egyptian Isis was worshiped as the queen of Heaven, as was the Mesopotamian goddess Ishtar. In the Hellenistic and Roman period, Artemis, the mother goddess of Ephesus, was called by that same name, as was Aphrodite-Venus.

The closest equivalent of the Israelite goddess Ashtoreth was the Canaanite goddess Ashtarte. To dishonor the goddess in the Hebrew text her name is altered, with the vowels replaced by the vowels for the Hebrew word for shame, *boshet*.

Wherever she was found, the queen of Heaven was worshiped as a fertility goddess. Numerous small images of nude goddesses have been uncovered by archaeologists at Israelite sites.

Solomon is credited with the introduction of Ashtoreth worship in Israel, an error that King Josiah would later seek to redress by destroying the shrines dedicated to her. The Judeans, however, resisted Jeremiah's efforts to put an end to the worship of their queen.

Their defiant reply to his efforts is recorded by Jeremiah: "Instead, we will do everything that we have vowed, make offerings to the queen of heaven and pour out libations to her, just as we and our ancestors, our kings and our officials, used to do in the towns of Judah and in the streets of

An Ancient Fingerprint

We read in the Book of Jeremiah that the prophet was assisted by a scribe by the name of Baruch: "Then Jeremiah called Baruch son of Neriah, and Baruch wrote on a scroll at Jeremiah's dictation all the words of the Lord that he had spoken to him" (Jeremiah 36:4). It is this very same Baruch whose fingerprint is thought to be known.

In a correlation with the biblical text, the name "Baruch" appears on an ancient seal known as a "bulla" unearthed at the City of David excavations. The bulla, a lump of clay impressed with a seal, was used to secure documents. A scroll would be tied with string and then sealed with clay to identify the owner.

The bulla found at the City of David is dated to the late seventh or sixth century B.C., the last years of the kingdom of Judah chronicled by the prophet Jeremiah. It reads: "Belonging to Berekhyahu, son of Neriyahu, the Scribe." Berekhyahu is the long form of the name Baruch, meaning "Blessed of Yahweh." The identification of this seal with the biblical Baruch is confirmed by the fact that Baruch's father is called Neriah—a variant of Neriyahu—in the Bible.

A medieval depiction of the prophet Baruch by Giotto Di Bondone. The Book of Baruch is a collection of prayers and poems attributed to Jeremiah's scribe.

The seal was found in a location that also fits with what we know of Jeremiah. It was discovered near what is known as the "stepped-stone structure" thought to be a retaining wall for David's palace in ancient Jerusalem. Jeremiah frequently appeared before the king of Jerusalem and would have been present in the same place where archaeologists uncovered the seal.

Another bulla bearing the same name was found, this one with a fingerprint on the edge. Since Baruch would have been the person to use this seal containing his name, there is little doubt that it is the fingerprint of the biblical personage Baruch.

In the Book of Jeremiah, the prophet states: "And I gave the deed of purchase to Baruch son of Neriah son of Mahseiah, in the presence of my cousin Hanamel, in the presence of the witnesses who signed the deed of purchase, and in the presence of all the Judeans who were sitting in the court of the guard" (Jeremiah 32:12).

It was during the signing and sealing of this document, or another like it, that the fingerprint of Baruch was preserved for all time.

Jerusalem. We used to have plenty of food, and prospered, and saw no misfortune" (Jeremiah 44:17).

Their repeated refusal to stop goddess worship brought condemnation from the Lord upon them: "I am going to watch over them for harm and not for good; all the people of Judah who are in the land of Egypt shall perish by the sword and by famine, until not one is left" (Jeremiah 44:27). Thus, the prosperity and fertility they hoped for by rejecting the Lord in favor of their goddess were irrevocably lost to them.

CAPTIVITY IN BABYLON

The Fall of Babylon

The Greek historian Herodotus, called the "Father of History," is one of our prime sources for what is known about the fall of Babylon. Herodotus lived a century after the time of Daniel and traveled widely in the East.

On his march to Babylon, Persia's King Cyrus was preparing to cross the Gyndes River with his army when one of his white horses fell into the swift current and was carried away.

The great city of Babylon was gradually abandoned when the Euphrates River, on which the city lay, changed its course. Here the river is shown at Dibsi Faraj, 60 miles south of Aleppo, Syria.

Furious that the river would dare take one of his prized steeds, he vowed to make it so tame that a woman could cross it without getting her knees wet. Temporarily forsaking his march on Babylon, Cyrus marked off 180 channels to be dug on either side of the river. The diverted water reduced the flow of the Gyndes to little more than a trickle.

Having taken his revenge, Cyrus resumed his march on Babylon, where the defenders of the great city were waiting for him. After attacking Cyrus' troops unsuccessfully, they retreated to within the massive city walls. Herodotus writes that the Babylonians were well prepared for a long siege, having accumulated enough food to last for years.

The siege of the city seemed to accomplish little, and Cyrus was beginning to despair when he remembered his experience with the Gyndes, setting a brilliant strategy in motion. The seemingly impenetrable walls of Babylon had one weak point, where the Euphrates River flowed under them on its course directly through the middle of Babylon.

Cyrus stationed his troops near where the river entered and exited the city. He then went upstream with his construction troops to a point where it was possible to divert the river. His men worked furiously, careful not to give themselves away, and soon the depth of the river was reduced to no more than the middle of a man's thigh.

Cyrus' troops waited until nightfall and waded into the city. While the people of the city were celebrating the feast of Belshazzar, dancing and enjoying themselves, the Persians entered Babylon by stealth.

A Fateful Night in Babylon

It was a story almost too fantastic to be true, or so thought many scholars, but new evidence is shedding light on the last evening in the life of King Belshazzar and his kingdom. ♥

We read in the Book of Daniel that Belshazzar made a great feast for a thousand of his lords. As the wine flowed, the king was in a boastful mood, and he ordered that the gold and silver vessels that his father, Nebuchadnezzar, had taken from the Temple of Jerusalem be brought out so that his guests could drink from them.

To use the sacred objects for drunken revelry was more than a show of contempt. To those present, the act would be yet another reminder of the humiliation that the Jews suffered in the conquest of their country and the carrying off of their temple treasures.

What happened next put an instant end to the festivities. As the glasses were filled and the gods of Babylon were praised, suddenly the hall fell silent. A finger appeared and began to write on the wall. No one present understood the meaning of the four words that appeared: *MENE, MENE, TEKEL, PERES.*

The text then describes Belshazzar's response: "The king was watching the hand as it wrote. Then the king's face turned pale, and his thoughts terrified him. His limbs gave way, and his knees knocked together" (Daniel 5:5–6). He immediately called for his magicians and diviners, promising the third place in his kingdom for whoever succeeded in interpreting the writing.

The wise men of Babylon, however, were unable to translate the writing. Then the queen suggested that Belshazzar summon Daniel, the prophet from Judah who years earlier had interpreted the visions of Nebuchadnezzar. Daniel was hastened to the banquet hall and told Belshazzar the meaning of the strange words.

The Writing on the Wall

At his fateful last feast, King Belshazzar called for the wise men and diviners of Babylon to interpret the four words—*MENE, MENE, TEKEL, PERES*—that mysteriously appeared on the wall of the banquet hall. He did so with the expectation that they would be able to decipher the message, as Babylon was renowned for explaining the hidden messages of omens.

Archaeologists have uncovered several ancient libraries containing large numbers of cuneiform tablets dealing with the subject of omens and how to interpret them. In ancient Babylon, enormous effort was devoted to collecting and archiving the meaning of cryptic signs. Dreams, extraordinary circumstances, the unusual behavior of animals, even patterns in the sky, smoke, or in oil on water—all were considered either good or bad omens of some future event.

It was considered vital that the omens be properly interpreted so that danger could be averted. If, for example, what was taken to be a sign appeared before a defeat in battle, whenever the same sign occurred before military conflict, it would be taken as a warning to avoid battle until a more favorable time.

Over time, thousands of signs and their supposed meanings were catalogued by the diviners of Babylon. But on the night of the fall of Babylon, when Belshazzar commanded his wise men to interpret the writing on the wall, the lists proved worthless. Nothing like this had ever happened before.

The message was one of doom: "MENE, God has numbered the days of your kingdom and brought it to an end; TEKEL, you have been weighed on the scales and found wanting; PERES, your kingdom is divided and given to the Medes and Persians" (Daniel 5:26–28). According to the text, Belshazzar was killed as Darius the Mede conquered Babylon.

The traditional setting for this story as told in the Book of Daniel is sixth-century B.C. Babylon. In the third century A.D., Porphyry, a philosopher and opponent of Christianity, challenged the sixth-century date for the book. Porphyry dated the Book of Daniel to 165 B.C., arguing that it foretold events so accurately that it must have been written after the events occurred.

With the rise of biblical criticism in the last century, this opinion became widely accepted among scholars, who adopted the view that the Book of Daniel represented a second-century B.C. Jewish national folktale containing little historical value. The fact that, up until the mid-nineteenth century, Belshazzar's name had been nowhere to be found outside the biblical text further lent support to the later date. Nebuchadnezzar was included in the ancient lists of Babylonian kings preserved by the Greeks. However, the name of the last native ruler of Babylon and successor to

Nebuchadnezzar was listed there as Nabonidus, not Belshazzar.

Then, in 1854, several small clay cylinders were uncovered in the temple of the moon god in Babylon. Only four inches long, each cylinder was inscribed with 60 or so lines of the wedge-shaped cuneiform writing used in ancient Mesopotamia. When deciphered, the text was found to be a prayer for good health and a long life for Nabonidus, who ruled Babylon from 555 to 539 B.C. The prayer also included mention of his eldest son, identified on the cylinder as none other than Belshazzar.

There was no longer any doubt that Belshazzar existed, but he was identified in the cylinder only as the king's son. The mystery deepened as several other references to Belshazzar were discovered in the following decades, and in every case he is identified as the king's son or as the crown prince, never as king.

And yet something was amiss. Legal documents from the sixth century B.C. uniformly include an oath only to the god and the king. The documents swearing by Nabonidus and his son Belshazzar were the only known exceptions to this standard practice. This implied a unique relationship between Nabonidus and Belshazzar.

Other evidence came to light regarding the two men from ancient Babylonia. It seems that Nabonidus was an eccentric ruler who spurned the usual gods of Babylon in favor of worshipping Harran and the moon god, Ur. Nabonidus abandoned Babylon for several years and resided at the distant oasis of Teima in northern Arabia. It was during Nabonidus' absence from the throne that Belshazzar ruled in his stead.

The word for king in Aramaic, the language of much of the Book of Daniel (some of the text is in Hebrew), is a broad term that can mean "governor" or "crown prince." This is precisely how Belshazzar functioned as the regent of Nabonidus.

This conclusion solves another puzzle in the story of King Belshazzar. We read that Belshazzar promised that whoever could read the writing on the wall would "rank third in the kingdom" (Daniel 5:7). Why would that person only be the third ruler in the kingdom? Why wouldn't he instead become the second ruler in the kingdom? The answer to the mystery appears to be that Belshazzar was already the second ruler, after Nabonidus. Thus, the highest position that could be offered to Daniel was that of third ruler over the kingdom.

It seems, then, that the story of Daniel fits well into the setting of Babylon in the sixth century B.C. There is no evidence outside of the Bible for the writing on the wall, nor could any be reasonably expected.

We do, however, have one last confirmation of the events of the Book of Daniel in the testimony of Greek historian Herodotus. Writing a century after the fall of Babylon, Herodotus confirmed that a festival was in progress at the very hour the Persians entered the city.

Left: *Rembrandt's rendition of Belshazzar's feast depicts the horror that attended the appearance of handwriting on the wall, which preceded the conquest of Babylon by the Persians that very evening.*

EZEKIEL'S MYSTERIOUS PROPHECY

When North Is Not North

One popular theory about the identity of Gog of the land of Magog is that these mysterious names make reference to Russia.

The basis for the theory is given in the prophecy of Ezekiel, which states that Gog and his confederates will descend upon Israel "from the remotest parts of the north" (Ezekiel 38:6). Indeed, if one takes a map of the world and draws a line north from Israel, it will go directly through Russia, thus appearing to confirm the theory.

In fact, the drawn line will pass near Moscow, Russia's capital city. This would seem to confirm another verse that identifies Gog as the "chief prince of Meshech and Tubal" (Ezekiel 38:3), which

Map showing the "fertile cresent" of the Middle East, which surrounds the Syrian and Arabian deserts

some take to refer to the Russian cities of Moscow and Tobolsk.

But is this what the Bible means by "north"? Not necessarily. In numerous instances, the Bible refers to an invasion from the north that actually originates from the east. An example of this is the warning of the prophet Jeremiah: "Raise a standard toward Zion, flee for safety, do not delay, for I am bringing evil from the north, and a great destruction" (Jeremiah 4:6).

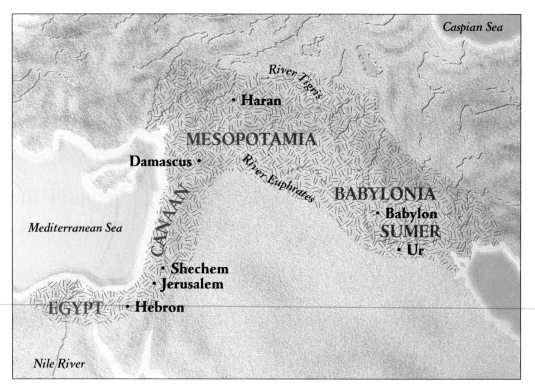

Jeremiah is here prophesying the destruction of Jerusalem by the Babylonians, which happened in 586 B.C. However, a quick check of the map shows that Babylon is not north of Israel, but rather directly east of it.

Similarly, Jeremiah foretells another defeat: "Egypt shall be put to shame; she shall be handed over to a people from the north" (Jeremiah 46:24). This prophecy came to pass in 605 B.C., when Pharaoh Neco II was defeated at Carchemish by the neo-Babylonians led by Nebuchadnezzar. Once again, however, the Babylonians lived not to the north, but to the east of Egypt.

Were the biblical writers so ignorant of geography that they mistakenly thought that Babylonia was to the north of Israel? The answer lies in the geography of the Middle East. The biblical world is sometimes called "the fertile crescent," which refers to the swath of arable land that curves upwards from the Tigris and Euphrates rivers in Mesopotamia, over to northern Syria, and then down into the Promised Land.

In the middle of this boomerang-shaped territory lie the Syrian and Arabian deserts. In Old Testament times, travelers from Mesopotamia to Israel would avoid a direct route through the inhospitable wasteland, instead following the fertile crescent, along which they had guaranteed access to food and water. This is the route, for example, that Abraham followed when he left Ur.

Ancient armies, which required considerable supplies of water, would attempt a desert crossing only at their peril. Like everyone else, the Babylonians marched along the fertile crescent on their way to conquer Israel, which meant that they entered the Promised Land from the north.

Field Marshals of the Final Battle

We read in chapter 38 of the Book of Ezekiel about the foreboding Gog of the land of Magog, who is summoned by the Lord to invade the land of Israel:

"After many days you shall be mustered; in the latter years you shall go against a land restored from war, a land where people were gathered from many nations on the mountains of Israel, which had long lain waste; its people were brought out from the nations and now are living in safety, all of them"(Ezekiel 38:8).

This invasion will take place in "the latter years," which is taken as a reference to the final battle at the end of the world. Many students of Bible prophecy believe that the modern state of Israel is the only viable historical possibility for the fulfillment of this passage.

If so, then the land of Israel can expect an invasion by the forces of Gog of the land of Magog. According to Ezekiel, Gog is the head of a confederation of forces that includes "Meshech" and "Tubal" and others: "Persia, Ethiopia, and Put are with them, all of them with buckler and helmet; Gomer and all its troops; Beth-togarmah from the remotest parts of the north with all its troops—many peoples are with you" (Ezekiel 38:5).

What is known of the identification of these strange names? The historical identity of Gog of the land of Magog is uncertain. Many scholars lean towards identifying Gog with a certain King Gugu, who is identified as Gyges, the king of Lydia around 660 B.C. Lydia was located in Asia Minor, in what is now Turkey.

The identity of Magog is even less certain. It is not even mentioned in Assyrian literature, our main source of information about the eighth and seventh centuries B.C.

Based on the similarity of the names, it has been speculated that Rosh, Meshech, and Tubal refer to Russia, Moscow, and Tobolsk. Identifying place names purely on the basis of a phonetic similarity is far from conclusive, however.

Rosh has also been identified with Assyria's Rashu, on the northwest border of Elam, now northwestern Iran. Tubal and Meshech are the people that the Assyrian inscriptions call *Tabal* and *Musku*, located in what is now modern Turkey. Of the remaining allies of Gog, Persia, Ethiopia, and Put (Libya) are easily identified, while Gomer was sometimes assumed to be East Germany, particularly by those who held to the Rosh/Russia identification.

Again, the Assyrians provide an alternative possibility. Gomer was known to them as the land of *Gimirrai*, a people who lived in Asia Minor, or modern Turkey, during the eighth century B.C.

The final name, Bet-togarmah, is associated with the Hittite *Tegarama* and the Assyrian *Til Garimmu*, a people also from central Asia Minor.

All of this indicates that the participants in the battle of Gog from the land of Magog come from a generally definable area stretching between northern Africa and eastern Turkey, including parts of Iran and Iraq, and perhaps extending into

southern Central Asia. It is no secret that many of the countries that occupy these ancient lands today have posed a military threat to Israel since its very inception.

Countdown to the Great Battle

*T*he timing of the battle of Gog of the land of Magog has been much debated among students of prophecy.

The Book of Ezekiel indicates that this great battle will take place after a great worldwide dispersion of the Jews, known as the Diaspora. The Jews are destined to return to their own land: "But you, O mountains of Israel, shall shoot out your branches, and yield your fruit to my people Israel; for they shall soon come home"(Ezekiel 36:8).

Historically, there have been only two possibilities for this prophesied return. The first is in the second century B.C., when Judea was controlled by the successors of the Greeks, known as the Seleucids. In 169 B.C., the Jews, horrified when Antiochus IV desecrated their Temple with a pagan altar, revolted against the ruler.

The Maccabean brothers led the charge against the Seleucids, whose weaponry included a herd of 32 elephants. With God on their side, the Maccabees were convinced that the powers of evil—which they equated with their Seleucid overlords—would be vanquished.

The Jews fought brilliantly, eventually triumphing over their foes and establishing the Hasmonean kingdom. Many of them undoubtedly thought the independent Jewish kingdom they had established was the fulfillment of Ezekiel's prophecy. Their messianic expectations would eventually fade, however, as the Hasmonean dynasty became torn with internal dissent. Rome intervened in 63 B.C., putting an end to the Jewish nation.

The second historical possibility for the return of the Jews to their homeland has occurred in modern times. In 1948, after nineteen hundred years of Diaspora, the Jewish people once again established an independent Jewish state in the land of Israel, despite fierce opposition from their Arab neighbors.

Many believe the modern state of Israel is the fulfillment of the ancient prophecy of Ezekiel, which speaks of a restored nation "where people were gathered from many nations on the mountains of Israel, which had long lain waste; its people were brought out from the nations and now are living in safety, all of them" (Ezekiel 38:8).

Whereas, during the Hasmonean period, the Jews returned from one nation (Babylon), the modern state of Israel is composed of Jews from more than 100 nations, thus fulfilling the prophesy that "many nations" would return.

Ezekiel also states that the Jews would return to a land "which had long lain waste," a fitting description of the land

Many believe that the ancient prophecy of Ezekiel has been fulfilled in the modern state of Israel as pictured above. Ezekiel's prophecy speaks of Israel as a place "where people were gathered from many nations..." (Ezekiel 38:8).

of Palestine until the influx of immigrants who planted fields and orchards and built modern cities in the nineteenth and twentieth centuries.

Finally, the reference to the people of Israel "living in safety" may refer to the safety that comes from military security. If so, then it is a fitting parallel to modern Israel. Few nations invest as much in their military as the Jewish nation, which requires all young men and women to serve in the army and which has repeatedly demonstrated its capabilities on the battlefield.

And yet, when all the evidence is presented, it still doesn't add up to absolute certainty. It is entirely possible that political changes or future military conflict in the unstable Middle East will change the geopolitical map into something quite different from the way it appears today.

It is also a very real possibility that the identification of the modern state of Israel with the return mentioned in Ezekiel is mistaken. After all, more than two thousand years ago, the Hasmoneans believed that they had good reason to think that they represented the fulfillment of Ezekiel's prophecy.

Consider also that the Hasmonean kingdom, which lasted more than a hundred years, was larger and more "religious" than modern Israel. The supreme Jewish council, known as the Sanhedrin, was in session at this time, and daily sacrifices were being offered in the Temple, none of which is taking place today in modern Israel.

All of these instances go to show that interpreting biblical prophecy requires two things: a thorough knowledge of the past and a cautious approach to the future.

THE RETURN FROM EXILE

Esther: Folklore or History?

The Book of Esther, the story of a narrowly avoided massacre set in fifth century B.C. Persia, is a favorite among Jews and is the biblical basis for the holiday of Purim.

Rabbis hesitated to include the Book of Esther in the Hebrew canon because it is the only book in the Bible in which the name of God is found. It was also the only biblical book not represented among the treasure trove of documents found at Qumran near the shores of the Dead Sea.

The value of the book eventually convinced skeptics, and Esther was included in the canon. It is an exceptional tale that beautifully characterizes virtue in the persons of Esther and Mordecai, at the same time portraying the ultimate in homicidal arrogance in the archvillain Haman.

In fact, the book is so well-plotted and entertaining to read that critics of the Book of Esther consider it little more than a Jewish folktale passed down through the centuries. However, from archaeological and historical sources, it now seems evident that the Book of Esther is soundly rooted in history.

The story begins with a lavish banquet in the palace of Xerxes, king of Persia. Queen Vashti is ordered to make an appearance and display her beauty to the assembled participants. She refuses and is deposed. The search begins for a new queen, and after a full year of beauty treatments—apparently standard procedure for Persian harems—Esther is chosen to succeed Vashti.

The story takes an ominous turn when Esther's uncle Mordecai, who sits at the gate of the city, learns that two of the royal bodyguards are plotting to assassinate the king. He informs Esther and the plot is thwarted.

Enter Haman the Agagite, a high official of Xerxes who becomes enraged when Mordecai does not bow down to him when he passes by. Learning that Mordecai is a Jew, he convinces King Xerxes that Jews are a disobedient people who should not be tolerated. Xerxes issues a proclamation that allows the murder and plunder of the Jews of Persia.

Mordecai prevails upon Esther to use her influence with the king to have the proclamation canceled. Esther gathers her courage to make her request, knowing full well the stakes: Under pain of death, no one is allowed to enter the presence of the king uninvited.

Esther is successful, and the decree against the Jews is ultimately rescinded. Haman is humiliated by being commanded to walk through the city, leading the royal steed on

which his adversary Mordecai is seated—an honor Haman thought was being reserved for himself.

It is a captivating story, wryly written and full of both the pitfalls of human nature and the triumph of forthrightness. But it is more than that. Numerous details of the story reflect an intimate familiarity with Persian life and culture of the fifth century B.C.

Some of the evidence is linguistic. Old Persian terms used in the book went out of use during the fourth century B.C.

Fifteenth-century artist Jacopo del Sellaio created this painting of the coronation of Esther at the palace of Persian king Xerxes.

This indicates that the book was written during the actual time when the events took place.

As for Mordecai, historical sources indicate at least one similar name, Marduka, who was a scribe at Susa. It was not unknown for foreigners to serve in the Persian court, as did Nehemiah, who served in the honored capacity of cup-bearer to the king (Nehemiah 2:1).

The Book of Esther describes Mordecai as sitting at the king's gate, an occupation that the modern mind might pic-ture as lowly or demeaning. But in ancient Persia, the entrance to the palace was an important administrative center for the royal court. The Hebrew word for "sit" may actually mean to occupy an official position, perhaps akin to serving in the palace guard. In any case, Mordecai's presence at the gate was more likely than not a sign of his importance.

King Xerxes' lavish banquet described at the beginning of the Book of Esther was held in "the third year of his reign." The reason for this is given by historical sources, which

The Persian Devil

No other foreign ruler is spoken of so highly in the Bible as King Cyrus of Persia. Isaiah speaks of God choosing Cyrus to accomplish his purposes. Indeed, it is Cyrus who sent the Jews back to their homeland with his blessing.

In the Book of Esther, another Persian king, Ahasuerus (Xerxes), is portrayed as a fair and just king who is persuaded by Esther to save the Jews from the evil Haman.

The Bible, however, says virtually nothing about the religion of the land of Persia. For that we must turn to other ancient sources. The religion of Persia is called Zoroastrianism, after a prophet who is said to have lived somewhere between 1500 and 600 B.C. It is a religion that, incidentally, continues to be practiced by a dwindling number of followers.

In Zoroastrianism, we have one of the clearest expressions of belief in a devil in pre-Christian times. A destructive spirit called Angra Mainyu is responsible for the evil in the world. Like the biblical Satan, Angra Mainyu, who rules from Hell, is the enemy of Ahura Mazda, the Creator and Wise Lord.

Ahura Mazda created an order of heavenly beings not unlike those described in Scripture. Similarly, Angra Mainyu is the leader of ranks of evil demons.

One fundamental difference separates the religion of Persia from that of the Bible. While Zoroastrianism looked forward to the ultimate triumph of good over evil, both forces are in some respects considered equal. Unlike Satan, Angra Mainyu is not a created being, but is co-eternal with Ahura Mazda.

Any such duality is rejected by the Bible, which teaches that all things, whether inanimate, animate, or spiritual, owe their existence to their creator, who alone is eternal.

record that, during Xerxes' first two years on the throne, he was occupied with rebellions in Egypt and Babylonia.

After Vashti's refusal at the banquet, we read that Xerxes consulted "the seven officials of Persia and Media, who had access to the king, and sat first in the kingdom" (Esther 1:14). The existence of this council, which served the Persian king, is confirmed by Greek sources.

There is one more historical detail that lends credence to the story of Esther. At the end of the book, we read that King Xerxes (called Ahasuerus in Esther) "laid tribute on the land and on the islands of the sea" (Esther 10:1). The only islands that the Persians are known to have controlled were in the Aegean Sea. In 480–479 B.C., the Persians fought unsuccessful battles to retain control of these islands.

Thus, the date for the setting of Esther in the third year of Xerxes' reign (482 B.C.) fits well within the historical context, and the Book of Esther remains a glorious account of triumph over the specter of persecution.

What Motivated Cyrus?

Cyrus the Great, king of Persia, overthrew the Babylonian empire in 539 B.C., an event that would bring about the return of the Jews to their homeland.

The tomb of Cyrus the Great at Pasargadae, in what is now southern Iran. Cyrus was renowned for his military exploits as well as his tolerance toward the peoples under his rule.

Shortly after ascending the throne, King Cyrus declared: "The Lord, the God of heaven, has given me all the kingdoms of the earth, and he has charged me to build him a house at Jerusalem in Judah. Any of those among you who are of his people—may their God be with them!—are now permitted to go up to Jerusalem in Judah . . ." (Ezra 1:1–3).

How did the Lord stir up the spirit of Cyrus to permit the Jews to return to Jerusalem? Some have suggested that Cyrus was aware of the prophecies of Isaiah, which foretold the return of the Jews and mention Cyrus by name: "Thus says the

Lord . . . who says of Cyrus, 'He is my shepherd, and he shall carry out all my purpose'; and who says of Jerusalem, 'It shall be rebuilt,' and of the temple, 'Your foundation shall be laid'" (Isaiah 44:28).

Precisely because of the references to Cyrus, many scholars reject the traditional dating of the writings of Isaiah to the eighth century B.C. in favor of a sixth-century date for at least the second part of the book (Isaiah 40–66). It is not possible, they point out, for Isaiah to have known of Cyrus more than 50 years before he was born. The Book of Isaiah must therefore have been written after the time of Cyrus.

However, the dating of the Book of Isaiah to the eighth century is supported by the ancient Jewish historian Josephus, who insisted that Cyrus did indeed know of the prophecies of Isaiah and of his foretold role in enabling the Jews to return to their land. Author of *The History of the Jews*, Josephus was intimately acquainted with the history of his people and had access to many source materials now lost. Josephus believed that the Book of Isaiah must have been written before Cyrus' time; in order for him to have read it, how could it be otherwise?

The prophet Daniel was still living during the early years of Cyrus' reign. His esteemed position would have made him a likely candidate to introduce Cyrus to the prophecies of Isaiah, particularly those regarding him. There is every reason to suspect that seeing his name in the ancient Jewish prophecies would have profoundly affected the Persian monarch, perhaps even enough to let the Israelites go.

A discovery made during the excavation of Babylon confirms the biblical account of Cyrus' freeing of captive peoples. The "Cyrus Cylinder," a ten-inch-long barrel-shaped cylinder made of clay, details the royal policy regarding captives: "[Cyrus] gathered all their [former] inhabitants and returned [to them] their inhabitations." Here we do have a nonbiblical reference to the "spirit" of Cyrus.

Darius, King of Persia

After Cyrus the Great decreed that the Jews should be allowed to rebuild their temple, their foes succeeded in delaying the project for decades. According to the Book of Ezra, the inhabitants of neighboring lands "bribed officials to frustrate their plan throughout the reign of King Cyrus of Persia and until the reign of King Darius of Persia" (Ezra 4:5).

With the ascension of Darius, work on the temple was finally begun, but not before the opponents of the Jews appealed to the Persian ruler. Ezra contains several fascinating letters of correspondence between the various parties and the Persian monarch. Darius had a search made of the royal archives and found the original decree of Cyrus, which permitted the rebuilding, thus settling the issue.

What do we know about this ruler who figures so prominently in the rebuilding of the Jewish temple? Fortunately, quite a lot. The Persians were skilled at chronicling their history, even though it presented their rulers in a positive light.

Darius, who reigned from 522 to 486 B.C., was the second in a line of succession after Cyrus the Great and his successor Cambyses. His rule of nearly forty years breathed new life into the Persian empire, which had been fragmented by revolt prior to his ascension.

This upheaval in the empire may be that which is referred to in the Book of Haggai, written during the time of the rebuilding of the temple. "For thus says the Lord of hosts: Once again, in a little while, I will shake the heavens and the earth and the sea and the dry land; and I will shake all the nations, so that the treasure of all nations shall come, and I will fill this house with splendor, says the Lord of hosts" (Haggai 2:6–7).

The correspondence between Darius and various parties preserved in the Book of Ezra indicates an efficient administration of the empire, a fact confirmed by history. Darius divided his empire into twenty provinces. He built major roads and established a uniform standard of weights and measures. He has also been credited with issuing the world's first currency. A gold coin known as the Daric was stamped with Darius' own likeness, showing him running and holding a spear and bow.

This relief at the ancient Persian city of Persepolis features King Darius and his son and successor Xerxes, known as Ahasuerus in the Book of Esther.

The Persian ruler carefully examined the conflict between the Judeans and their opponents, and he paid deference to the decrees of his predecessors. This indicates an empire that observed at least some semblance of a legal system.

Despite his considerable achievements, Darius also presided over one of the worst defeats of the Persian empire, at the hands of the Greeks at the Battle of Marathon in 490 B.C. The battle marked a turning point in Persian history, after which the empire entered a period of permanent decline.

New Testament: Politics and Sects

The religious and political struggles occurring in Judea during the first century are a reflection of the various philosophies of several sects and parties that were active at that time. The Pharisees, who controlled the synagogue, were the most influential group overall, though the Sadducees, the party of the rich and powerful, held the most privileged positions in society. Also part of the spectrum were the scholarly Essenes, the revolutionary Zealots, and the Herodians, supporters of Herod Antipas.

In this rendition in stained glass from Worcester Cathedral in Worcester, England, Herod Antipas questions Jesus.

THE FIRST CENTURY

Why Is the New Testament Written in Greek?

Alexander III of Macedon received his designation "the Great" from the Romans. They recognized the genius of Greek civilization, which was his gift to much of the then-known world. Indeed, the Romans themselves could do no better than to adapt wholesale much of Greek culture. Even Roman mythology was, in large part, a latinized version of the Greek pantheon. The Greeks gave the world the concept of the *polis*, the well-planned city, which the Romans eagerly adopted and spread throughout the Empire. And for centuries Greek was the *lingua franca*—the language of commerce and diplomacy—of the ancient world.

In 336 B.C., the 20-year-old Alexander succeeded to the Macedonian throne following the assassination of his father, Philip II. By 334 B.C., Alexander had united the Greek city-states under his control and led his army across the Hellespont (in what is now Turkey) to confront Persia, the dominant Eastern power of the day. Although outnumbered three to one, Alexander achieved a surprise victory over the Persians and soon drove them from Asia Minor and the Mediterranean.

Before continuing his Asian campaign, which would eventually take him to the Indus River and beyond, Alexander realized he needed to secure his southern flank. That meant occupying Syria-Palestine and Egypt along the eastern Mediterranean. In 332 B.C., Alexander marched down the Mediterranean coast, driving the Persians out of the Levant.

According to Jewish tradition, Alexander went to Jerusalem and met with the Jewish High Priest. If this is true, this was

In a surprise victory over the Persian army, Alexander waged battle across the Hellespont, driving the Persians from Asia Minor and the Mediterranean.

his only foray into the hill country of Judea—which would have been of little consequence in his grandiose ambitions. But as Alexander's armies continued their eastward march, until, on the plain of the Ganges, they refused to go any farther, the influence of Hellenism would be indelibly stamped upon the land of Judea.

After Alexander's death in 323 B.C., his generals divided up the Levant, with Ptolemy taking control of Egypt and Seleucus getting Syria. For nearly two centuries the rival kingdoms of the Seleucids and Ptolemies vied for control of Palestine until an independent Jewish kingdom was reestablished in 142 B.C. under the Maccabees.

Under Greek control, self-governing cities had sprung up to replace ancient Semitic cities, and despite efforts to cleanse the land of foreign influence, many Judean towns would retain their Greek names for centuries to come. It was only at the Arab conquest in the seventh century that Scythopolis would again revert to its Semitic name of Beth-shan. In the twentieth century, Shechem would still be called Nablus—an adulteration of the Greek "Neapolis."

As a result of Hellenistic influence, the art and architecture of the Jews became more refined. They also adapted the Greek style of tombs. But what may very well have been the most prevalent and enduring legacy that Greece bestowed upon the Jews was their language. As a result, the Septuagint, a Greek version of the Hebrew Bible, was translated from Hebrew in the mid-third century B.C.

Although the early Christians in Judea were Jewish, the Greek language had become so universally accepted that it was used instead of Hebrew in the writing of the New Tes-

Alexander the Great was a brilliant soldier and conquerer, while spreading Greek language, culture and ideas everywhere his armies went.

tament. It has been suggested that the Greek language was in part responsible for the rapid spread of the Gospel, as Greek was understood among the educated classes throughout the known world. Thus the language of Alexander conquered far more than his armies ever did.

An Adventurer and Scholar

Outside of the New Testament, our primary source of knowledge about first-century Judea is the Jewish historian Josephus, whose life was full of fascinating exploits and adventures—if what he writes about himself can be believed.

Josephus was born in A.D. 37 into a well-established priestly family in Jerusalem. Educated in a rabbinical school, he became an authority on the law by the time he was 14 and was routinely consulted by his seniors. By the age of 16 he was studying the major Jewish religious parties—the Pharisees, the Sadducees, and the Essenes—to decide which of these to join.

Not quite ready to make up his mind, Josephus spent three years in the desert meditating with a hermit before returning at age 19 as a Pharisee. The next seven years passed uneventfully in priestly duties, but at age 26 he was sent to Rome on a minor diplomatic mission and became shipwrecked on the way.

By the time he returned home in A.D. 66, Judea was on the eve of revolt against Rome. The country was divided into

six regional commands. Although Josephus was a priest and scholar, he was appointed commander of Galilee. It was through a series of unusual circumstances that this appointment came, as he was hardly qualified to be a military leader.

But Josephus rose to the occasion, leading his men bravely in defense of their fortress at Jotapata. However, after two months siege, Jotapata was about to fall. Josephus and the

The Jewish historian Josephus lived during the first century A.D. His **Jewish Wars** *and* **Antiquities of the Jews** *are our primary sources on the Great Jewish Revolt of A.D. 66–70.*

last of his men were hiding out in a cave, where they decided to commit mass suicide rather than surrender to the Romans.

Josephus suggested they organize the task by drawing lots. One by one his men had their throats slit until only he and another man were left. As Josephus later says, this was due either to luck or divine providence.

Deciding that suicide was not the most attractive alternative, Josephus convinced the other man that they would be better off surrendering after all, and they were brought before Vespasian, commander of the Roman legion. While all expected Josephus to be executed, or sent in chains to Rome, once again he managed to save himself. He surprised Vespasian by playing the seer and prophesying that Vespasian was destined to become emperor of Rome.

The commander was curious about this prophet as well as intrigued by him. Vespasian kept Josephus at his headquarters for the next two years, during which time Nero was dethroned and Vespasian proclaimed emperor. Josephus remained in the entourage of Vespasian's son Titus, who completed the conquest of Judea. Josephus' presence during the destruction of Jerusalem was the basis for his riveting eyewitness account of the siege.

Scholars debate the accuracy of Josephus' account of his exploits during the Jewish revolt. It is likely that some of what he wrote was intended to justify his own conduct in deserting to the Romans, while tactfully avoiding offending his captors.

After the war, Titus granted Josephus an estate outside Jerusalem in reward for his services. However, having angered his fellow Jews because of his dealings with Rome, he wisely decided to leave the country.

In Rome, Josephus was granted citizenship and a lifetime pension, and he was given Vespasian's private home to live in. It is here that he spent the rest of his life recording the history of his homeland, Judea. In gratitude for the privileges bestowed upon him, Josephus took the family name of the ruling Flavius dynasty as his own, and so Joseph of Matthias became Flavius Josephus.

The Herodians

We read in the Gospel of Matthew that, along with the Pharisees, representatives from a party called the Herodians came to Jesus and said: "Teacher, we know that you are sincere, and show deference to no one; for you do not regard people with partiality, but teach the way of God in accordance with truth. Is it lawful to pay taxes to the emperor, or not?" (Mark 12:14). Jesus' answer amazed them: "Give to the emperor the things that are the emperor's, and to God the things that are God's" (Mark 12:17).

The question revealed their basic sympathies: As their name indicates, they were supporters of Herod Antipas, who ruled in Judea after the death of his father, Herod the Great.

The Herodians supported Herod to a much greater degree than the Pharisees and the Sadducees. Why this was so is not known with certainty. The Herodians may have been a small group with close, perhaps familial, ties to their rulers.

The question was meant to trip up Jesus with either one or another of the sects and parties of first-century Judea. On the one hand, Antipas would have been keenly interested in hearing about anyone advocating "tax revolt" in his kingdom. If Jesus' answer could have been taken in such a way, one can assume that the Herodians would have wasted no time in reporting him. On the other hand, the Zealots, a sect with considerable popular sympathy, abhorred the idea of paying taxes to Rome. If Jesus' words could be understood as lending support to the ruling powers, he would have alienated the populace. That his answer brilliantly silenced both sides is a testimony to the divine inspiration that guided him.

On another occasion, after he silenced those who opposed his ministry, we read: "The Pharisees went out and immediately conspired with the Herodians against him, how to

Herod's Family Tree

Students of the Bible are sometimes confused by the various rulers named Herod mentioned in the New Testament. The name "Herod" became a title assumed by Herod the Great's descendants, much like the Roman emperors after Julius Caesar were called "Caesar."

The family tree of Herod the Great was sparser than it would have been had he not murdered so many of his own family. Among his victims were his Hasmonean wife Miriam, their two sons Alexander and Aristobulus, and Antipater, a son by another of his wives.

After Herod died, his three surviving sons fought for control over his domain. Augustus Caesar intervened, resolving the dispute by dividing the kingdom into three parts. Archelaus was given Judea, Samaria, and Idumea, along with the lesser title of "ethnarch."

Fear of Archelaus was the reason why the Holy Family went to live in Nazareth in Galilee, which was bequeathed to Archelaus' younger brother Antipas.

Referred to as "that fox" by Jesus (Luke 13:31–32), Antipas was responsible for the death of John the Baptist.

Philip, son of Herod by Cleopatra, received the extreme northern territories of Batanea, Trachonitis, and Auranitis. Little is known about his rule, which was apparently uneventful and peaceful.

Herod Agrippa was the grandson of Herod the Great. He was raised in Rome and in A.D. 41 was awarded Judea and Samaria to rule. He persecuted the early Christians. Under his brief rule, James, the son of Zebedee, was beheaded and Peter was imprisoned. Acts 12 relates how Agrippa was struck down suddenly while addressing a crowd in the theater at Caesarea in the year A.D. 44.

The last of the Herodian dynasty to rule in Judea was Agrippa's son, Agrippa II. In Acts 25, Paul appears before Agrippa II while imprisoned in Caesarea. Agrippa II sided with his Roman benefactors during the Jewish Revolt of A.D. 66–70, after which he thought it prudent to move to Rome, where he died sometime after A.D. 93.

destroy him" (Mark 3:6). So began the plotting that would eventually culminate in Jesus' crucifixion.

Sadducees:
The Aristocratic Party

*I*n first-century Judea, the Sadducees were the party of the rich and powerful. Their name in Hebrew means "righteous ones," a reference to their claim to be the descendants of Zadok, the high priest in the days of Solomon. They were ❦

in charge of the Temple and the daily sacrifices, and they participated in the Jewish court, or Sanhedrin.

The Sadducees were the ultimate power brokers of Judea. They cultivated good relations with the ruling powers, which in turn kept them in power, and they wanted nothing to threaten their privileged position in society. In the New Testament, they are presented as constant opponents of Jesus. Whereas the Gospels record some positive encounters between Jesus and individual Pharisees, his dealings with the Sadducees are all negative.

Jesus would have had little in common with the Sadducees. Jewish historian Josephus describes the Sadducees as elitist and boorish. They encouraged students to argue with their teachers, and they recommended harsher punishments for crimes. He limits the influence of the Sadducees to a few wealthy and powerful families. The majority of the people sided with the Pharisees.

In contrast to the Pharisees, the Sadducees accepted only the authority of the Pentateuch, the first five books of the Hebrew Bible. However, the Sadducees

French artist James J. Tissot's rendition of the Pharisees and Sadducees coming to test Jesus. The theological adversaries found common ground in their opposition to Jesus. ❦

rejected the immortality of the soul, and this led to a dispute with Jesus when they attempted to ensnare him with a complicated question about marital states in the resurrection.

Jesus' reply indicates how misguided he believed them to be: "Is not this the reason you are wrong, that you know neither the scriptures nor the power of God? For when they rise from the dead, they neither marry nor are given in marriage, but are like angels in heaven. And as for the dead being raised, have you not read in the book of Moses, in the story about the bush, how God said to him, 'I am the God of Abraham, the God of Isaac, and the God of Jacob'? He is God not of the dead, but of the living; you are quite wrong" (Mark 12:24–26).

Jesus often grouped the Sadducees and Pharisees together and condemned both sects for their hypocrisy and incorrect teachings. The two groups are presented in the Gospels as coming together to challenge Jesus. This indicates that, despite their differences—which were significant—they had more in common with each other than with the prophet from Galilee.

Pharisees: The Separated Ones

The Pharisees were the most influential political/religious movement in the Judea of New Testament times. They were respected as the teachers of Jewish law, and they controlled the central Jewish institutions of the synagogue and the Sanhedrin, or religious court.

Most scholars believe the name "Pharisee" means "the separated ones." In all likelihood, this was intended to suggest that they separated themselves though their close attention to ritual purity and dedication to the law.

They scrupulously practiced tithing, contributing a set portion of all that they possessed, including food. This prompted the criticism of Jesus: "Woe to you, scribes and Pharisees, hypocrites! For you tithe mint, dill, and cummin, and have neglected the weightier matters of the law: justice and mercy and faith. It is these you ought to have practiced without neglecting the others" (Matthew 23:23).

The Pharisees accepted the divine inspiration of the Hebrew Bible. They were noted for their authoritative interpretations of Jewish law, and for their simple way of life. They believed in angels and demons, the afterlife, and the resurrection of the body.

The Gospels portray the Pharisees as being in opposition to Jesus, who publicly called them hypocrites, but there were also positive encounters. On one occasion, he commends the response of a scribe, most of whom were Pharisees: "When Jesus saw that he answered wisely, he said to him, "You are not far from the kingdom of God" (Mark 12:34). We also know that the Pharisee Nicodemus visited Jesus by night, asking him questions, and after the crucifixion he brought the spices with which to anoint Jesus' body.

Nowhere are we told the process by which one became a Pharisee. Josephus claims to have been one, although he criticizes them on certain points. Likewise, the Apostle Paul mentions on several different occasions that he was formerly a Pharisee. The word is perhaps better understood as representing a broad-based movement rather than a rigidly defined sect such as, for example, the Essenes.

Rabbinical literature discusses Shammai and Hillel, the founders of the two great first-century schools of the Phar-

Belgian artist Jacob Jordaens' depiction of Jesus disputing the Pharisees, the most influential religious/ political party in first-century Judea.

isees. However, these stories are dated from A.D. 200 or later, leading some scholars to question whether they present an accurate portrayal of the movement in the time of Jesus.

What *is* certain is that, nearly 2,000 years later, the term "pharisee" has come to convey for most people a negative connotation, used to describe a person who is hypocritically self-righteous.

Legions in Judea

No Roman legions were stationed in Judea until they were brought there to suppress the First Jewish Revolt. Only after the uprising were they permanently stationed in the land.

When they were not at war, the Roman legions were put to good use and in effect became construction battalions. The remains of their presence and work can still be seen. Legion X Fretensis took part in the conquest of Jerusalem by Titus in 70 A.D. and established its headquarters there. Many fragments of tiles have been found in the Old City stamped with the initials of this legion.

The emperor Hadrian sent several legions to put down the Second Jewish Revolt of A.D. 132–135. This revolt was even more violent than the First Revolt. Historians note that at this same time an entire Roman legion—the 25th from Egypt—disappeared from history. When the commander of the legions made his customary report to the Senate upon his return to Rome, instead of the customary greeting, "The emperor and the legions are well," he could only state, "The emperor is well."

Legion X Fretensis took part in that campaign and afterward constructed a number of public works projects commissioned by the emperor Hadrian. The most enduring of these is an impressive aqueduct extending from Caesarea, some 15 miles north, to springs in the Haifa range; parts of it can still be seen today. An

This aqueduct at Caesarea Maritima is built on two independent foundations. The first channel was built by Herod the Great (37–4 B.C.); the second was added a century and a half later by the Roman Emperor Hadrian.

inscription found attached to the aqueduct read: "Imperator Caesar Traianus Hadrianus Augustus has made (this aqueduct) by a detachment of Legion X Fretensis."

Evidently, the Tenth Legion was aided in this massive construction project by another legion. At Megiddo, in the valley of Esdraelon, not far from the northern end of the aqueduct, an ancient village named el-Lejjun preserves the name "Legion." The remains of a Roman camp were located nearby, in which was found another telltale tile stamped with the abbreviation "LEGVIF" for Legion VI Ferrata.

Jewish Freedom Fighters

*U*nlike the Pharisees and Sadducees, who had come to a grudging acceptance of Roman rule, and the Essenes, who withdrew from active participation in Jewish society, the Zealots dreamed of revolution.

Under military occupation, Judea in the first century was ripe for an extreme nationalistic movement like the Zealots. Roman-appointed tax collectors bled the populace, while their rulers—Herod the Great and his sons who succeeded him—lived in splendor.

Zealots were fierce opponents of the Roman occupation of Judea, which began in 63 B.C. They taught that God alone was the rightful king of Israel. Submitting to any other power was treason, and payment of taxes to foreign power was idolatry. The Zealots preferred death to the yoke of Roman occupation.

According to Josephus, the movement began in A.D. 6 when the sons of Judas the Galilean, Jacob and Simeon, led a revolt over a census that Rome was conducting for taxation purposes. That revolt was crushed, but as discontent grew, the movement continued to gain followers.

The word "Zealot" appears in the New Testament on only two occasions, both with reference to Simon the Zealot, one

The Arbel cliffs overlooking the Sea of Galilee. Here, in 38 B.C., as King Herod was eliminating all political opposition, the supporters of his opponent Antigonus leaped to their deaths rather than submit to his rule.

of the disciples of Jesus. Some suggest that, when used for Simon, the epithet "Zealot" merely refers to the older sense of the word: one who is devoted to the law and zealous for God. Others believe the word would have had too close an association with the nationalistic movement for it to be used in the traditional sense.

There may be one other indirect reference to the Zealots in John's Gospel, where he uses a word in reference to Barabbas that Josephus used to describe the Zealots. This would be entirely in character, for Barabbas was an insurrectionist, opposed to all government authority. If so, the enthusiasm that the crowd showed for having Barabbas released instead of Jesus is an indication of the popularity of the Zealots.

In the decades after Jesus, the Zealots grew ever bolder, and it was their influence that was responsible for pushing Judea over the brink in A.D. 66, when the fateful Jewish Revolt against Rome began. The Jews fought bravely and had some initial success, but were eventually overwhelmed by the iron fist of Rome.

Josephus records that, as the Roman legions closed on Jerusalem, it was the Zealots who refused any talk of surrender, slaying those who attempted to talk peace with the enemy. Even when the Temple Mount was captured in A.D. 70 and the city was burning, the Zealots fought on to the last man.

After the fall of Jerusalem, the Zealots were still not finished. Hundreds escaped to Masada, Herod's desert fortress on the shores of the Dead Sea. There, after a year's siege, Masada fell and the last of the Zealots met their bitter end.

Roman Rule

*I*n 63 B.C., Pompey and his Roman legions put an end to the civil war in Judea. This marked the beginning of centuries of Roman rule, which lasted throughout the period of the New Testament and the early Church. Roman domination ended in the seventh century, when the Byzantines were defeated by Arab armies marching under the Islamic crescent.

In the time of Augustus, the ruling emperor when Jesus was born, the Roman Empire had an estimated population of between seventy and ninety million, spread out across much of the known world. All this required efficient administration—which, fortunately, Augustus excelled at. He instituted major reforms that brought stability to Roman politics and society.

The three major institutions of ancient Rome were the emperor, the Senate, and the army. It was not possible to become emperor without the allegiance of the army, and every emperor was wary of his generals. This proved to be the undoing of many Roman commanders, including Mark Antony and Pompey before him.

Before Augustus, the emperor and the Senate had often been at odds. When Julius Caesar assumed dictatorial powers, he attempted to abolish the Senate, which fled to Greece. Augustine trimmed the size of the Senate and appointed its new members, but also granted it new powers.

One such power-sharing was the division of the empire into Imperial and Senatorial provinces. The Senate had jurisdiction over one group of provinces, which were closer to home and peaceful. The Imperial provinces, on the other hand, were farther away and required a military presence. In this, Augustine shrewdly kept the upper hand, for by directly administrating the provinces where the legions were, he maintained control over that vital institution.

At any given time, Rome fielded numerous legions that were scattered throughout the empire as needed. Each legion consisted of 6000 men—on paper at least—and was composed of 10 cohorts of 600 men each, more or less the equivalent of the modern battalion. In Acts 10:1, Cornelius is called "a centurion of the Italian Cohort, as it was called."

The commander of a cohort was called a tribune, one of which, Claudius Lysias, is mentioned by name in Acts 23. Paul learns of a plot to kill Claudius and sends a young boy to warn him. The tribune took immediate action: "Then he summoned two of the centurions and said, 'Get ready to leave by nine o'clock tonight for Caesarea with two hundred soldiers, seventy horsemen, and two hundred spear men. Also provide mounts for Paul to ride, and take him safely to Felix the governor'" (Acts 23:23–25).

The centurion, an officer in command of 100 or more soldiers, completed the chain of command in the Roman army. Centurions were usually chosen from among the ranks for their courage and reliability. Several centurions are mentioned in the Gospels and Acts. Curiously, each is presented in a positive light, which is more than could be said about many of the religious leaders of the Jews.

Jesus healed the servant of a centurion in Capernaum, and when he saw the soldier's faith he declared: "Truly I tell you,

Roman soldiers sometimes threatened and extorted money from civilians (Luke 3:14). On the other hand, every mention of Roman centurions (commanders of 100 men) in the New Testament presents them in a positive light.

in no one in Israel have I found such faith" (Matthew 8:10). All three of the Synoptic Gospels mention the conversion of the centurion at the foot of the cross who, impressed by what he saw and heard, concluded that Jesus was both innocent and divine.

In the Book of Acts, the first Gentile convert to the Christian faith is the "god-fearing" centurion Cornelius. Later, another centurion named Julius treats Paul kindly when he is charged with accompanying the apostle to Rome.

James Tissot's rendition of the healing of the ten lepers. Of the ten, only one returned later to thank Jesus for his healing.

The Samaritans: Second-Class Jews

On his way to Jerusalem, Jesus entered a village and was approached by ten lepers: "Keeping their distance, they called out, saying, 'Jesus, Master, have mercy on us!' When he saw them, he said to them, 'Go and show yourselves to the priests.' And as they went, they were made clean. Then one of them, when he saw that he was healed, turned back, praising God with a loud voice. He prostrated himself at Jesus' feet and thanked him. And he was a Samaritan" (Luke 17:13–16).

The words "he was a Samaritan" were likely used to shame the Jewish listener, by whom the Samaritans were considered inferior—pretenders who were not true Jews. Though the origins of the Samaritans are not certain, it is believed that they were Jews who, centuries before the time of Jesus, intermarried with Gentiles and thus were not of pure Jewish descent.

The Jews looked down upon the Samaritans with contempt and avoided their territory. The ancient Jewish route from Galilee to Jerusalem skirted Samaritan territory, and it was here, as he "was going through the region between Samaria and Galilee" that Jesus encountered the lepers.

It was the Samaritan who returned to Jesus and gave praise to God. A man who was a double pariah—both for his leprosy and his race—was the one who received Jesus' praise and blessing: "Rise up and go; your faith has made you well."

Interestingly, this was not the first time Jesus praised a Samaritan. Earlier in the same Gospel, we read the famous parable of the good Samaritan, who helped a man left for dead after a priest and a Levite refused to help. Priests and Levites served in the Temple and occupied lofty positions in ancient Jewish society.

Once again, as was typical of the ministry of Jesus, we find him showing his disapproval of those who sought adulation and commending those whom we would not expect to be praised.

A Clash of Cultures

*T*he Apostle Paul's missionary journeys took him to Athens, the capital city of the Greeks. While Paul was waiting for his companions, "he was deeply distressed to see that the city was full of idols" (Acts 17:6).

After preaching the Gospel in the marketplace, Paul was approached by several philosophers who had been debating with him and who had decided that he needed a larger hearing: "So they took him and brought him to the Areopagus and asked him, 'May we know what this new teaching is that you are presenting? It sounds rather strange to

us, so we would like to know what it means" (Acts 17:19–20).

We read that the "strange teaching" that Paul was preaching was "the good news about Jesus and the resurrection" (Acts 17:18). But why should this teaching have been so incomprehensible to the Athenians? The answer lies in how the Greeks and the Romans after them viewed the world around them—what philosophers call a "worldview."

The Romans, who followed Greece on the stage of world history, were a practical people concerned more with empire-building than philosophical speculation. We find in Rome no equivalent to Mars Hill, the gathering place of philosophers in Athens where Paul was brought to explain his beliefs.

As a result, Rome added little to the philosophical worldview of its predecessors. It adopted Greek mythology wholesale, giving Latinized names to the Greek gods: Zeus became Jupiter; Hermes was renamed Mercury; Aphrodite became Venus; and so on.

Underlying the popular mythology of Greece and Rome was a more formal philosophical worldview, which for the Greeks since the time of Plato was built upon the belief that an individual consisted of two distinct parts: a physical body as well as an immaterial, eternal soul.

At first glance, this seems to have a lot in common with how Christians look at the themselves and the world. After all, does not the Bible teach that humans have a soul, or spiritual nature, as well as a body? Indeed it does, but here is where the similarity ends.

The Greeks considered the material world to be of little value. Instead, it was an evil to be escaped. However, salvation, if the Greeks considered this concept at all, had nothing to do with sin or with one's relationship with God. The only thing people needed to be "saved" from was the body itself, which had become entrapped in the material world.

The key point here is that, in the Greco-Roman worldview, the body was of no lasting importance. It was only a shell to be discarded, a chain that imprisoned the soul. The great schools of Greek philosophy had little interest in preserving or healing the body, only escaping it.

Thus, the Greeks and Romans could not fathom the idea that the body was destined to be resurrected. The teaching that Jesus of Nazareth had been resurrected from the dead was to them even more incomprehensible: "When they heard of the resurrection of the dead, some scoffed; but others said, "We will hear you again about this" (Acts 17:32).

As in other places in the Greco-Roman world where Paul preached, we read that "some of them joined him and became believers." These new Christians were the beginning of a movement that would grow despite persecution and one day conquer the Roman Empire.

QUMRAN

The Essenes

*T*he Essenes were members of a Jewish sect that existed in Judea between the mid-second century B.C. to the end of the first century A.D. They numbered approximately 4,000 members—almost all males—who lived in monastic communities throughout the land.

The Essenes are believed to have originated in Babylon after the fall of Jerusalem. They reacted against what they saw as the moral laxity of the Jewish religious establishment, dedicating themselves to the strict observance of the Torah, the body of wisdom and law contained in Jewish Scripture.

Scholars have pieced together the story of how the Essenes came to live in remote areas. Some believe that the settlement at Qumran near the shores of the Dead Sea was an Essene community. After the successful Maccabean revolt of 167–164 B.C., some Essenes returned to Judea, bringing with them their ideas about religious reform. They were shocked by what they viewed as the compromise of pure Judaism on the part of the leaders of the rebuilt Temple. Their indignation won few converts, but one of these, who came to be known as the Teacher of Righteousness, was a member of the influential Sadok family, from whose ranks the high priest had traditionally come.

The Teacher of Righteousness was already favorably inclined toward the various reforms that the Essenes advo-

The Essene Creed

Josephus, who lived in Judea in the first century, was raised to be a rabbi— a Jewish religious teacher— and briefly joined the Essenes. He recorded the rigid vow that the Essenes took at the beginning of the common meal:

"Before touching the communal food, he must swear terrible oaths, first that he will revere the Godhead, and secondly that he will deal justly with men, will injure no one either of his own accord or at another's bidding, will always hate the wicked and cooperate with the good, and will keep faith at all times and with all men—especially with rulers, since all power is conferred by God. If he himself receives power, he will never abuse his authority and never by dress of additional ornament outshine those under him; he will always love truth and seek to convict liars, will keep his hands free from stealing and his soul innocent of unholy gain, and will never hide anything from members of the sect or reveal any of their secrets to others, even if brought by violence to the point of death. He further swears to impart their teaching to no man otherwise than as he himself received it, and take no part in armed robbery, and to preserve the books of the sect and in the same way the names of the angels. Such are the oaths by which they make sure of their converts." (Josephus, *The Jewish War, II*, 145.)

cated when he assumed the office of high priest between 159 and 152 B.C. However, the hopes of the Essenes were dashed when he was deposed by the Jewish leader Jonathan. After losing the power struggle in Jerusalem, the Teacher of Righteousness joined the Essenes and soon became their leader.

Some of the writings of the Teacher of Righteousness were preserved among the Dead Sea Scrolls found at Qumran. They portray him as a man of intense religious conviction who harbored deep resentment toward the religious establishment. He and his followers chose to live apart from Jewish society rather than endure what they viewed as its many corruptions.

From Josephus we learn something of their strict way of life, which was marked by the avoidance of all luxuries and pleasures. The Essenes typically rose before dawn for prayers. After working in the morning, they dressed in linen garments and partook of a ritual bath. Afterward, they ate their midday meal, then worked until evening when they ate again in total silence.

Earning the full privilege of joining the sect required a probationary period of several years and the swearing of allegiance to the community. Upon becoming a member, the successful candidate was given the emblems of the community: a white robe and belt, along with a tool for digging holes in the earth when he relieved himself.

The law was of central importance to the Essenes, and they studied it twenty-four hours a day in overlapping shifts of ten hours each. The Essenes were also preoccupied with the endless copying of Biblical manuscripts and the writing of their own religious commentaries. Many of these documents, discovered hidden in caves along the Dead Sea, have furnished a wealth of information for historians and biblical scholars.

Who Lived at Qumran?

*I*n 1947, the world was stunned by the discovery of ancient biblical manuscripts in caves along the northwest shores of the Dead Sea. In the search to find who may have hidden the scrolls, attention soon focused on the nearby ruins of Qumran, named after a dry gorge.

It would not be until 1953, several years after Israel's War of Independence, that the ruins would finally be excavated. From the beginning, it was widely believed that the site had been occupied by the Essenes, an austere Jewish monastic sect that was opposed to the religious establishment in Jerusalem.

Archaeologists uncovered what they believed to be the remains of a religious community, including a "scriptorium," a room with a long table presumably used for copying the scrolls found in nearby caves, and a "refectory," used for communal meals. Two *mikvot* (ritual baths) were found as well, indicating that members performed ceremonial bathings.

The painstaking process of piecing together, identifying, and deciphering the tens of thousands of manuscript fragments continues decades after their discovery between 1947 and 1956.

The Discovery of the Century?

*I*f the treasures listed in the Copper Scroll are ever located, the find will surely rank among the most exciting of modern archaeological discoveries.

The story of how the Copper Scroll was found is itself a fascinating one. The first ancient scrolls at Qumran on the shores of the Dead Sea were discovered in 1947. The search of other caves in the cliffs along the sea was disrupted by war, as Israel and its neighbors fought over the very territory where the first scrolls were found.

The fighting and subsequent political uncertainty over who would control the area did not prevent its native inhabitants, the Ta'amirah Bedouin, from engaging in their age-old profession of hunting for ancient artifacts to sell. Eventually, pieces of scrolls began showing up in the antiquities market, leading archaeologists to suspect that the bedouins, who knew the area intimately, had found other scroll-bearing caves.

In 1952, Jordan's Department of Antiquities began a search of caves in the area, which led to the finding of what is known as "Cave 3." The chamber contained many fragments of leather scrolls similar to those that had been found in other caves. Far more important, however, were the two rolls of copper found in a corner by themselves.

The two rolls turned out to be two halves of the same document, on which Hebrew script had been punched. Scholars were eager to unroll and read the scroll, but soon discovered that it was too brittle to open.

Used to working with ancient scrolls made of leather and papyrus, scholars were at a loss as to how to open the Copper Scroll. Finally, after deliberating for three years, it was decided that it would be taken to England, where it was painstakingly sawed into twenty-three sections and photographed.

As with many ancient artifacts, the Copper Scroll fared better for the nearly two thousand years it lay stored in a cave than it has in the decades since being removed. The scroll is composed of extremely pure copper with only about one percent tin, which has prevented severe oxidation. Unfortunately, however, the edges have begun to crumble, and some of the worst damage is on either side of the saw cuts.

Cave 4 at Qumran is located across a small gully from the main settlement. Originally a dwelling, it became the repository for 40,000 fragments of biblical documents.

In recent years, some scholars have rejected the identification of Qumran as an Essene religious community. These scholars point out that Josephus, the first-century Jewish historian who is one of our primary ancient sources of information about the Essenes, never mentions that they had a community at Qumran.

One suggestion is that the site was a winter villa, similar to those in nearby Jericho. During winter, the wealthy in Jerusalem would escape the cold of the central hill country, many of them traveling to Jericho to enjoy its mild climate. Supporting this thesis are the delicate blown glass, finely cut stone urns, painted pottery, and elegant column bases found at Qumran. Such fineries, it is argued, would be out of place in a monastic community.

But while poverty was obligatory for individual Essenes, the community itself did acquire material goods. It's also possible that some of the expensive items were donated to the community by wealthy patrons. On the other hand, almost all of the pottery used at Qumran was of a cheap, common variety that one would not expect to find in an affluent villa.

Yet another idea is that Qumran was a military fortress. There is what appears to be a fortified tower at the site, and signs of battle, including Roman iron arrowheads from the destruction of the site in 68 A.D.

However, many structures—even farmhouses—had towers in ancient days, and it makes sense that an isolated religious community would want to protect itself against marauders. Later Christian monasteries in the region were built like fortresses for much the same reason. Even more damaging to the military fortress thesis is the fact that the settlement at Qumran has no outer defensive wall and is easily accessible from almost every side.

The death knell to the view that Qumran was either a villa or a military fortress is the scrolls themselves. Found in caves near the site, almost all are religious in nature. What use would either a military fortress or a villa have for such a hoard?

Furthermore, the vast cemetery adjoining the settlement would have been out of place next to a villa or a military fort. But it does fit with the original thesis that Qumran was a long-term community of about 200 people who lived their lives, died, and were buried on a bleak plateau overlooking the Dead Sea.

The Enigmatic Copper Scroll

In 1952, in a cave near the barren shores of the Dead Sea, a mysterious document was found that continues to baffle scholars and treasure hunters alike.

Though identified with the famous discoveries of biblical documents at Qumran, the Copper Scroll is unique. Unlike the leather and papyrus manuscripts and fragments at Qumran, the Copper Scroll, measuring approximately eight feet long and 11 inches wide, is made of unusually pure copper.

The scroll dates to before the destruction of Jerusalem in 70 A.D., and the Hebrew script in which it is written differs from that of the other Qumran documents. Also unlike the

The monument known as Absalom's Tomb is one of the sites mentioned in the Copper Scroll as containing hidden treasure.

others, it makes no pretense at being a religious document.

Rather, it appears to be an ancient treasure map. The scroll details dozens of hiding places—64 to be exact—containing fabulous quantities of treasure. The scroll begins without introduction, listing the various locations, followed by the quantities of valuables at each one.

The sum total is staggering. Scholars estimate the amount of silver, gold, and other valuables hidden at the sites to weigh as much as 174 tons. This initially caused many scholars to conclude that the Copper Scroll was the result of some ancient scribe's overactive imagination. But if it was fraudulent, it was a complex and expensive hoax. Copper was a high-priced commodity. And why hide the scroll in a remote cave where it would not be found for almost 2,000 years?

It has been pointed out that ancient documents from Jewish folklore—which few interpret literally—also describe the concealment of the treasure from the so-called First Temple. But these writings are very different, relating the legendary acts of famous figures such as Jeremiah in hiding the treasure.

A Treasure Too Fabulous to Be True?

Many scholars have begun to consider the possibility that the Copper Scroll is a genuine list of treasures hidden in Judea before the end of the First Revolt (66–70 A.D.). Some have connected these riches with the treasury of Jerusalem's Temple. One problem remains: the sheer volume of these treasures.

The scroll lists approximately 4,630 talents of gold and silver, with each talent weighing between 25 and 75 pounds. By twentieth-century standards, that seems like an incredible amount.

The evidence from ancient literature and inscriptions tells the story of a vastly different age when precious metals were used as currency and were hoarded by nations in great quantities. Some of these records refer to treasures seized by conquerors; others list the contents of national treasuries. Still others detail the tribute paid by one country to another— normally exacted in gold and other precious metals.

Surprisingly, when compared to other ancient records, the amounts of precious metals listed in the Copper Scroll are not unthinkable for their day. If all of the precious metals described in the Copper Scroll were converted to gold according to their relative value, the total would come to 39 tons.

Greek historian Herodotus provides us with our first statistics regarding the wealth of the ancient world. He lists the annual income of Persian kings as 39 tons of gold, virtually the same amount of wealth as listed in the Copper Scroll. But there's more—much more.

The treasure that Alexander the Great found at the Persian capitals of Persepolis and Susa amounted to the more than 800 tons, dwarfing what is listed in the Copper Scroll. The treasury of Athens in 432 B.C. is said to have contained 21 tons of gold; while in 347 B.C., the equivalent of 127 tons of gold were found in the treasury at Delphi. Sizable amounts of precious metals are known to have existed in Judea during that period as well. Herod the Great is said to have left more than three tons of gold to Augustus Caesar and his cronies.

There is little chance that any of Herod's money made its way into the Temple treasury, but other sources of income remained. The Temple was, after all, a tax-collecting body, gathering tithes from the Jews year after year, century after century.

If the cryptic riddles contained in the Copper Scroll are ever deciphered, perhaps the treasures it describes can still be found.

By contrast, the Copper Scroll appears to be a no-nonsense, unembellished list that, unlike the others, does not include descriptions of any famous relics from the Jewish past. Accordingly, the scholarly consensus has cautiously come around to the possibility that the Copper Scroll is indeed describing locations where treasure is buried.

The various descriptions of the sites add to the mystery. The first location, for example, is "in the ruin that is in the Valley of Achor." It is thought that, in the first century, the Valley of Achor was north of Jericho in Wadi Nuwei'imeh. But what is the "ruin"? It may be the name of a village in the valley with a similar name.

The mystery continues to deepen as the directions to the treasure are given: "Beneath the steps that enter to the east, forty cubits west: a chest of silver and its articles. Weight: 17 talents." Scholars disagree as to the weight of a talent at that time, with the possibilities ranging from 25 to 75 pounds.

The second location is apparently near the first: "In the funerary shrine, in the third course of stones: 100 gold ingots." The mention of a funerary shrine suggests a town, perhaps no longer inhabited.

The third description suggests that another location is in view: "In the large cistern that is within the Court of the Peristylion, in a recess of its bottom, sealed in the entrenchment opposite the upper door: 900 talents." A peristyle is a small round courtyard surrounded by a colonnade. One would expect to see a sophisticated structure such as this in a larger metropolis such as Jerusalem.

Some have suggested that the third treasure location is somewhere inside the Temple Court. But if the purpose of the Temple Scroll was to hide the treasure from the Romans, who were intent on conquering Jerusalem, it is unlikely that it would be hid in the eye of the impending storm. Indeed, the Temple was destined to be completely destroyed by Titus' legions.

The list continues, identifying locations around Judea said to contain large amounts of treasure. Some of the descriptions of locations have groups of Greek letters of unknown meaning—and which scholars have been unable to interpret.

Further compounding the mystery is the last location listed on the scroll. Instead of treasure, this site is said to contain "a duplicate of this document and an explanation and their measurements and a precise reckoning of everything, one by one." It appears, then, that this duplicate scroll, which has not been found, may be necessary to interpret the descriptions of the other locations.

Undeterred, adventurers have gone spade in hand throughout the land looking for the buried treasure. Alas, nothing has been found, not even in the most recognizable of sites, such as the monument known as Absalom's tomb in the Kidron Valley of Jerusalem.

One intriguing theory suggests that the Copper Scroll is actually a list of tithes to the Temple treasury. The terms "contribution" and "tithe" appear throughout the scroll. In addition, at least one of the locations is found on the estate of the priestly Hakkoz family, to whom was entrusted the Temple treasury after the exile. The fourth location reads: "In the cave that is next to the fountain belonging to the House of Hakkoz, dig six cubits. (There are) six bars of gold."

We find a reference to this family in the Book of Ezra that: "On the fourth day, within the house of our God, the silver, the gold, and the vessels were weighed into the hands of the priest Meremoth son of Uriah" (Ezra 8:33).

The Book of Nehemiah provides the final connection, referring to "Meremoth son of Uriah son of Hakkoz" (Nehemiah 3:4). Thus, the Hakkoz family mentioned in the Copper Scroll was responsible for the treasure of the Temple.

Jewish law specified that if the tithe could not be taken to Jerusalem for political or other reasons, it was to be stored in Genizah—a hidden place for sacred objects. Judea was in extreme turmoil during the years of the First Revolt (66–70 A.D.), which falls within the accepted dating of the Copper Scroll. This would explain the reason for hiding the treasure in various locations rather than taking it to the Temple treasury.

The question will likely not be solved until the codes in the scroll are deciphered or the elusive second scroll is found. Until then, the Copper Scroll will likely remain one of the most mysterious treasure maps of all time.

Eating and Drinking at Qumran

Providing food and water in a desert environment presents unique challenges, which the Essene community at Qumran met in resourceful ways.

One of the rooms excavated in the compound at Qumran sheds light on the eating habits of inhabitants. In an adjoining storeroom, more than 700 bowls were found, carefully arranged in piles of a dozen. Other assorted eating and drinking utensils, including 210 plates and 75 beakers, were found here as well.

Archaeologists have pieced together the diet of the community. It consisted of bread, wine, and as the main course, a bowl of cooked meat. The meat was mutton, beef, or goat, and would usually be boiled but sometimes roasted. Curiously, the leftover bones were carefully buried after being covered with broken pieces of pottery. This suggests that at least some of the meals had a ritual significance.

In a desert area such as the region of the Dead Sea, obtaining sufficient quantities of water is a concern of utmost importance. Qumran solved the problem with an ingenious system that included a dam, an aqueduct, and cisterns.

Unlike the bone-dry region around the Dead Sea, the hill country of Judea received significant precipitation during the winter months. After a particularly heavy rainfall, the water would drain into the normally dry wadi systems running down to the Dead Sea. These would fill with water, in some cases turning into raging torrents as they raced down to the sea, located 1,300 feet below sea level.

Qumran lay on a plateau at the head of one of these gorges, Wadi Qumran. Above the settlement, a dam was built across the wadi, which would fill with water during floods. The water was diverted into an aqueduct leading to Qumran, where it filled cisterns that supplied the community with water.

This water system was quite sophisticated. A filtration pool was built into the aqueduct to remove the fine sand that would clog it. The sand sank to the bottom, while the clear water flowed into channels that diverted water throughout the settlement. Similar filtration basins provided the same service for individual cisterns.

The steps leading down to a mikvah, *or Jewish ritual bath, at Qumran. The inhabitants of Qumran immersed themselves in cold water to ritually purify themselves before eating.*

The water system also served the ritual baths known as *mikvot.* The Essenes were required to perform ritual baths before entering the refectory.

Oddly enough, the excavation at Qumran uncovered no buildings that had been used as living quarters. Where, then, did the Essenes live? Given their austere lifestyle, scholars assume that the Essenes inhabited the numerous caves in the vicinity, or that they lived in tents or other temporary shelters.

Archaeologists excavated a scriptorium where the Essene scribes worked copying their sacred manuscripts. Two inkwells containing dried ink were found among the debris of this room. The settlement also contained a complete pottery workshop, including a circular pit for a potter's wheel and kilns for firing the earthenware. The large jars in which some of the scrolls were found were likely made here.

When they completed their work on earth, the members of the community were buried in a nearby cemetery. Of those excavated, the vast majority are adult males. The severity of life in such a hostile environment is indicated by the average life span of less than forty years.

NEW TESTAMENT: GOSPELS

On the pages of the Gospels—the "good news" of evangelists Matthew, Mark, Luke, and John—we follow the life of Christ from his birth and baptism, through the practice of his ministry, to his final days on earth, culminating in his death and resurrection and his ascension to Heaven. The Gospel writers include many accounts of miracles in their narratives, emphasizing how trust in God brings salvation, even in the face of chaos and despair.

Jesus during Palm Sunday as depicted in St. Mary's Cathedral in Winnipeg, Manitoba, Canada.

THE KING IS BORN

The Anointed One

The Hebrew word "messiah" means to "smear" or "anoint." The high priest Aaron and his sons were consecrated to the priesthood by anointing with oil. Saul, the first king of Israel, was called "the anointed of the Lord"— a title that became synonymous with king.

Little is known about the method of anointing. According to Jewish tradition, olive oil was poured on the head and rubbed on the forehead in the form of a cross. The anointing signified that the priest or king was endowed with the spirit of God and that he was chosen by God to fill his office. After the prophet Samuel anointed Saul, he told him that "the spirit of the Lord will possess you, and you will be in a prophetic frenzy along with them and be turned into a different person" (1 Samuel 10:6).

Unlike rulers of some other cultures in the ancient Near East, the Israelite kings never claimed divine honors. There was, however, a transformation that took place when the king was anointed. At the anointing of Saul, we read that "after (Saul) turned away to leave Samuel, God gave him another heart; and all these signs were fulfilled that day.

King Solomon, called the wisest man who ever lived, ruled during Israel's Golden Age. This depiction of him is found in St. Mary's Basilica in Minneapolis, Minnesota.

When they were going from there to Gibeah, a band of prophets met him; and the spirit of God possessed him, and he fell into a prophetic frenzy along with them" (1 Samuel 10:9–10).

Through disobedience, Saul eventually forfeited his anointing, and the Lord chose a new king. Samuel was sent to Bethlehem, and after finding David "took the horn of oil, and anointed him in the presence of his brothers; and the spirit of the Lord came mightily upon David from that day forward" (1 Samuel 16:13).

However, Saul still ruled, and his antagonism towards David grew into open, murderous hostility. David was forced to flee with his compatriots to the wilderness of Engedi. Such was his respect for the one who had been anointed that when he had opportunity to kill Saul he refused, saying: "The Lord forbid that I should do this thing to my lord, the Lord's anointed, to raise my hand against him; for he is the Lord's anointed" (1 Samuel 24:6).

David's son and successor, Solomon, failed to observe another requirement of the Lord's anointed, to rule with care as a shepherd cares for his sheep: "And he shall stand and feed his flock in the strength of the Lord" (Micah 5:4). Solomon's grandiose building projects and his greatly expanded empire required high taxes, forced labor, and military conscription. His rule fulfilled the lament of the prophet Samuel when the Israelites first demanded to have a king over them:

"These will be the ways of the king who will reign over you: he will take your sons and appoint them to his chariots and to be his horsemen, and to run before his chariots . . .

He will take your daughters to be perfumers and cooks and bakers.

He will take the best of your fields and vineyards and olive orchards and give them to his courtiers.

He will take one-tenth of your grain and of your vineyards and give it to his officers and his courtiers.

He will take your male and female slaves, and the best of your cattle and donkeys, and put them to his work.

He will take one-tenth of your flocks, and you shall be his slaves.

And in that day you will cry out because of your king, whom you have chosen for yourselves; but the Lord will not answer you in that day" (1 Samuel 8:11, 13–18).

The ideal of the anointed king was never fully realized in any of the kings of Judah or Israel. Indeed, it was often trampled underfoot by a succession of unrighteous kings. It would be left to one who was yet to come, the future Messiah, who would become the fulfillment of the ideal king.

When Did Jesus Live?

The Gregorian calendar, instituted by Pope Gregory XIII in 1582 and still used for civil purposes around the world today, is correct to within one day in 20,000 years. However, the pivotal date of the Gregorian calendar—the birth of Jesus Christ—cannot be fixed with precision and is incorrect by several years.

The Gospels provide several details about the life of Christ that help date his birth and death. We read in the Gospel of Luke that the events of Jesus' birth occurred "in the days of King Herod of Judea" (Luke 1:5). The Herod that Luke is referring to, known as "Herod the Great," ruled Judea from 37 B.C. to his death in 4 B.C. Since Herod was alive when Jesus was born, Jesus could not have been born after Herod's death in 4 B.C.

A further clue is found in the Gospel of Matthew, where we read: "In the time of King Herod, after Jesus was born in Bethlehem of Judea, wise men from the East came to Jerusalem, asking, "Where is the child who has been born king of the Jews? For we observed his star at its rising, and have come to pay him homage" (Matthew 2:1–2).

Herod, determined to eliminate any potential threat to his rule, inquired of the chief priests and scribes where this "king of the Jews" was to be born. He learned that the Scriptures prophesied that the Messiah was to be born in Bethlehem. Meanwhile, the wise men, having been warned of Herod in a dream, eluded him.

Infuriated, Herod then "sent and killed all the children in and around Bethlehem who were two years old or under, according to the time that he had learned from the wise men" (Matthew 2:16).

Why were the children aged "two and younger" killed? Herod may have shrewdly learned that the wise men saw the star announcing the birth of the Messiah and began their

journey as early as two years before the event. Not knowing exactly when in that time frame the birth occurred, he decided to take no chances and so ordered the slaughter of all children age two and younger. However, the Holy Family escaped the slaughter, having departed for Egypt also after they, too, were warned in a dream.

Herod presumably did not receive the wise men in his final months. It was during these months that he had become deathly ill and was preoccupied with finding a cure for his various ailments. If are to we assume that the wise men arrived in Jerusalem a year or so before Herod's death, Jesus' birth could be placed between 5 B.C. and 7 B.C.

Scholars differ as to the length of Jesus' earthly ministry. Here we are given clues by the biblical text. Luke tells us: "Jesus was about thirty years old when he began his work" (Luke 3:23).

In addition, at least three Passovers (celebrated once a year) are mentioned in the Gospels as having taken place during Jesus' ministry. This would indicate a life span of about 33 years.

When was Jesus crucified? Astronomical data related to the dates for the Jewish Passover in the first century A.D. also suggests that the Passover of Jesus' trial and crucifixion was either that of A.D. 30 or 33.

We also learn from Luke's Gospel that John the Baptist began his ministry: "In the fifteenth year of the reign of Emperor Tiberius, when Pontius Pilate was governor of Judea, and Herod was ruler of Galilee" (Luke 3:1). The Herod mentioned here is not Herod the Great, but his son

Antipas, who ruled in Galilee and who inherited the title "Herod."

The fifteenth year of the Emperor Tiberius was in A.D. 28–29. John baptized Jesus in that year, which also marked the beginning of Jesus' ministry. As already mentioned, the Gospels allude to at least three Passovers, which would fit chronologically with a date of A.D. 33 for Jesus' crucifixion.

However, the matter remains unresolved, with some scholars maintaining that the period of Jesus' ministry was actually one year rather than three, and holding for a crucifixion date of A.D. 30. Whatever the exact date, it is certain that the crucifixion of Jesus took place between A.D. 26 and 36, when Pontius Pilate was prefect of Judea.

No Room at the Inn

The Christmas season is a special time of year around the world, with its wintry manger scenes in straw-filled wooden barns. However endearing the images they inspire may be, in the light of history and biblical evidence, these re-creations are somewhat fanciful.

The New Testament does not tell us the time of year Jesus was born and gives no indication that the event occurred in December. We do, however, have one clue that the time of year could not have been winter. The Gospel of Luke states that, "In that region there were shepherds living in the fields, keeping watch over their flock by night" (Luke 2:8).

In Palestine, the grain crops are grown in winter during the rainy season. Animals are not permitted in the fields during the growing season because they would trample the stalks. After the grain is harvested, the sheep and goats are allowed to graze the stubble and fertilize the fields.

The birth of Jesus was first celebrated on December 25 in the fourth century. Up until then, that date marked the weeklong revelry of the Saturnalia, one of the most popular festivals of ancient Rome. The festival was a celebration of the winter solstice, which occurs December 21. After the empire became Christianized, the pagan festival was transformed into a Christian holiday.

The familiar nativity picture of Mary and Joseph being turned away from the inn at Bethlehem is likewise inaccurate. We read in the Gospel of Luke that Mary delivered Jesus and laid him in a manger "because there was no place for them in the inn" (Luke 2:7).

The Greek word that was translated as "inn" actually means a "guest room" or "dining room." Luke uses the word only one other time, in his description of the Last Supper of Jesus before his crucifixion. The word he uses for the "guest room" in which they celebrate the Passover, elsewhere described as a "large room upstairs, already furnished" (Luke 22:11–12), is the same Greek word used in the story of Mary and Joseph.

There would have been walled enclosures in the countryside where shepherds and travelers could find shelter with their animals. But hotels or inns would have been unknown in first-century Judea. People traveled infrequently, and when they did, they would plan to stay with relatives.

Pope Gregory instituted the Gregorian calendar, which is still used for civil purposes around the world.

The one exception was Jerusalem, whose population could double during the Passover feast. Those who had no relative in the city to stay with made other arrangements for lodging. It is in this context that we read about the "guest room" that Jesus and his disciples used to celebrate their Passover.

The reason for Mary and Joseph's trip to Bethlehem was to register for the census decreed by Caesar Augustus. This meant that the town was filled with travelers like themselves, who were returning to their place of origin for the census.

It is likely that, upon arriving in Bethlehem, Joseph and Mary went to their relatives looking for lodging. However, the "guest room" was occupied. It is also possible that their prospective hosts did not realize how far along Mary was in her pregnancy.

We are not told exactly where they ended up staying. That the newborn babe Jesus was placed in a "manger"—a stone feeding trough—indicates they found shelter with the animals.

We must not suppose that this was a massive-beamed barn like that portrayed by European artists. Even today, the area around Bethlehem has many caves used to shelter animals. In olden times, homes in Palestine were often built over natural caves that were enlarged to provided a secure place for animals to stay. As an alternative, some homes were built with a separate first-floor area where animals were kept.

Mary and Joseph may have been offered a place in one of these interior "stables" by their apologetic hosts, who had nothing else to offer.

A Star in the East

*F*or centuries, astronomers and students of the Bible have pondered a strange celestial event described in the Gospel of Matthew:

"In the time of King Herod, after Jesus was born in Bethlehem of Judea, wise men from the East came to Jerusalem, asking, 'Where is the child who has been born king of the Jews? For we observed his star at its rising, and have come to pay him homage'...Then Herod secretly called for the wise men and learned from them the exact time when the star had appeared...When they had heard the king, they set out; and there, ahead of them, went the star that they had seen at its rising, until it stopped over the place where the child was" (Matthew 2:7–9).

The identification of the star is complicated by the uncertainties over when Jesus was born, which is generally estimated

Spanish artist Jose Ribera's rendition of the adoration of the shepherds. The manger was actually a stone-cut feeding trough for animals.

Italian artist Fra Giovanni da Angelico here depicts the arrival of the magi to worship the Christ child. The magi may have learned about the coming of the Messiah from the large Jewish community in Babylon.

It is thought that the tail of the comet helped to "point" the way towards Bethlehem. However, in the ancient Near East, comets were considered evil omens, not signs of good tidings, as the birth of Jesus was intended to be. It is also difficult to imagine how Halley's Comet would have pointed to Bethlehem.

Another explanation for the star was the possible sighting of the planet Jupiter near the star Regulus. Astrologers in ancient Mesopotamia considered Jupiter to be the "king" planet. Since Regulus also means "king," the conjunction of the two would have been significant. Also, Regulus is in the constellation Leo, which is the astrological sign of the ancient tribe of Judah. This conjunction, however, occurred a year after the death of Herod the Great and may be too late to fit the chronology of the nativity story.

as occurring between the years 8 and 4 B.C. In those years, several celestial events of note took place that various scholars suggest may have been the "star" that the wise men saw.

One theory is that the star was none other than Halley's Comet, which would have been visible in the fall of 12 B.C.

Another possibility was first suggested by the seventeenth-century astronomer Johann Kepler. He correctly calculated that three alignments of Jupiter and Saturn occurred in 7 B.C. Astronomers now know that the first one took place in May of that year. This would have been a highly significant event, considering that Saturn is the ruling planet of Judah. Also, the alignment took place in the constellation Pisces, known as "The House of the Hebrews."

Even more momentous was a near-alignment of Mars, Jupiter, and Saturn in September of 6 B.C. This is a rare event, occurring only once every 800 years.

One final possibility comes from records kept by Chinese astronomers, who reported a new star in the constellation Capricorn in the spring of 5 B.C. This star—likely a nova—was visible for 70 days, appearing several hours before sunrise in the East. However, this location would have been the opposite of Matthew's star, which guided the wise men; they came "from the East" and journeyed westward.

The suggested theories for the identity of the star, while intriguing, remain to varying degrees unsatisfactory, for they fail to account for the star's precise guidance of the wise men to Bethlehem. Thus, there remains the possibility that the star was part of a miraculous event separate from these other, natural, phenomena.

Messianic Expectations

*T*he age into which Jesus was born was one of heightened expectation of the coming Messiah. The Jewish people eagerly awaited their coming king, who would put an end to Roman domination and bring about the spiritual renewal of their nation.

Several Messiah candidates are mentioned in the New Testament and in the writings of the Jewish historian Josephus. The first of these was John the Baptist, who began preaching and baptizing in the region of the Jordan River. We read

that the crowds of people who came out to see him were "filled with expectation, and all were questioning in their hearts concerning John, whether he might be the Messiah" (Luke 3:15).

John steadfastly denied that he was the Messiah, telling the people: "I baptize you with water; but one who is more pow-

This depiction of John the Baptist, bowing in worship before Jesus, is from the Kirk in the Hills, Bloomfield Hills, Michigan.

Heinrich Hoffmann's painting "The Lord's Image."
While many hoped that Jesus was the political Messiah,
Jesus said, "My kingdom is not of this world."

erful than I is coming; I am not worthy to untie the thong of his sandals" (Luke 3:16).

Another Messiah figure named Theudas appeared on the scene after the time of Jesus, during the rule of the procurator Cuspius Fadus (A.D. 44–46). According to Josephus, Theudas led a large crowd to the Jordan River, where he promised to repeat Joshua's miracle by commanding the river to dry up, after which he would lead his followers across.

Fadus sent a squadron of cavalry against the fanatics, who were gathered on the riverbank waiting for the miracle to transpire. Many were taken prisoner, and their leader Theudas was killed. His severed head was brought back to Jerusalem.

This episode is also mentioned in the Book of Acts, where the Pharisee Gamaliel cautions his fellow members of the Sanhedrin against taking extreme action against the Apostle Peter: "Fellow Israelites, consider carefully what you propose to do to these men. For some time ago Theudas rose up, claiming to be somebody, and a number of men, about four hundred, joined him; but he was killed, and all who followed him were dispersed and disappeared" (Acts 5:35).

In his speech, Gamaliel gave another example of a false Messiah: "After him Judas the Galilean rose up at the time of the census and got people to follow him; he also perished, and all who followed him were scattered" (Acts 5:37). Josephus mentions Jacob and Simeon, the sons of Judah the Galilean, who attempted to lead a revolt under the procurator Tiberius Alexander (A.D. 46–48). Alexander had the sons of Judah crucified.

Josephus records that, under the procurator Felix (A.D. 52–59), an Egyptian gathered thousands of disciples who followed him up to the Mount of Olives, where he promised to crumble the walls of Jerusalem and deliver the Roman garrison into their hands. He promised to then rule as king over the nation. Felix sent soldiers against them, massacring many, but their leader managed to escape, never to be heard from again.

This event is mentioned in Acts, when the Apostle Paul is arrested in the courtyard of the Temple. The Roman commander suspects Paul is the Egyptian who got away. Then, after he hears Paul speak Greek, the commander remarks: "Then you are not the Egyptian who recently stirred up a revolt and led the four thousand assassins out into the wilderness?" (Acts 21:38).

Finally, Josephus also reports that, during the rule of the procurator Festus, an anonymous self-styled prophet promised salvation to all who would follow him into the desert. Soldiers were dispatched to dispel the gathered crowds with force, killing the prophet along with a number of his followers.

The large numbers that followed these would-be Messiah figures speaks to the widespread longing among the Jewish people for a Messiah who would bring political liberation from the hated Romans.

Throughout Jesus' ministry, many hoped Jesus would be the political Messiah they were waiting for. The Gospel of John records what happened when Jesus explained the profoundly spiritual nature of his ministry: "Because of this many of his disciples turned back and no longer went about with him" (John 6:66).

Their hopes would not die, though. As Jesus was approaching Jerusalem the week of his arrest, the people laid down palm branches, a Jewish messianic symbol, on the path before him, unmindful of what he tried to tell them: "My kingdom is not of this world."

Where Is Herod's Tomb?

*T*he notorious monarch Herod gave himself the name "Herod the Great." Among his grandiose building projects was a series of fortresses in the wilderness. These strongholds were not constructed to protect against foreign invasion, for Herod faced few if any external threats.

Rather, the fortresses served primarily for Herod's personal protection. During his long reign, Herod made many enemies among his Judean subjects, and the fortresses served as places to hide in the event of a coup attempt in Jerusalem.

One of Herod's most impressive desert strongholds is the Herodium, visible today as a lone, flat-topped mountain on the edges of the wilderness east of Bethlehem. The site held nostalgic value for the Idumean king: In 40 B.C., Herod's political opponents in Jerusalem took advantage of a

ered, Herod made his way to Rome, where he was proclaimed "King of the Jews."

The memory of this battle and his mother's near-fatal accident so impressed Herod that he returned 20 years later to build a fortress on the site of the earlier battle. As usual, Herod was determined to make this another grandiose construction and spared no expense making the Herodium another impressive construction project. To increase the height of the hill on which the fortress was built, he leveled a nearby hill and added the rubble to the base of the Herodium.

The remains of the solid round tower in the Herodium is a possible location for the tomb of Herod. The tower, originally 140 feet tall, overlooked the Judean desert.

Parthian invasion of nearby Syria to stir revolt in Judea. Forced to flee for his life with his immediate family, Herod fought a rear-guard battle at the site.

During the fight, his mother was critically injured when her chariot overturned. Fearing that her injuries were fatal, Herod tried to commit suicide but was restrained. His entourage made it safely to Masada. While his mother recov-

On top of the artificial mountain, he constructed seven-story-high cylindrical walls with four massive towers. The tallest, which served as Herod's private keep, had three levels of living space and soared 100 feet above the walls. The Herodium was equipped with the usual Roman amenities to which Herod had become accustomed, including a bathhouse, a columned hall, and dining room. On the grounds below, a lavish palace was constructed, complete with a swimming pool and formal, Roman-style gardens.

Out of all the sites of his building projects around the land of Judea, it is the barren wilderness setting of the Herodium that Herod chose for his burial. Josephus describes Herod's last agonizing days as he sought relief at the hot springs of Machaerus on the eastern shores of the Dead Sea. He finally succumbed at his palace at Jericho. An elaborate funeral procession accompanied Herod's solid gold bier to the Herodium, where, according to Josephus, Herod was interred.

Thus Herod met his end. But for archaeologists, the mystery of where he was buried is one that is very much alive. Beginning in the 1970s, the Herodium has been systematically excavated. Archaeologists hoped to find Herod's tomb but were unsuccessful in their efforts to do so.

A possible location for Herod's tomb was the round tower that served as his keep, but initial examination determined that the base was solid. However, that conclusion has recently been challenged with the use of new techniques for discovering hidden chambers.

The round tower was examined using two different advanced sensing technologies, geophysical radar and ground-penetrating sonar devices, both of which indicated the presence of a chamber 8 to 10 feet in diameter inside the tower.

The same high-technology sensing equipment discovered unexplored subterranean chambers underneath a building at the base of the Herodium. Fragments of beautifully carved stones, which might have been part of a mausoleum, were found in this area.

It may well be that Herod's tomb was looted and destroyed after his reign and nothing remains to be found. Technical difficulties and financial constraints have prevented the excavation of these newly discovered possible locations of Herod's tomb. Archaeologists still dream of finding the solid gold bier and other treasures buried with the "King of the Jews."

The Burial of Herod

*I*n his book *The Jewish War*, the historian Josephus records how Archelaus, the newly proclaimed king of Judea, attended to the burial of his father:

"Everything possible was done by Archelaus to add to the magnificence: He brought out all the royal ornaments to be carried in procession in honor of the dead monarch. There was a solid gold bier, adorned with precious stones and draped with the richest purple. On it lay the body wrapped in crimson, with a diadem resting on the head and above that a golden crown, and the scepter by the right hand. The bier was escorted by Herod's sons and the whole body of his kinsmen, followed by his spearmen, the Thracian Company, and his Germans and Gauls, all in full battle order, headed by their commanders and all the officers, and followed by five hundred of the house slaves and freedmen carrying spices. The body was borne twenty-four miles to Herodium, where by the late king's command it was buried. So ends the story of Herod."

A Controversial Passage From Josephus

Among the references made by ancient writers regarding Jesus of Nazareth, none is more remarkable or controversial than that recorded by the historian Josephus in his *History of the Jews*:

> *"About this time there lived Jesus, a wise man, if indeed one ought to call him a man. For he was one who wrought surprising feats and was a teacher of such people as accept the truth gladly. He won over many Jews and many of the Greeks. He was the Messiah. When Pilate, upon hearing him accused by men of the highest standing amongst us, had condemned him to be crucified, those who had in the first place come to love him did not give up their affection for him. On the third day he appeared to them restored to life, for the prophets of God had prophesied these and countless other marvelous things about him. And the tribe of the Christians, so called after him, has still to this day not disappeared."*

This passage, known as Josephus' "Testimonium," appears to be an astounding testimony to Jesus being the Messiah—and of his resurrection—by a non-Christian ancient source. To some, it would have been unthinkable for a Jewish historian to make such an admission.

Therefore it has been suggested that this particular passage must have been altered at some later date to include the dis-tinctly Christian elements. As Josephus' works were preserved and handed down to us by the Church, there would have been ample opportunity for the texts to be secretly revised.

One thing, however, is certain: The Testimonium cannot be dismissed as being simply a late fabrication. The text is quoted in its entirety by the fourth-century Church historian Eusebius in his work *History of the Church*. Eusebius was known to be a meticulous scholar, who thoroughly researched his sources. Despite his obvious enthusiasm for defending and furthering the Gospel, there is no evidence that Eusebius willfully used fraudulent source material to prove his point.

It is then left for some unknown Christian scribe in the time before Eusebius to have supposedly altered the text to include what he believed to be some critical details about the life of Christ. But this assumes a willingness to engage in and condone an obvious fraud on the part of those in the early Church, contrary to the fundamental moral axioms of their faith. The Church did not depend upon secular historians for proof of their most important doctrines, and it is difficult to fathom the purpose in attempting to change the original text.

Unfortunately, as no other ancient manuscript versions of the passage are available for comparison, a definitive resolution to the controversy surrounding Josephus' Testimonium may never be reached. However, even if the disputed references to the Messiah and the resurrection are found to be a later inclusion, the passage remains a valuable confirmation by a secular source of the historical existence of Jesus Christ.

MINISTRY IN GALILEE

A Prophet Without Honor

Nestled along the northern shores of the Sea of Galilee at the foot of the Korazin Valley are the remains of an ancient fishing hamlet by the name of Kefar Nahum ("village of Nahum"). Known as Capernaum by readers of the New Testament, this village was overshadowed by larger cities on the lake, such as Magdala and Tiberius to the south.

This is where Jesus went to live after the people of Nazareth rejected him. We read in the Gospel of Luke that the enraged inhabitants of the city tried to throw him off a cliff after he applied the prophecy of Isaiah to himself:

"The Spirit of the Lord is on me, because he has anointed me to preach good news to the poor. He has sent me to proclaim freedom for the prisoners and recovery of sight for the blind, to release the oppressed, to proclaim the year of the Lord's favor" (Luke 4:18–19).

Much effort has gone into attempting to understand what Jesus meant by these words. Some see Jesus' use of this passage—which speaks of "freedom for the prisoners" and releasing the oppressed—as a manifesto for insurrection against the heavy-handed Roman occupation of Palestine. Indeed, many in Jesus' day were looking for a messiah figure who would lead such a revolt. History records several candidates including Judas Maccabeus and Bar Kochba, who led the Jewish people in bloody uprisings.

Jesus lived in Capernaum after Nazareth rejected him. The inhabitants were outraged when Jesus applied Isaiah's prophecy to himself.

However, Jesus steadfastly refused to allow himself to be cast as a political messiah. This is evident from his rebuke to those who came to arrest him in the Garden of Gethsemane (Luke 22:52): "Am I leading a rebellion, that you have come with swords and clubs?"

Later, when questioned by Pontius Pilate as to whether he considered himself to be the king of the Jews, he replied: "My kingdom is not of this world. If it were, my servants would fight to prevent my arrest by the Jews... my kingdom is from another place" (John 18:36).

If, by quoting Isaiah, Jesus was not advocating revolution, then what was he talking about? We find the key in his response when questioned about the kingdom of God:

"The kingdom of God does not come visibly, nor will people say, 'Here it is!' or 'There it is!' because the kingdom of God is within you" (Luke 17:20–21). By this Jesus was indicating that his mission on earth was primarily a spiritual one. His intent was not to lead a political revolt but to revolutionize men's hearts.

After his rejection in Nazareth, we have no indication in the Gospels that Jesus ever returned there. From then on, Capernaum is referred to as Jesus' "home" (Mark 2:1) and "his own town" (Matthew 9:1). Capernaum, along with Korazin on the heights above the water and nearby Bethsaida, form what Bible scholars call the "evangelical triangle"—the geographical region where Jesus conducted much of his ministry.

Modern-day pilgrims to the Holy Land can visit each of these three sites at the northern end of the Sea of Galilee. ❦

But even there, Jesus' ministry did not have the intended effect:

"Then Jesus began to denounce the cities in which most of his miracles had been performed, because they did not repent. 'Woe to you, Korazin! Woe to you Bethsaida! If the miracles that were performed in you had been performed in Tyre and Sidon, they would have repented long ago in sackcloth and ashes... And you, Capernaum, will you be lifted up to the skies? No, you will go down to the depths. If the miracles that were performed in you had been performed in Sodom, it would have remained to this day. But I tell you that it will be more bearable for Sodom on the day of judgment than for you" (Matthew 11:21,23–24).

Jesus wanted his miracles to have a life-transforming effect on those who experienced them. But all too often this was not the case. Given the large number of miracles that the Gospels say he performed, and the small geographic area of Galilee, there could not have been many extended families that were not touched by Jesus' ministry.

And yet many rejected Jesus' message, fulfilling his proverb that "a prophet has no honor in the prophet's own country" (John 4:24).

The Magnificent Caesarea Maritima

The story of how Herod acquired the site of Caesarea Maritima is shrouded in mystery. In 31 B.C., Octavian—who was given the name Augustus by decree of the

Roman Senate—completed his revenge on the murderers of Julius Caesar by defeating Mark Antony at the Battle of Actium.

King Herod of Judea, who up until then had supported Anthony, had an uncanny ability to curry favor with whoever was in power in Rome. He wasted no time switching allegiances, traveling to Rome laden with gifts for the new emperor.

Perhaps because he was impressed with the gall of the upstart Herod, Augustus decided he was just the man to look out for his interests in the defiant land of Judea, which had come under direct Roman control in 63 B.C.

Besides being one of the cruelest taskmasters the Jews ever had, Herod the Great was a shrewd businessman. He realized the local spices and other agricultural products could fetch three or four times the normal price in Rome if he could beat the Egyptian ships sailing from Alexandria in the spring. Unfortunately, there was no serviceable natural harbor along the whole coast of Judea.

Not one to let obstacles stand in his way, Herod built a port and named his new city Caesarea Maritima in honor of

Excavated ruins at Caesarea Maritima, a magnificent accomplishment of Herod the Great, who built an artificial harbor along a stretch of the Mediterranean where no natural harbor existed.

Is This the House of St. Peter?

We read in the Gospel of Matthew that, arriving in his adopted hometown of Capernaum, Jesus entered Peter's house, and "saw his mother-in-law lying in bed with a fever; he touched her hand, and the fever left her, and she got up and began to serve him" (Matthew 8:14–15).

Excavations at Capernaum have uncovered a number of enclosed dwellings called *insuli*, which accommodated extended families of up to a hundred persons. These were large walled areas composed of rooms surrounding a central courtyard.

Archaeologists believe they may have found the *insuli* that housed Peter's extended family. One of the enclosed dwellings contained a room that was set apart from the others. Dating to the first century A.D., it was the only room at Capernaum to have plastered floors and walls. At least six layers of plastered pavements were found, indicating that the area was well-used over an extended period of time. It is

Archaeological excavations at Capernaum discovered an ancient church built over this insuli, or walled enclosure, which may have been the home of the Apostle Peter.

thought that religious gatherings took place in this room.

Late in the fourth century, a wall was built around this room. Christian graffiti was found on plaster chunks that had fallen face down from this wall. The names Peter, Jesus, God, and Christ were found, as well as liturgical expressions such as *Amen* and *kyrie eleison*.

Interestingly, the presence of different languages indicates the site was a place of pilgrimage. The Spanish Sister Egeria wrote in 384 that "in Capernaum the house of the prince of the apostles has been made into a church, with its original walls still standing." By the fifth century, an octagonal church was built over the site, prompting a visitor to write in 570 that "the house of St. Peter is now a basilica."

That structure was eventually destroyed, and Capernaum lay abandoned until recent excavations brought the ancient site of Peter's house to light.

Augustus. The addition of "Maritima" was necessary to distinguish the city from Caesarea Philippi at the foot of Mount Hermon in northern Israel. One of Herod the Great's most ambitious building projects, Caesarea was the first artificially created port in the ancient world. It required the creation of a massive breakwater that extended nearly a third of a mile out into the sea.

Two developments in the ancient world made the building of such a port possible. The first was the invention by Roman engineers of a waterproof concrete that hardened underwater. The ingredient that made this possible was a volcanic sand known as *pozzolana*, a bonding agent similar to portland cement.

Secondly, in 25 B.C., a few years before Herod began building Caesarea, a Roman engineer and architect named Vitruvius published a treatise entitled *On Architecture*. The book set forth the "state of the art" in Roman architecture and discussed harbor construction among other things. Herod's engineers probably had access to this book.

The city had the usual amenities that expatriate Romans favored, including a theater seating several thousand and a stadium for racing horses. Caesarea even boasted a sewer system designed to flush each day with the tides. Blocks of warehouses stored local produce until it could be loaded for shipment to Rome.

Several significant incidents in the New Testament occurred in Caesarea. Herod Agrippa was struck down in the theater, and the Apostle Peter was sent there to meet the Roman centurion Cornelius, who would later become the first Gentile convert to the new Christian faith. Paul passed through

Caesarea several times, staying at the home of Philip the Evangelist, before being imprisoned and sent to Rome.

At the onset of the First Jewish Revolt in A.D. 66, tensions between Jews and Gentiles led to the desecration of the synagogue in Caesarea. Josephus records that as the result of this revolt 20,000 Jews were killed in the ensuing riots.

From Caesarea, revolt spread around the land until Vespasian, sent from Rome, arrived with his legions to regain the land. Later, when his son Titus completed the subjugation of Judea, he returned to Caesarea with Jewish captives. During the victory celebrations, 2,500 of these prisoners perished in gladiatorial games in the theater.

The Healing Pool

*H*idden among the maze of dusty narrow streets in the Old City of Jerusalem lies a medieval cloister. Behind its high walls stands the magnificent Church of St. Anne, the finest example of a Crusader church still standing in the Holy Land.

Next to the church are the impressive ruins of the ancient Pool of Bethesda spoken of in the Gospels. It was there that Jesus healed a man who had been an invalid for 38 years: "When Jesus saw him lying there and knew that he had been there a long time, he said to him, 'Do you want to be made well?' The sick man answered him, 'Sir, I have no one to put me into the pool when the water is stirred up; and while I am making my way, someone else steps down ahead of me.'

Jesus said to him, 'Stand up, take your mat and walk.' At once the man was made well, and he took up his mat and began to walk. Now that day was a sabbath" (John 5:6–9).

Biblical scholars have long puzzled over the story of the healing at the Pool of Bethesda. For one thing, the excavated pool did not have "five porches" as stated in the biblical text. And how was it possible to lower people into the huge basins, nearly 50 feet deep?

In 1950 the mystery of the Pool of Bethesda was solved by archaeologists. A pagan sanctuary to the healing god Aesclepius, a minor but popular Greek god, was uncovered adjoining the Pool of Bethesda. The shrine dated to the time of Jesus and was identified by the unearthed image of a serpent coiled around a pole, the symbol of the Aesclepian Cult (the symbol is familiar to us today as the symbol of the American Medical Association).

In each of the more than 200 Aesclepian shrines scattered throughout ancient Greece and Rome, the infirm would follow much the same prescribed ritual. After offering a sacrifice in a temple devoted to Aesclepius, they would immerse themselves in a ritual pool. Following that, they ❦

James J. Tissot's rendition of The Pool of Bethesda. Also known as "The Healing Pool," it is associated with a mysterious and miraculous healing.

The Pool of Bethesda lies within the present walls of the Old City of Jerusalem, and is viewed here below the remains of a Byzantine church built over the pool.

would ingest a hallucinogenic substance and retire to a darkened, cave-like niche. The drug-induced dreams that would follow formed the basis for a priest's diagnosis.

At the Pool of Bethesda, these excavated underground chambers are clearly visible surrounding a small pool. These discoveries fit well with the details of the biblical text. The Aesclepian temple at the Pool of Bethesda also accounts for the reason a "great number of disabled people" were gathered there: The site had become a healing shrine, and people believed miraculous things could happen there.

No Greater Faith

*I*n the Gospel of Luke, we read that Jesus was approached by the elders of Capernaum as he was entering the city. The fishing village on the shores of the Sea of Galilee had become his adopted home and was more appreciative of his ministry than was Nazareth, where he grew up. Indeed, hundreds of years after the time of Jesus, Capernaum would be known for its large population of believers in the Prophet from Galilee.

The miracle of Jesus healing the centurion's servant is depicted in a window of Christ Church Cathedral, Oxford, England. The dour expressions on some of the faces may be a reaction to Jesus' praise of the centurion's faith.

ordinary request. The Jews hated the Roman occupiers of their country with a passion. That hatred resulted in two ferocious revolts that would level the country and destroy the Jewish nation.

So why did the Jewish elders come to Jesus on behalf of a Roman military commander? The answer is given in their own words: "This man deserves to have you do this, because he loves our nation and has built our synagogue" (Luke 7:4–5).

Visitors to Capernaum today can view an imposing structure of white limestone that stands in the midst of the black basalt buildings of the ancient town. This synagogue, dated to the fourth century, is built over the original synagogue that Jesus knew and the elders referred to.

The adventurous visitor can explore the nearby fields where the partially excavated remains of a Roman military camp can be found hidden in the overgrowth. Recent excavations have uncovered a Roman-style bathhouse and other large, well-constructed buildings.

The elders of Capernaum came to Jesus to ask him to heal the deathly-ill servant of a Roman officer, or centurion. To our twentieth-century minds, this may not seem unusual. But given the political tensions of the day, it was an extra-

The Sea of Galilee Boat

In 1986, when the Sea of Galilee was at its lowest level in memory, archaeologists identified a number of previously unknown anchorages around the sea, indicating a thriving fishing industry in ancient times.

In January of that year, two brothers from Kibbutz Ginosar on the shores of the sea noticed the oval outline of what appeared to be a boat in a mud bar that had been exposed by the receding waters. News reports soon trumpeted the discovery of what was dubbed the "Jesus boat." Archaeologists dated it to between 100 B.C. and A.D. 100, declaring it the first ancient ship ever found in the Sea of Galilee.

The rising water level threatened to endanger the salvage operation as archaeologists sought the best means to remove the fragile remains from the seabed. Using new techniques in marine excavation and preservation, they encased the boat in polyurethane and floated it to shore.

The boat is almost certainly the same type Jesus and his fishermen disciples would have been familiar with. Twenty-six feet long and seven feet wide, the boat is built with wooden joints, which

This 26-foot-long boat was discovered submerged in mud in the Sea of Galilee. Although there is no evidence linking it to Jesus and his disciples, it has been dated to between 100 B.C. to 100 A.D.

is characteristic of this period. It had been repaired on several occasions, indicating it had a long life.

The boat was probably decked with storage areas below. It may have been in the hold created by such a deck that Jesus was resting in the Gospel story of a storm on the Sea of Galilee: "A great windstorm arose, and the waves beat into the boat, so that the boat was already being swamped. But he was in the stern, asleep on the cushion; and they woke him up and said to him, 'Teacher, do you not care that we are perishing?' He woke up and rebuked the wind, and said to the sea, 'Peace! Be still!' Then the wind ceased, and there was a dead calm" (Mark 4:37–39).

Sources indicate that ships of this size had a crew of five. Josephus refers to such ships holding as many as 15 people. Jesus and his 12 disciples would have fit comfortably into such a boat.

While no direct evidence connects the Sea of Galilee boat with Jesus, he or his disciples may have seen it or even ridden in it. Capernaum, his adopted hometown, was just a few miles north along the shore where the boat was found.

This is where the sick servant of the centurion lay. Jesus went with the elders to the camp to visit him. However, "the centurion sent friends to say to him, Lord, do not trouble yourself, for I am not worthy to have you come under my roof; therefore I did not presume to come to you. But only speak the word, and let my servant be healed. For I also am a man set under authority, with soldiers under me; . . . When Jesus heard this he was amazed at him, and turning to the crowd that followed him, he said, 'I tell you, not even in Israel have I found such faith.' When those who had been sent returned to the house, they found the slave in good health" (Luke 7:6–7, 9–10).

One need only recall how the Jewish people had been chosen by God from among the nations to imagine how Jesus' observation must have stung them. He may have intended this illustration to spur his countrymen on to a deeper piety.

A Special Mountain

*T*he view from Mount Tabor is one of the most spectacular in all of Israel, looking out over a panorama of biblical history. To the south rise the heights of Mount Gilboa, framing the northern reaches of the broadest and most fertile valley in the land. There, at the foot of Gilboa by a spring that can still be seen, is where Gideon encamped before delivering Israel from the Midionites. Later, Saul met his end there in his futile bid against the Philistines.

In the distance, barely visible in the haze on the back slopes of the Carmel Range, lies the ancient site of Megiddo, which ❧ lends its name to the valley. Megiddo also gives its name to the most celebrated battle yet to be, for "Armageddon" comes from two Hebrew words meaning "mountain of Megiddo." Napoleon once stood there and proclaimed the site an ideal location for just such a battle.

Across the valley from Megiddo is where the opening shots of another battle were fired 2,000 years ago, resulting in the victory of the Kingdom of God over the forces of evil. Mount Nazareth, bearing the same name of the place Jesus grew up, rises from the northern edge of the valley, nestling the tiny hamlet.

Not far from the foot of Mount Tabor, on the hill called Moreh, the village of Endor was located. It is to the witch of Endor that a frightened Saul went concealed on his last fateful night.

And it is at the hill of Moreh where two of the most dramatic healings recorded in the Bible occurred, separated by nearly a thousand years. The miracles occurred in two tiny villages on opposite sides of the hill. The one facing Tabor is still in existence and bears the same name as recorded in the biblical text.

We read that Jesus "went to a town called Nain, and his disciples and a large crowd went with him. As he approached the gate of the town, a man who had died was being carried out. He was his mother's only son, and she was a widow; and with her was a large crowd from the town. When the Lord saw her, he had compassion for her and said to her, 'Do not weep.' Then he came forward and touched the bier, and the bearers stood still. And he said, 'Young man, I say to you, rise!'" (Luke 7:11–14).

Since Byzantine times Mount Tabor has been one of the two traditional sites of the transfiguration of Jesus. The other is Mount Hermon, to the north.

The Raising of Lazarus

In chapter 11 of the Gospel of John, we read "a certain man was ill, Lazarus of Bethany, the village of Mary and her sister Martha" (11:1). Jesus was in the wilderness of the Jordan River when he was told of his friend's sickness. He did not leave immediately, although Bethany would have been perhaps a day's journey away.

It is only after Lazarus has died that Jesus goes to Bethany. In a foreshadowing of the miracle he would perform, he told his disciples: "For your sake I am glad I was not there, so that you may believe. But let us go to him" (11:15). If Jesus arrived when Lazarus was still alive, the miracle would have been one of healing. Instead, a greater miracle was performed in Bethany.

It is significant that Jesus delayed three days, arriving on the fourth. According to Jewish custom, the spirit of the dead person hovers over the body for three days before departing. This tradition may have arisen because of instances when those who appeared to be dead, but

In the fourth century a Byzantine church was built over the tomb of Lazarus on the eastern slope of the Mount of Olives. A later Crusader church further obscured much of the original rock, some of which can still be viewed in the inner chamber.

were actually in a comatose state, revived later in the tomb. By waiting three days, Jesus was rebutting those who might claim that Lazarus was not truly dead.

When Jesus approached the tomb, "he cried with a loud voice, 'Lazarus, come out!' The dead man came out, his hands and feet bound with strips of cloth, and his face wrapped in a cloth. Jesus said to them, 'Unbind him, and let him go'" (11:44). Some have speculated that Jesus was careful to specify Lazarus' name when he commanded him to come forth because if he had not, all the dead would have arisen.

The Arab village of al-Azariyeh, several miles east of Jerusalem, marks the site of Bethany. The name reflects the Greek "Lazarion," meaning "the place of Lazarus." Archaeological excavation has uncovered a cemetery dating from the first century, and in the fourth century a church was built over a specific rock-cut chamber thought to belong to Lazarus. The tomb remains empty.

Raising people from the dead is the most dramatic recorded miracle that Jesus performed. It is a great demonstration of his power and authority, and we only find it in a few instances in the Gospels.

Nain was one of dozens of villages in Galilee that Jesus passed through. While only a few hours walk across the valley from Nazareth, there is no indication that he knew the widow of Nain or her son. And yet he was moved to comfort her.

Telling the woman grieving for her son not to weep was a surprising thing for anyone to say to a mourner in the midst of a funeral procession. But Jesus had other plans for this funeral. Although there is no indication in the text that he was recognized, or that anyone requested his assistance, we read that on Jesus' command the dead man "sat up and began to speak, and Jesus gave him to his mother" (Luke 7:15).

We then read of the reaction of the people of Nain: "Fear seized all of them; and they glorified God, saying, 'A great prophet has risen among us!' and 'God has looked favorably on his people!' (Luke 7:16). The cry of the people of Nain that a great prophet had risen among them was not a common expression of the times. Who, then, was the "great prophet" that they thought had appeared to them?

The spectacular miracle that the inhabitants of Nain witnessed stirred an ancient memory within them, for this was not the only time someone had been raised from the dead on the hill of Moreh. Hundreds of years earlier, another prophet performed a similar miracle on the other side of the knoll on which Nain lay.

To this day a village in the same geographic location recalls the biblical town that was a way station for the journeys of the prophet Elisha. In those days—as today in the Middle East —houses were not gabled but flat, and in the hot summertime, people would often sleep on the roof to enjoy the cool evening breezes.

A woman from the village of Shunem built Elisha a room on the roof of her house so that he could have a place to rest whenever he passed through the area. In gratitude, the prophet performed his first miracle for the woman, who was childless. Her joy over the gift of a son, however, turned to despair some years later when the young boy suddenly died.

Upon learning of the tragedy, Elisha wasted no time in going to the boy: "When Elisha came into the house, he saw the child lying dead on his bed. So he went in and closed the door on the two of them, and prayed to the Lord. He got down, and immersed himself in fervent prayer. He got up, walked once to and fro in the room, then got up again and bent over him; the child sneezed seven times, and the child opened his eyes. Elisha summoned Gehazi and said, 'Call the Shunammite woman.' So he called her. When she came to him, he said, 'Take your son.' She came and fell at his feet, bowing to the ground; then she took her son and left" (2 Kings 4:32, 35–37).

Perhaps this episode of raising the young boy from the dead is the incident that the people of Nain associated with the dramatic miracle they had witnessed when Jesus raised the dead young man. Elisha was the "great prophet" who they thought had been resurrected in the person of the miracle worker in their midst.

JESUS' FINAL DRAMA

The Notorious Pontius Pilate

Up until A.D. 6, Palestine was in the firm control of Herod the Great, followed by his son and successor, Archelaus. After Archelaus was deposed, Rome was concerned about the security of the land bridge between Africa and Asia. To keep the rebellious population in check, Rome annexed Judea as a province and governed it through a series of prefects, or governors.

The fifth of these was Pontius Pilate, who ruled from A.D. 26 to 36. He came to power at a time when Jews were being persecuted in Rome and in the adjoining province of Egypt. Pilate wasted no time in taking the same harsh tactics, and his actions led to a confrontation shortly after he took office.

Wherever Rome ruled, images of Caesar, known as standards, were displayed in military camps and headquarters. However, these standards greatly offended the Jews, who believed any such image worship constituted idolatry. Pilate's predecessors respected the Jewish sensibilities and did not bring the standards up to Jerusalem.

Josephus relates how Pilate had the standards brought to Jerusalem under the cover of darkness. When the Jews discovered them the next morning, the city erupted into riots. A huge mob rushed to Pilate's headquarters in Caesarea and demanded that the standards be removed. When he refused, the crowd staged a giant sit-in around his residence.

The next day, Pilate summoned the crowd to the stadium, had soldiers surround them, and threatened them with death unless they ceased their protests. At his nod, the soldiers drew their swords to show he meant business. To Pilate's amazement, instead of yielding to his ultimatum, the Jews fell to the ground and bared their necks, saying they preferred to die rather than see their law trampled on.

The Jews won that round. Pilate ordered the standards to be removed from Jerusalem. But there would be other tests of will between Pilate and his unwilling subjects.

Josephus records that Pilate stirred up further trouble by taking funds from the Temple treasury to build an aqueduct. This time when the Jews protested, he was better prepared. He had his soldiers dress in civilian clothing and mix with the crowd that gathered outside his residence in Jerusalem. When he gave the signal, they took out their weapons and killed many of the protesters.

Each of the Gospels has references to Pontius Pilate and his role in Jesus' trial and crucifixion. Given Pilate's dislike for the Jews, it is somewhat surprising that he agreed with their demand that Jesus be put to death. The Gospels make his uncertainty clear when he says: "You brought me this man as one who was perverting the people; and here I have examined him in your presence and have not found this man guilty of any of your charges against him" (Luke 23:14).

The date of Jesus' crucifixion is not certain, but it is known that Pilate ruled for several more years until another crisis

Italian artist Antonio Ciseri's rendition of Pontius Pilate presenting Jesus to the crowd with the words "Ecce Homo" (Here is the man).

brought his rule to an end. This crisis was caused when he ordered a group of Samaritan worshipers who had gathered on Mount Gerizim cruelly attacked, supposing them to be preparing for a revolt. The Samaritans complained to Pilate's immediate superior, Vitellius, governor of Syria, and Pilate was ordered to give an account in Rome. Few of his subjects mourned his leaving, and he soon disappeared from history.

The Cross of Christ

C rucifixion was a brutal form of capital punishment used by the Romans as a deterrent against the most serious crimes and to keep rebellious provinces in check. The historian Josephus called it the "most wretched of deaths."

An Inscription to Pilate

I n 1961, the only known inscription mentioning Pontius Pilate was found among the ruins of Caesarea Maritima along the Mediterranean coast of northern Israel. It happened while an Italian archaeological team was excavating the theater, which was dated to the third and fourth century A.D.

Builders in ancient Israel made use of materials from ruined structures whenever possible. Since most buildings were constructed from stone, this saved the trouble of quarrying new blocks.

It was one of these blocks in secondary use that gave us Pilate's inscription. When archaeologists were examining the seats of the theater, they turned one of

the stone blocks over and found the following inscription in Greek: "Pontius Pilate, Prefect of Judea, made and dedicated the Tiberium to the Divine Augustus."

The word "prefect" (*praefectus*) is the Latin word for governor. A "Tiberium" is a temple or shrine honoring the Roman emperor Tiberius Claudius Caesar Augustus. The one mentioned in the inscription has not been found.

This inscription mentioning Pontius Pilate, uncovered in 1961 at Caesarea Maritima by Italian archaeologists, provided the first archaeological confirmation of Pilate's existence.

Andrea Mantegna depicts the crucifixion in this medieval Renaissance painting. Many archaeologists believe that Golgotha was part of a quarry located just outside the first-century walls of Jerusalem.

Artistic images of Jesus carrying a square-cut cross to Golgotha are most likely incorrect. While there were several varieties of crosses on which the victims were hung, in most cases the condemned man carried only the crossbar, the central post often being the trunk of a tree.

Since wood was scarce in Jerusalem, both the tree and the crossbar were likely reused. Josephus records that, during

the siege of Jerusalem in A.D. 70, the Romans were forced to gather wood from ten miles away for their siege machinery.

A highly visible site was chosen for crucifixions to make an example of the victim. In Jerusalem of Jesus' day, one such site was called Golgotha, meaning "the place of a skull." The Gospels indicate that Jesus was put to death along a highway, for we read that, "Those who passed by derided him, shaking their heads" (Matthew 27:39).

Sentence was typically carried out immediately. Upon arriving at the site of crucifixion, the condemned man was stripped and flogged. He was then placed on the ground and roped or nailed to the crossbar, which was then lifted into place.

One feature of the cross reveals the true cruelty of crucifixion. There was a small wooden block or "seat" placed beneath the buttocks to support the weight of the torso. This was not to provide comfort for the victim, but to prolong his agony. To breathe, the condemned man had to push himself up on his nailed feet, causing terrible pain. Death resulted by asphyxiation from the weakening of the diaphragm and the chest muscles.

The Romans evidently learned from experience that the doomed men died too quickly to suit their purposes. The

After Jesus died on the cross, Joseph wrapped him in a linen cloth, put him in a tomb, and rolled a stone in front of the entranceway.

The Crucified Man

There are nine references to crucifixion in the writings of Josephus, but until 1968, no physical specimen of a crucified man was known to exist. In that year, a burial tomb excavated at Givat HaMivtar, north of Jerusalem, was found to contain the skeletons of a young man and woman.

When the man was examined, he was found to have a four and one-half inch iron spike through his left heelbone, indicating he had been crucified. The nail was not removed before burial because the tip was bent, apparently from hitting a knot in the cross, making removal difficult. According to Jewish custom, the dead had to be buried before sunset, and there may not have been time to remove the nail.

A block of wood was attached to the head of the nail, probably to prevent it from being wrenched out by the victim. From this evidence, scholars have sketched what the crucifixion of the man from Givat HaMivtar probably looked like. His feet were likely nailed on either side of the upright post. The man's fingers and wrists gave no sign of traumatic injury, thus indicating that his arms were tied to the cross rather than nailed.

The legs of the crucified man from Givat HaMivtar had not been broken before he expired. When it was convenient for death to be hastened, the soldiers would break the legs of the condemned man. This made it impossible for the man to push up and gasp for breath, and he would quickly suffocate. However, the Gospel of John records that "when they came to Jesus and saw that he was already dead, they did not break his legs" (19:33).

block was provided so that they would not collapse from their agony and suffocate prematurely. A crucified man would often hang on the cross for days, expiring slowly from a combination of dehydration, exposure, and the effects of his scourging.

We read that "they offered him wine to drink, mixed with gall; but when he tasted it, he would not drink it" (Matthew 27:34). The meaning of "gall" is uncertain. Some equate it with the hemlock poison that Socrates drank. If so, it was an offer to Jesus to help put an end to his suffering, which he refused. Others suggest the liquid may have contained opium, given to him according to Jewish custom.

The Romans put a placard around the neck of the condemned man on which his offense was written. We read in the Gospels that Pilate had an inscription put on the cross that read: "Jesus of Nazareth, the King of the Jews."

However, the Jews objected to Pilate's choice of words, because it seemed to confirm what they had so strenuously denied: "Then the chief priests of the Jews said to Pilate, 'Do

There were three women present during the crucifixion. Mary his mother, his mother's sister, and Mary Magdalene were all by Jesus' cross.

not write, "The King of the Jews," but, "This man said, I am King of the Jews.'" Pilate answered, 'What I have written I have written'" (John 19:19, 21–22).

There is little evidence to suggest that Pilate's stubbornness on this point was due to any conviction regarding who Jesus was. In all likelihood, Pilate was making a statement to the effect of: "Look what a sorry king these despicable Jews have."

Where Is the Tomb of Jesus?

There are two main possibilities in Jerusalem for the site of the crucifixion, burial, and resurrection of Christ. The first is the Garden Tomb, which was discovered by the British General Charles Gordon in 1883 while he was visiting Jerusalem. General Gordon noticed caves in the side of a hill just outside the walls of Jerusalem that gave the impression of the eye sockets of a skull. He thought that this hill was Golgotha, where Jesus was crucified, since "Golgotha" means "skull."

Subsequent excavation of the area revealed a tomb cut into the same hill. Above the tomb was what appeared to be the sign of the cross. Nearby was a large cistern that some believed was used to water an ancient garden

A typical first-century rolling stone, a safeguard against robbers, can be seen in this rock-cut tomb in the Shephela region of Israel.

at the site. The theory that a garden may have exsisted there would coincide with the Gospel of John, which mentions that Mary mistook Jesus for a gardener, indicating the tomb was in a garden.

The Garden Tomb is a lovely place to contemplate the Gospel events. However, the tomb itself is the same age as an Iron Age tomb complex located on the property of St. Stephen's Church next door. This means that the Garden Tomb was carved hundreds of years before the time of Christ and could hardly qualify as the "new tomb" of Joseph of Arimathea.

Scores of tombs have been found outside the walls of Jerusalem, as well as dozens of Byzantine monastic sites. It is likely that the Garden Tomb was the site of a monastery in the centuries after Christ and that the tomb was reused for Christian burial.

The other possible site for the crucifixion, burial, and resurrection of Christ is the historic Church of the Holy Sepulcher. Although the church is inside the present-day walls of Jerusalem, it was outside the walls of the city that existed in the days of Jesus.

Archaeological soundings in the Church have confirmed that the site was used as a quarry until the first century B.C., when it was filled in and used as a garden or orchard. Several tombs dating from the first century A.D. confirm that the area was used as a cemetery in the time of Jesus.

German painter Carl Julius Milde's rendition of the three women at Jesus' tomb. According to Gospel accounts, they were the first witnesses to the empty tomb.

But the most powerful evidence that this is the site of Jesus' burial is historical. The fourth-century historian Eusebius records an unbroken list of bishops of Jerusalem from the time of Christ to this day. It is unlikely that the location of the most important event of Christendom would have been forgotten.

The Roman emperor Hadrian contributed unwittingly to the preservation of the site of Jesus' death and resurrection. After his legions suppressed the Second Jewish Revolt of A.D. 132–135, Hadrian banned Jews from the destroyed Jerusalem and rebuilt it as a Roman city, which he named Aelia Capitolina. He also changed the name of the country from Judea to Palaestina, or Palestine.

Hadrian attempted to remove all places of Jewish and Christian worship in Jerusalem. One of these was the place revered as the tomb of Christ. Hadrian ordered it covered with a massive platform and a temple to the goddess Venus. Ironically, in attempting to obliterate the Christian holy place, he instead permanently marked the site of Calvary under the temple.

Less than two hundred years later, Constantine the Great converted to Christianity and wasted no time in commissioning the bishop Macarius to build a basilica commemorating the death and resurrection of Christ.

There was little doubt in anyone's mind where the actual location was. Even though the church could have been built in an open area nearby, Constantine insisted that it be built upon the exact site. Accordingly, the pagan temple was destroyed and underneath was found the tomb believed to be that of Jesus.

The basilica erected over that tomb is known today, after considerable alterations through the centuries, as the Church of the Holy Sepulcher.

The Burial Cloth of Christ?

*P*eople have been fascinated by a mysterious artifact called the Shroud of Turin, which some claim to be the burial shroud of Jesus. After more than two decades of careful investigation and scientific analysis, there still is no consensus as to the shroud's authenticity.

The Shroud of Turin has a long and colorful history. It has been suggested, for example, that the shroud is the same cloth as the sixth-century *mandylion*, or face cloth, of Edessa (modern Urfa, in Turkey). The image of Christ was allegedly displayed on the *mandylion*, which was brought to Constantinople in the tenth century. The *mandylion* remained in Constantinople as late as the thirteenth century, after which it disappeared from history. Some believe that it was transferred to Europe, where it eventually became known as the Shroud of Turin.

The cloth known as the Shroud of Turin appeared in 1357, when it was exhibited in the village of Lirey in northern France. In 1460, the shroud passed into the hands of the House of Savoy, which held legal title to it until 1983. The shroud was partially burned in 1532, when fire swept through the chapel in the castle at Chambery, where it was kept in a silver chest. The image, however, was largely undamaged.

Approximately 45 years later, the shroud was brought to the city of Turin in northern Italy, where it resides today in the Royal Chapel of the Cathedral of St. John. The chest in which it is held requires three different keys to open it, and the shroud is exhibited only on rare occasions. The shroud has only been on public display nine times in the past two centuries. On the four hundredth anniversary of the shroud's arrival in Turin, it was viewed by more than three million people over a six-week period.

Although the shroud was exhibited frequently during the late medieval and Renaissance periods, doubts about its authenticity exist. Whether these doubts are the product of actual evidence or whether people are too overwhelmed by the shroud to accept it is irrelevant. While scholars and the faithful are equally in awe of the shroud's mystique and history, the Church never officially proclaimed it to be Jesus' actual burial cloth. A number of Church pronouncements through the centuries exhibited caution regarding the origin of the shroud.

The first scientific indication of the unusual nature of the shroud came in 1898, when it was photographed with glass-plate negatives. It was discovered that the image on the plate was a positive, an anomaly that, if faked, was produced hundreds of years before the invention of photography.

In 1973, a group of European scientists was permitted to inspect the shroud in order to recommend how best to preserve it. Upon examining the shroud, the scientists were divided in their opinions concerning its authenticity.

A year later, two U.S. Air Force scientists processed some photographs of the shroud with a computer image analyzer used to transform satellite photographs into three-dimensional topographical reliefs. To the scientists' surprise, a relatively undistorted three-dimensional image was produced by the analyzer. This would have been impossible if the image on the shroud had been painted on the fabric.

This was the beginning of the Shroud of Turin Research Project (STURP), involving more than 30 researchers from various highly respected scientific institutions in the United States. The scientists ranged from confirmed believers to agnostics in their religious beliefs.

The first problem that the STURP team tackled was the alleged bloodstains on the shroud. In 1973, Italian specialists were unable to confirm that the stains were blood. However, after running a series of sophisticated experiments, two experts on the STURP team concluded that the stains were in fact made by blood.

Some continued to disagree, claiming that the alleged bloodstains are from iron-oxide pigment painted on the linen. The iron-oxide theory, however, has to date not been verified by scientific analysis.

It has also been pointed out that the bright red color of the bloodstains suggests they are of relatively recent origin. Others, however, have expressed the theory that the shroud may have been washed with soapwort, a plant used as a detergent in antiquity. Soapwort has a preservative effect upon blood cells.

Other evidence appears to tie the shroud to the land of Israel. Scientists removed pollen spores embedded in the shroud that are native to the area of the Dead Sea and other parts of Palestine.

In 1978, during a rare public exhibition, the Shroud of Turin is here displayed in the San Giovanni Cathedral in Turin, Italy. Scholars continue to be divided over the date and origin of the shroud.

In James J. Tissot's rendition "The Holy Face," the imprint of Jesus' face is clearly visible on the Shroud of Turin.

In the 1980s, investigators also found calcium carbonate (limestone) particles on the shroud. Microscopic examination revealed that the particular type of limestone was not the more common calcite, but travertine argonite deposited from springs.

Argonite is also the type of limestone common to the hill country of Judea, so investigators decided to obtain limestone samples from ancient tombs in Jerusalem. Both the limestone particles on the shroud and the samples from Jerusalem tombs were tested by a device called a high-resolution scanning ion microprobe. The graphs produced by the microprobe revealed that the samples were an unusually close match, indicating that the shroud had at one time been in a Jerusalem tomb.

However, this positive evidence was seemingly overturned in 1988, when the Vatican permitted a few pieces of thread from the shroud to be tested by a method of carbon-14 dating using accelerated mass spectrometry. Three laboratories working independently arrived at a date of origin for the shroud between 1260 and 1390. These scientific findings seemed to confirm the theory that the shroud had been created around 1350 by Geoffrey de Charny, a French knight who was hoping to attract pilgrims to his newly built church.

In spite of that conclusion, the mystery of the shroud continued as other researchers pointed out that the image itself contains extraordinarily precise physical details that only the most accomplished medieval artist could have hoped to attain. However, there are no brush strokes or pigments visible on the surface of the shroud, indicating that the linen was not painted.

In addition, the carbon-14 dating of the shroud has been challenged on the basis of new research. Scientists have discovered that various microbes can cover ancient artifacts with plasticlike coatings that significantly alter the results of carbon-14 analysis. That, combined with the minuscule amount of fabric tested, increased the possibility that the initial carbon-14 test results were invalid.

What seems clear is that the image of a man estimated to be just under six feet tall, weighing 175 pounds, and between the ages of 30 and 35 has been inexplicably imprinted on the surface of the fabric. While the faithful and the skeptics continue to disagree concerning whose image it may be, further investigation may someday establish with more certainty the date—and authenticity—of the Shroud of Turin.

The Spear of Longinus: Legend or Myth?

*I*n a shadowy back corridor of the ancient Church of the Holy Sepulcher in Jerusalem, which the Emperor Constantine built in the fourth century A.D., is a small shrine unnoticed by most tourists. The shrine is dedicated to Longinus, identified by tradition as the Roman centurion who plunged his spear into Christ at his crucifixion.

Throughout the centuries, legends have arisen and mysterious powers have been attributed to the spear. It is said that whoever possesses the lance "holds the destiny of the world in his hand—for good or for evil." Remarkably, the influence of the spear has been traced to one of the most cataclysmic periods of the twentieth century.

After Jesus died on the cross, a soldier pierced Jesus with a spear and according to the Bible, blood and water poured from his side.

According to folklore, the spear acquired its supernatural powers when it touched the holy blood of Jesus. Tradition has it that while the spear was in the possession of Constantine, he won his famous victory at the Milvian Bridge outside Rome, which paved the way for his ascension to the Imperial throne. It is also alleged that in the following centuries the spear was in the various hands of the emperors Justinian and Charlemagne, as well as assorted German emperors. And this was what was responsible for their successes. The spear could be a curse as well as a blessing. Again, according to tradition, when the spear left the hands of both Constantine and Charlemagne they died shortly afterward.

In modern times one relic above all others has come to be associated with the spear of Longinus: the Maurice Spear, which resides in the Hofburg Museum in Vienna. It was there, back in the early part of the century, that an obscure artist named Adolf Hitler became familiar with the spear and the legends surrounding it. He reportedly would spend hours at the museum, entranced by the spear and its supposed powers.

Despite the fact that the known history of the Maurice Spear cannot be traced earlier than the eleventh century A.D., Hitler was convinced that it was the actual spear of Longinus. And he would not—could not—forget it. In 1939, after the failed artist had risen to become *Reichsfuehrer*, Austria was annexed by Germany. Hitler wasted no time. The same evening in which he made his triumphal entry into Vienna, Hitler directed his entourage to the Hofburg Museum and spirited away the Maurice Spear.

The Bones of Caiaphas Discovered

The Gospels record that on the night of Jesus' arrest he was taken to "Caiaphas the high priest, in whose house the scribes and the elders had gathered" (Matthew 26:57).

During a mockery of a trial, various false witnesses were introduced but failed to corroborate their stories. Caiaphas asked Jesus directly whether he was the Messiah: "Jesus said to him, 'You have said so. But I tell you, From now on you will see the Son of Man seated at the right hand of Power and coming on the clouds of heaven.' Then the high priest tore his clothes and said, 'He has blasphemed! Why do we still need witnesses? You have now heard his blasphemy. What is your verdict?' They answered, 'He deserves death.'" (Matthew 26:64–66).

Thus the Gospels indicate that Caiaphas was a leader in the plot to have Jesus put to death. Little is known of him outside the New Testament, other than that he apparently served as high priest from about A.D. 18 to A.D. 36.

In 1990, workmen building a water park outside the Old City of Jerusalem broke into an ancient burial cave dating from the first century A.D. Inside were the remains of 12 ossuaries, ornately carved limestone containers that served as secondary repositories for bones. In the first century, it was common Jewish custom to deposit the body in a tomb until the flesh decayed, after which the bones were collected and put into an ossuary.

To date, many ossuaries have been found in the Jerusalem area. However, this particular discovery caused a sensation when two of the accompanying inscriptions included the name Caiaphas. The full text of one of the inscriptions was deciphered to read: "Joseph, Son of Caiaphas." The obvious clue given by this deciphered text marked the first archaeological confirmation of the existence of the high priest who was instrumental in having Jesus condemned to death.

This ancient cistern on Mount Zion marks the site of the house of the high priest Caiaphas, where Jesus was detained and questioned before the crucifixion.

Hitler was convinced that the spear—the *Heilige Lance*—would confer great powers upon him. And so he ensured that the spear remained in Nazi possession. And, as fate would have it, during the next few years it seemed as though nothing could stand in the way of the Third Reich. Much of Western Europe fell to the Nazis, whose triumphant armies stood at the English Channel and reached nearly to the gates of Moscow.

When Hitler's fortunes changed and the tide turned against the Nazis, the pilfered Maurice Spear was hidden for safe-keeping. In the heart of Bavaria lies a 900-foot tunnel, carved several hundred feet beneath the Nuremberg Fortress; it became home to Hitler's amulet. Until the end, Hitler persisted in the belief that his fortunes would rise again, as long as he possessed what he believed to be the spear of Longinus.

And, in an odd twist of fate, that is exactly what happened. At the end of April 1945, United States armed forces swept into Nuremberg. Shortly afterward they discovered the hid-

Adolf Hitler, considered by some to be the Antichrist, believed that the Maurice Spear would endow him with great and even supernatural powers.

den entrance to the tunnel and found vast treasures stolen from the museums of Europe. At exactly 2:10 P.M. on April 30, the United States took possession of the *Heilige Lance*. Within two hours Adolf Hitler would be dead.

THE HOUSE OF GOD

Quarrying Stones for Herod's Temple

*T*he Temple Herod built for the Jewish people was one of the most impressive buildings of ancient times. Even today, the visitor to Jerusalem can see the enormous blocks,

some weighing as much as 50 tons, used in its massive retaining wall. It was an enormous project requiring great manpower and materials.

The Jews were hesitant to permit Herod to dismantle the modest Temple that Zerubbabel had rebuilt hundreds of years earlier. What if he razed the building and then went

The Indestructible Temple Mount

On Mount Moriah in Jerusalem stands one of the most imposing structures of the ancient world, a massive structure called the Temple Mount. Towering above the Kidron Valley, it covers a quarter of the area of the ancient city.

The Temple that Jesus knew was called the Second Temple. The first—Solomon's—was destroyed in 586 B.C. by the Babylonians. In 520 B.C., under Zerubbabel, the Temple was rebuilt on a modest scale. This structure was used until the time of Herod the Great.

Herod decided to construct an edifice that would be as much of a lasting tribute to himself as it was to the God of his Jewish subjects. Not content to rebuild Zerubbabel's Temple, Herod decided in 20 B.C. to double the area. At a size of 24 football fields, the Temple Mount would be the largest man-made platform in the ancient world.

Such a massive structure required the kind of technical innovation at which the Romans excelled. The lower

This recreation of the Temple built by Herod the Great for the Jewish people is part of the model of Jerusalem at the Holyland hotel in Jerusalem.

end of the platform, for example, could not merely be filled in with rubble lest the walls burst out from the pressure. To solve the problem, the southern end of the Temple Mount was built upon huge vaulted structures known traditionally—but erroneously—as "Solomon's Stables."

As prophesied by Jesus, the Temple itself was destroyed by the Romans in A.D. 70. The Temple Mount was razed and a temple to Jupiter was built upon the site. That structure is long gone, and the Temple Mount is now dominated by the Muslim al-Aksa Mosque and the Dome of the Rock shrine.

The immense foundation and retaining wall of the Jewish Temple, however, have withstood the ravages of time and continue to dominate the vista of the Old City. Tour guides point out the colossal limestone blocks, some of which are 40 feet in length and weigh as many tons. They were joined so masterfully—without cement—that not even a piece of paper can be slipped in between the blocks.

back on his promise to build the new Temple? Only after Herod promised to have all of the materials prepared for the new Temple did they agree to have the old structure dismantled.

As part of his preparations, Herod employed 10,000 workmen, including 1,000 priests who were trained as masons. They were necessary to build the inner temple, to which only priests were allowed access.

The stone used to construct the Temple came from quarries around Jerusalem, some of which can still be seen. The stone was freed from the rock by hammering wooden beams into chiseled grooves. The pressure was sufficient to break the rock free. The next step was squaring off the stones to specific dimensions, after which the smaller blocks were placed on wagons and transported to the Temple site.

The larger blocks, weighing many tons, could not be placed on carts, so Herod's Roman engineers developed special techniques to move them. The stones were placed on rollers and then pulled to the site. According to Josephus, at least 1,000 oxen were used to complete the task. The known quarries were at a higher elevation than the Temple site, and using gravity made moving the stones easier.

Once the stones arrived, they had to be put into position—no mean feat, considering that stones weighing 80 tons were positioned at least 100 feet above the foundations. To lift stones of that size was beyond the capability of the most sophisticated engineering equipment of the day.

In fact, the stones did not have to be lifted to such a height. Scholars believe that, as the 16-foot-wide walls were laid

course by course, each successive layer became the construction platform for the next. The blocks for each course would arrive from the higher elevation at the northern end of the site and were moved down to their position. The base of the Temple Mount is still visible today, supporting the great Dome of the Rock, a holy site for Muslims. The fine workmanship of Herod's stonemasons can be seen: Their blocks are smoother and better carved than blocks from later periods that are also in these walls.

The remaining retaining wall is 40 courses high, or the height of a 15-story building. It was originally significantly higher. The project took decades to complete. Herod began building around 20 B.C., and the main construction was done by Jesus' day. However, it was not until A.D. 64 that the Temple was finally completed and dedicated.

All the effort to create what Josephus calls "the most wonderful edifice ever seen or heard" would soon come to naught. In A.D. 70, six years after being dedicated, the Jewish Temple was completely destroyed by the conquering Romans.

The Fall of Jerusalem

During the final week before his crucifixion, Jesus was coming out of the Temple with his disciples when they pointed out to him the magnificence of the structure. They were no doubt shocked by his reply: "You see all these, do you not? Truly I tell you, not one stone will be left here upon another; all will be thrown down" (Matthew 24:2).

How the Walls Came Tumbling Down

Jesus' prophecy that Herod's Temple would be "thrown down" (Mark 13:1–2) was fulfilled in A.D. 70 when a Roman legion under Titus conquered Jerusalem, thus ending the First Jewish Revolt. Knowing the proportions of Herod's Temple, scholars have puzzled over how such a massive stone structure could have been completely destroyed.

Although most of the building materials of the Temple have long disappeared, much of the retaining wall can still be seen today. This wall holds the secrets as to what happened to the structure above it.

The stones of the retaining wall of the Temple are beautifully trimmed with beveled edges. The outside face was joined so perfectly without mortar of any kind that even today a piece of paper cannot be fit between many of the joints. The engineers, realizing that limestone expands as its moisture content increases, were careful to leave space behind the surface of the blocks to allow for expansion.

Normally, the expansion and contraction occurs without harming the rock. However, when the Romans took Jerusalem, overzealous soldiers set fire to the Temple, against the orders of their commander Titus.

It was this fire that doomed the building. As the limestone was rapidly heated, the moisture in the rock could not escape quickly enough. The result was that

In A.D. 70, as prophesied by Jesus, the walls of the Jewish Temple came tumbling down. Here, excavated stones from the Temple lie along the Western retaining wall of the Temple Mount.

the superheated moisture caused the blocks to explode, collapsing the walls of the Temple. Only the retaining wall below survived the conflagration.

ing infants in those days! For there will be great distress on the earth and wrath against this people; they will fall by the edge of the sword and be taken away as captives among all nations; and Jerusalem will be trampled on by the Gentiles, until the times of the Gentiles are fulfilled" (Luke 21:20, 23, 24).

The Jewish historian Josephus, who witnessed the fall of Jerusalem firsthand, describes the siege in horrendous detail. In the spring of A.D. 70, an enormous army commanded by Titus, totaling almost 80,000 men, set up camp around Jerusalem.

The city was swarming with refugees and pilgrims who,

This detail of Roman soldiers carrying away the menorah—or ritual candle stand—after the destruction of Jerusalem in A.D. 70 appears on the Emperor Titus' victory arch in Rome.

despite the war, had come to celebrate Passover. All pleas to surrender were rebuffed by the inhabitants, who had supreme confidence in the city's defenses. On the south, Jerusalem was protected by steep cliffs, and on the more vulnerable north side, a series of three massive walls stood between the defenders and the Romans.

The Gospel of Luke provides more details of the destruction of the Temple: "when you see Jerusalem surrounded by armies, then know that its desolation has come near... Woe to those who are pregnant and to those who are nurs- ▼

Titus gave the order to attack. The Roman artillery included siege engines that battered the walls and stone throwers that could hurl 100-pound rocks as far as 600 feet. Day and night the city underwent a ferocious bombardment.

To the dismay of the defenders, it took just two weeks for the Roman siege machines to break through the outermost northern wall. In another five days, the second wall was breached. Titus was sure the city would surrender, but its inhabitants spurned his attempts to get them to do so. Sending Josephus to plead with his countrymen met with no success.

The battle began anew. All Judeans caught outside the city were summarily executed. Hundreds were nailed to crosses in full view of their comrades within the city. The practice was halted only when there were no more trees left.

Inside the city, food became scarce. Josephus records that the hunger of the inhabitants of Jerusalem became so great that they ate old hay and chewed their belts and shoes. Many people died of starvation, but there was no place to bury the dead, so the bodies had to be thrown over the walls. Soon, thousands of corpses lay rotting along the town's perimeter.

The Romans finally succeeded in breaking through to the Temple, which was soon set ablaze. From there, they swept down into the rest of the city and began a horrible slaughter. Of the estimated 600,000 men, women, and children in Jerusalem at the beginning of the siege, only 97,000 prisoners were accounted for.

To ensure that Judea would not rise up again, the tenth Roman legion was stationed in the city for the next 60 years. Nevertheless, the flames of revolt would be stirred up once more in A.D. 135 with the Bar Kochba Revolt, which brought even more devastating consequences.

New Testament: Acts

Chronicling the beginnings of the Christian Church, the Book of Acts, also known as the Acts of the Apostles, begins with the ascension of Jesus. The event transformed the disciples and launched them on the mission that Jesus had given them: to spread the word of God "in Jerusalem, in all Judea and Samaria, and to the ends of the earth." Many lost their lives, but not before the seeds of Christianity had been planted throughout the world.

This depiction in stained glass of Jesus calling Matthew is from St. Peter's Lutheran Church in Ottawa, Ontario.

TO THE ENDS OF THE EARTH

How Did Judas Iscariot Die?

*I*n the Gospel of Matthew, we read that, after betraying Jesus, Judas repented and went back to the Jewish authorities in an effort to return 30 pieces of silver paid him to lead ❦ the way to Jesus: "He said, 'I have sinned by betraying innocent blood.' But they said, 'What is that to us? See to it yourself'" (Matthew 27:4).

The Temple officials refused to take the money back because it was considered "blood money" and therefore unsuitable for an offering to God. Judas then threw down the pieces of silver in the Temple and "went and hanged himself" (Matthew 27:5).

The Book of Acts, however, gives a somewhat different account of how Judas died. The Apostle Peter is reminding the disciples of the circumstances of Jesus' betrayal and states how Judas died: "...for he was numbered among us and was allotted his share in this ministry. (Now this man acquired a field with the reward of his wickedness; and falling headlong, he burst open in the middle and all his bowels gushed out. This became known to all the residents ❦

of Jerusalem, so that the field was called in their language Akeldama, that is, Field of Blood) (Acts 1:18–19).

How, then, did Judas die—by hanging, or as a result of his bowels bursting? An examination of the probable area where his death occurred indicates that he may have suffered both of those calamities.

The despair of Judas after realizing the full extent of his betrayal, contrasted with the indifference of the priests, is here portrayed by English artist Edward Armitage.

The Luck of the Draw

In the first chapter of Acts, we read how the disciples chose a replacement for Judas: "And they cast lots for them, and the lot fell on Matthias; and he was added to the eleven apostles" (Acts 1:26).

Lots are mentioned throughout Scripture as a means of determining divine will, as Proverbs states: "The lot is cast into the lap, but the decision is the Lord's alone" (Proverbs 16:33). The Promised Land was divided by lot, as was the Temple priests' order of service.

The Urim and Thummim were also a means used by the priests to inquire of the Lord. Scripture does not describe the exact method of their use. They may have been shaped stones inscribed with symbols that were put into a vessel and then shaken until one jumped out, or perhaps they were drawn from a bag.

Saul used Urim and Thummim to determine who had broken his vow in a battle with the Philistines: "Then Saul said, 'O Lord God of Israel; why have you not answered your servant today? If this guilt is in me or in my son Jonathan, O Lord God of Israel, give Urim; but if this guilt is in your people Israel, give Thummim.' And Jonathan and Saul were indicated by the lot, but the people were cleared. Then

Dice used in the ancient world were much the same as their modern counterparts. In ancient Israel, casting lots was a common way of determining God's will.

Saul said, 'Cast the lot between me and my son Jonathan.' And Jonathan was taken" (1 Samuel 14:41–42).

The Book of Joshua relates how Achan, son of Zerah, hid stolen booty in his tent, which was the cause for the initial defeat of the Israelites when they attacked the city of Ai. While lots are not specifically mentioned as being used by Joshua to determine the guilt of Achan, the method is similar: "So Joshua rose early in the morning, and brought Israel near tribe by tribe, and the tribe of Judah was taken. He brought near the clans of Judah, and the clan of the Zerahites was taken; and he brought near the clan of the Zerahites, family by family, and Zabdi was taken. And he brought near his household one by one, and Achan son of Carmi...was taken" (Joshua 7:16–18).

To the Western mind, the use of lots appears to be reliance upon blind chance, but the ancients believed that God revealed his will through such means. In fact, the use of lots was preferable to making a decision based on reasoning, because it removed the possibility of human error in determining the will of God.

One might be tempted to picture Judas hanging from gallows, such as those pictured in Western films. But such a contraption would have been unknown in ancient Israel. Indeed, hanging was not used as a form of execution, although the corpses of those put to death by stoning or the sword were sometimes hung afterward from a convenient tree.

The historian Eusebius and the early Church father Jerome mention that the site of Judas' hanging was known in their day (circa 330 A.D.). We can expect the early Christians in Jerusalem to have remembered the site, and, together with the location of other significant events, passed this knowledge along to succeeding generations.

The site of Akeldama has been preserved through the centuries by the Monastery of St. Onuphrius, located on a steep hillside in the Hinnom Valley outside the walls of the Old City of Jerusalem. Today, as very likely in ancient times, gnarled olive trees dot the steep hillsides and cliffs of the Hinnom. Judas may have come to a place such as this outside the city walls to hang himself.

It is easy to picture what might have happened. After tying the noose to the branch of a tree overlooking the Hinnom, Judas would have jumped to his death. Perhaps the rope did not hold, and his body hurtled and tumbled down the cliff and was disemboweled by a sharp rock or other obstruction below.

In an attempt to assuage his own guilt, Judas tried to return 30 pieces of silver given to him for betraying Jesus. The money was not accepted by the Jewish authorities and Judas hanged himself.

A Death in the Theater

Herod Agrippa I, the grandson of Herod the Great, ruled over Judea between A.D. 41 and 44. He maintained good relations with the Jews, but persecuted Christians. He was responsible for the beheading of James, the son of Zebedee, and for the imprisonment of the Apostle Peter.

Theaters such as this one at Bet Shean are an impressive reminder of Rome's presence in Palestine.

Agrippa's sudden and unexpected end came at Caesarea and is recorded in the Book of Acts: "On an appointed day Herod put on his royal robes, took his seat on the platform, and delivered a public address to them. The people kept shouting, 'The voice of a god, and not of a mortal!' And immediately, because he had not given the glory to God, an angel of the Lord struck him down, and he was eaten by worms and died" (Acts 12:21–23).

In his *History of the Jews*, Josephus describes the final scene of Agrippa's life in detail. He was in Caesarea to preside over games held in honor of the emperor. In some cultures, to be held up as a god was not uncommon for monarchs, but for pious Jews it was blasphemous. Acts states that he was "eaten by worms and died." Josephus concurs that he died shortly afterward from an unknown intestinal disease.

Standing in the theater at Caesarea, one can picture the dramatic scene. Agrippa, dressed in a glittering robe decorated with pieces of bright gold, would have been standing with his back to the sea. The sun rising over the top of the theater would have cast his robe in a brilliant light, hence the cry of the people as he addressed the crowd: "The voice of a god, and not of a mortal!" (Acts 12:22).

That he accepted their adulation instead of refusing it may have earned him the divine wrath that cost him his life.

A Short and Brutal Reign

After the birth of Jesus, the Holy Family fled to Egypt, having been warned in a dream that Herod the Great was about to search for them. Later, after Herod died, Joseph was told in another dream to return to Israel:

"Then Joseph got up, took the child and his mother, and went to the land of Israel. However, when Joseph heard that Archelaus was ruling over Judea in place of his father Herod, he was afraid to go there. And after being warned in a dream, he went away to the district of Galilee" (Matthew 2:21–22).

Other ancient historical sources shed light upon why Joseph avoided returning to Judea. The story begins 10 years earlier when Archelaus began his tumultuous 10-year reign in Judea. Archelaus was no more accepted by the Jews than was Herod the Great, and after a brief attempt to win them over, he resorted to harsh tactics that exceeded those of his father.

Not long after the beginning of his reign, Archelaus suppressed a mob protest by force, killing 3,000 people in Jerusalem. Tensions grew as representatives from the elders were

We read that "Herod put on his royal robes" and addressed the assembled crowd in the theater at Caesarea (Acts 12:21). During his address he suddenly became ill and died shortly afterward.

sent to Rome to demand that Archelaus be removed.

As Archelaus went to appear before Caesar to defend himself against his accusers, violence erupted back home in Judea. It was the time of the feast of Passover, and an enormous crowd gathered in Jerusalem—not to celebrate the feast, but to seize control of the city in protest of Archelaus' rule.

As revolt spread across the land, Quintilius Varus, the Roman legate of Syria, came swiftly with three powerful legions to restore order. After a series of pitched battles, Judea was once more subdued. In retribution, Varus crucified 2,000 of the rebels. These events were taking place when Joseph was returning from Egypt. He wisely decided to skirt the troubles in Judea, settling in the Galilean village of Nazareth.

Archelaus survived this test of his authority, but continued to exercise brutality toward his opponents. In his ninth year, after further emissaries were sent to Rome to demand his removal, Archelaus was banished to Vienne in Gaul. Thus began the age of direct Roman rule in Judea.

Worship and Angels

The Bible portrays angels as glorious and powerful beings that, on occasion, have unintentionally caused people to attempt to bow down and worship them.

In Chapter 19 of the Book of Revelation, John reacts to a series of amazing visions shown to him by an angel: "Then I fell down at his feet to worship him, but he said to me, 'You must not do that! I am a fellow servant with you and your comrades who hold the testimony of Jesus. Worship God! For the testimony of Jesus is the spirit of prophecy'" (Revelation 19:10).

On this occasion, as in every other in the Bible when men bowed down before angels, John was immediately prevented from worshiping him. The angel referred to himself as a "fellow servant" of the apostle, thus putting himself on the same level—that of the creature rather than the creator. Despite the angel's message, his appearance was so awe-inspiring that later John bows before him again and once more has to be reprimanded.

The polytheistic religions of Greece and Rome, as well as the nations surrounding Israel, believed in the existence of many deities. In sharp contrast to this was the biblical worldview, according to which God alone is eternal. He stands

Tissot's "The Angel's Rebuke" portrays one of the instances in the Bible when men mistakenly attempted to bow down before angels who remind them that God alone is to be worshiped.

apart from his creation, which includes the angelic realm, humankind, and animals.

There are fundamental distinctions between the different living beings in the created order as well. Humans are charged with the oversight of creation. This means mankind may use plants, animals, and the earth itself for its own purposes, but it must also respect them as God's creation.

The relationship between humans and angels is more complicated. The Bible indicates that in the present age the angels occupy a higher order than mankind. In referring to the human race, the writer of the Book of Hebrews quotes the Old Testament: "You have made them for a little while lower than the angels" (Hebrews 2:7).

The Scriptures testify that angels indeed have powers beyond that of mortal man. However, in the age to come, the faithful will no longer occupy a place under the angels. The writer of Hebrews completes his quotation and explains it: "'You have crowned them with glory and honor, subjecting all things under their feet.' Now in subjecting all things to them, God left nothing outside their control" (2:7–8).

The Apostle Paul states: "Do you not know that we are to judge angels—to say nothing of ordinary matters?" (1 Corinthians 6:3)

This verse, however, obviously refers to judging the fallen angels, and need not be taken to imply a general superiority over the angelic realm. Only man has been uniquely created in the image of God, with a spirit and the capacity to choose between good and evil.

Fallen angels seek to deceive mankind, as the Apostle Paul states when speaking of false teachers: "For such boasters are false apostles, deceitful workers, disguising themselves as apostles of Christ. And no wonder! Even Satan disguises himself as an angel of light. So it is not strange if his ministers also disguise themselves as ministers of righteousness. Their end will match their deeds" (2 Corinthians 11:13–15).

The extraordinary powers that angels possess caused the Apostle John and others in the Bible to sometimes mistake them for God. It is a testimony to the faithfulness of these beings—and to the power of God—that they unfailingly refused to permit for a moment what would clearly be a blasphemous act.

The Seed of the Church

After his resurrection, Jesus gave his disciples the marching orders that countless of his followers have taken to the ends of the earth: "Go therefore and make disciples of all nations, baptizing them in the name of the Father and of the Son and of the Holy Spirit, and teaching them to obey everything that I have commanded you" (Matthew 28:19–20).

According to historical sources and Church tradition, this command was carried out with amazing speed as the Gospel

Opposite Page: *The Apostle Peter asked to be crucified upside down since he was not worthy to be crucified in the same manner as the Lord.*

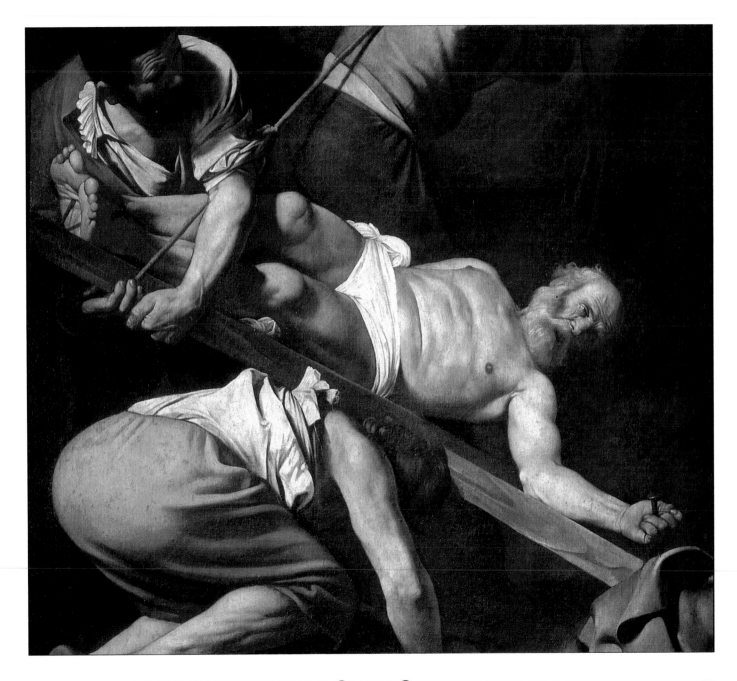

was preached throughout the known world. In the course of fulfilling their mission, many of Jesus' early disciples spread the faith at great personal cost, giving rise to the ancient saying that "the blood of the martyrs is the seed of the Church."

Jesus foretold how Peter's life would end: "Very truly, I tell you, when you were younger, you used to fasten your own belt and to go wherever you wished. But when you grow old, you will stretch out your hands, and someone else will fasten a belt around you and take you where you do not wish to go" (John 21:18–19).

The New Testament gives some indications that the final journeys of the Apostles Peter and Paul were to Rome, where they suffered imprisonment and death. In his first epistle, written from the Roman capital, Peter relates that he was "a witness of the sufferings of Christ, as well as one who shares in the glory to be revealed" (1 Peter 5:1).

In his second letter to Timothy, Paul reveals his thoughts about his coming martyrdom: "As for me, I am already being poured out as a libation, and the time of my departure has come. I have fought the good fight, I have finished the race, I have kept the faith. From now on, there is reserved for me the crown of righteousness, which the Lord, the righteous judge, will give me on that day, and not only to me but also to all who have longed for his appearing" (2 Timothy 4:6–8).

The early Church father Eusebius confirms that Peter and Paul died at the hands of Nero around the time of the infamous fire of A.D. 64, which consumed much of the city. When Peter was told he was to be crucified, the same pun-

ishment as was given to Jesus, he said he was unworthy and asked to be crucified upside down. According to ancient sources mentioned by Eusebius, the tombs of Peter and Paul were located on the Vatican hill, under what is now the Basilica of St. Peter.

We learn from Polycarp of Smyrna, who knew the Apostle John, that the "beloved disciple" lived at Ephesus in Asia Minor until the time of the Emperor Trajan (98–117 A.D.) There he is said to have continued being a witness for the Christian faith, teaching and, on one occasion, raising a man from the dead. The Church father Tertullian mentions that John was eventually taken to Rome and cast into a cauldron of boiling oil, only to escape without harm.

James, the son of Zebedee, was said to be the first disciple of Jesus to be martyred, being put to death by Herod Agrippa in A.D. 44. However, in other accounts from later sources, James is said to have made a trip to Spain, where he became the country's patron saint. The alleged place of his burial was a major pilgrimage site during the Middle Ages.

James, the brother of Jesus, remained in Jerusalem. Josephus states that James was stoned to death in A.D. 62. However, a source recorded by Eusebius claims that James was cast down from the pinnacle of the Temple—an estimated 140 feet in height. When he survived this fall, he was clubbed to death.

Other disciples went far and wide preaching the Gospel message. We know, for example, that Mark went to Alexandria and that Thaddeus went to Edessa, in what is now Turkey.

Perhaps the most intriguing story is the one told about Thomas. The apocryphal Acts of Thomas, written in the third century, claims that he evangelized as far as India, where he founded a church. He is alleged to have worked as a carpenter, performed miracles, and to have died a martyr's death.

To this day, a unique group of Syrian Christians, known as the "Christians of St. Thomas," exist among a population that is 97 percent non-Christian. They live in Malabar, on the southwest coast of India, and claim to be the descendants of those converted by the apostle, who lies buried near Madras. This claim has been confirmed with a high degree of probability by modern scholars of Christian history.

A Window of Opportunity

For much of Rome's history, the *Pax Romana* (Roman peace) was more of an ideal than a reality. Rome often found itself either threatened militarily by belligerent nations or plagued by political unrest or unstable leaders. Rarely was there able leadership, efficient administration, and external peace that lasted for any length of time.

One such time was during the Julio-Claudian dynasties, extending from before the birth of Christ to the end of the first century and encompassing the time of Jesus and the apostles. Jesus was born during the reign of Augustus Caesar (27 B.C.–A.D. 14), who rose to prominence during one of Rome's most tumultuous periods, at the time of the civil wars that followed the assassination of Julius Caesar in 44 B.C.

Augustus, whose original name was Octavian, gained control over the West while his rival Mark Antony ruled the East from Alexandria. In 31 B.C., their armies battled at Actium in Greece, resulting in the defeat and eventual suicide of both Antony and his consort Cleopatra.

During the reign of Augustus, the Roman Empire was established with him as the first emperor. Augustus was an extremely capable administrator who brought many needed reforms to the empire. One of these was to divide the dominion of Rome into Senatorial and Imperial provinces. Senatorial provinces were generally peaceful, while Imperial provinces generally were located in outlying regions that had rebellious subjects.

Judea fulfilled both of these requirements, with the result that in 6 A.D. it became an Imperial province. This meant being governed by the firm hand of prefects backed by a strong military garrison. Though discontent with Rome was widespread, leading to the rise of fervently anti-Roman groups like the Zealots, there would be no major uprising until the First Jewish Revolt, which began in A.D. 66.

In A.D. 14, the long reign of Augustus came to an end with his death, and the throne passed to Tiberius, the son of his consort Julia. Tiberius continued Augustus' efficient administration and was also a capable military commander. However, like Augustus before him, he avoided war by not attempting to expand the borders of the empire.

During this time, the *Pax Romana* was maintained, which brought distinct benefits for the first Evangelists who spread the Gospel throughout the empire. Travel was secure on good roads, parts of which can still be seen today. In addi-

An ancient sculpted head of the Roman Emperor Augustus (31 B.C.–14 A.D.), who inaugurated an era of order and prosperity that lasted throughout his long reign.

An exception to this era of stability was the succession of Tiberius' demented grandnephew Gaius (Caligula) in A.D. 27. He was hardly mourned when the ruinous four years of his reign came to an end and the empire was in firm hands once again—the hands of Gaius' uncle Claudius, who continued the efficient administration of Augustus and Tiberius. It was largely during his rule that the ministry of the Apostle Paul took place.

Agrippina, Claudius' fourth wife, poisoned him in A.D. 54 so that her son from a previous marriage, Nero, could take the throne. The first casualties of Nero's rule were the early Christians. In A.D. 64, Rome was largely destroyed by fire, and the conflagration that destroyed 10 of the 14 wards of the city was conveniently blamed on the Christians. It is during this time that the Apostles Paul and Peter are believed to have been martyred.

With Nero's increasingly unpredictable behavior, Rome's golden age of stability came to an end. After his death by suicide in A.D. 68, confusion ruled as the throne changed hands three times in one year in the midst of civil war. Vespasian, the first of the Flavian dynasty, was brought from suppressing the Jewish revolt in Judea to become emperor.

During the rule of Vespasian's son Domitian (A.D. 81–96), the situation of Christians deteriorated, and some persecution was reported. Trajan, fourth in a line of Vespasian's successors, became Caesar in A.D. 98. Whereas before the Christians suffered sporadically, under Trajan began the first systematic persecution of the Church. Some scholars

tion, at this time, Greek was the main language of the Roman world. The writing of the New Testament in Greek made it accessible to every corner of the empire.

believe that the persecution described in the Book of Revelation, written by the Apostle John at the end of the first century, reflects the rule of Trajan.

However, the formative decades of the Church were over by this time. The new faith of Christianity had become a force to be reckoned with.

Ancient Mariners

*S*ince the dawn of recorded history, men have taken to the seas. The earliest references to ships come from the Old Kingdom of Egypt, where as early as 2650 B.C., cedar logs were brought from Phoenicia on ships more than 170 feet in length. Egyptian reliefs also picture ships being used for military invasions and for ferrying captives.

A tomb painting from Thebes dated to the fifteenth century B.C. depicts sailing vessels with the same components familiar to mariners today, including masts with crow's nests, plus large rectangular sails, rudders, and oars.

Ships are also depicted in Assyrian reliefs as early as the eleventh century B.C., when Tiglath-pileser I sought to extend his power westward to the Mediterranean. From the time of Sennacherib, around 700 B.C., a three-decked warship is depicted with two levels of rowers and an upper deck where armed warriors sat.

Curiously, we have few pictures of the ships of the Phoenicians, who were renowned as masters of the sea. A large,

sophisticated sailing vessel is beautifully depicted on a second-century B.C. sarcophagus. Its large square sail is unfurled from the mainmast, and a flag hangs from the high curled stern.

At the time of the New Testament, the Roman Empire was in command of the seas. A relief now in the Vatican depicts a warship that was propelled not by sails, but by 36 oars on two levels. The ship had an estimated crew of more than 200, with an outside gangway, main deck, and raised platforms for three levels of fighting men. With an estimated length of 103 feet and a displacement of 81 tons, the ship was of moderate size for its time.

While we have few pictures of Phoenican ships, some tiles such as this one have been preserved.

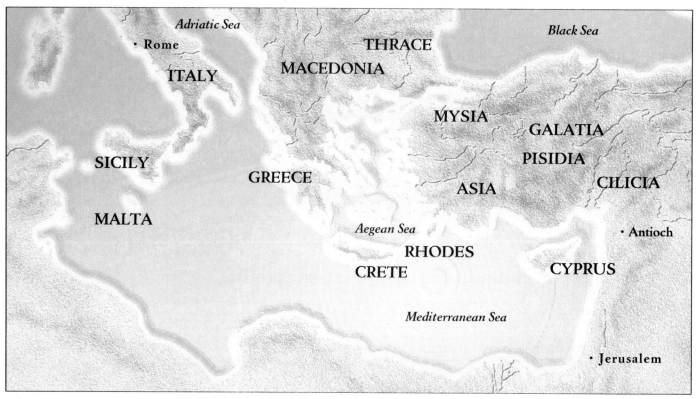

The Mediterranean Sea was tumultuous indeed during Paul's famous sea journey. The story of Paul's navigation and shipwreck of Malta is told in the Book of Acts.

Until the development of scuba-diving equipment, our knowledge of ancient ships was limited to references in contemporary literature and pictorial representations. However, today underwater archaeology has located the remains of hundreds of ancient sailing vessels built between the seventh century B.C. and the seventh century A.D. Among the most famous of these finds was the so-called Galilee Boat, which was discovered in 1985 and dated as belonging to the time of Jesus. Rowed by four men, the vessel could hold up to 15 people.

Cargo is invariably found at the sites of underwater wrecks. Grain, oil, and wine were common foodstuffs transported by sea. The remains of dried fish, nuts, olives, and pitch have also been found. Unlike the hull of a ship, which eventually disintegrates, the barrels and clay jars used as containers for foods and liquids have survived through the centuries.

Several ships uncovered were more than 100 feet long. The largest was about 140 feet, with a length-to-beam ratio between three to one and four to one.

Shipwrights favored fir, cedar, or pine in the construction of hulls, but would use whatever wood was available. Since exposure to the elements decays wood, no intact ships have been found. However, a few hull bottoms, protected by the sea floor and overlaying cargo, have survived. They tell us much about how Greek and Roman ships were constructed.

Unlike the modern technique of shipbuilding, which begins with a skeleton to which an outer wooden or metal skin is fastened, the ancients used the opposite method. A shell of planks was first crafted, joined by close-set mortars and interlocking joints. Into this sturdy shell a set of frames was then inserted and attached with wooden dowels, making for an immensely strong hull.

This type of construction was necessary for the often treacherous waters of the Mediterranean, a sea that is practically littered with ships that failed to reach their destinations.

Shipwrecked off the Island of Malta

*I*n Chapter 27 of Acts we read the story of Paul's famous sea journey, during which he was shipwrecked off the island of Malta. Paul's experience was not unusual—the Mediterranean was a notoriously hazardous sea to navigate, especially in winter, as the countless wrecks under its waters testify.

There were two main kinds of large seagoing vessels in the ancient world: warships and merchant ships ferrying various kinds of cargo. Passenger ships were unknown in the first century. On his way to Rome, Paul likely traveled on large ships of the type commonly used to bring grain from the provinces to feed the citizens of Italy.

Such cargo ships had a minimum of space available for passengers. Staterooms are mentioned rarely in ancient sources and in any case would have been reserved for wealthy travelers or official personnel. Paul and his companions must have spent most of their time on deck with the common passengers.

In stormy weather, they would have had to crowd below deck amidst the cargo and the foul air, with the hatches battened above them. When the storm raged for days, as it did on Paul's journey, conditions below must have been terrible.

After 14 days of storm, the crew of Paul's ship suspected they were near land. This was likely due to the sailors' experience in sensing the fragrances of trees and other plants that are often noticeable offshore. We read that four anchors were let down astern, with others ready at the bow.

Underwater archaeology has located hundreds of ancient anchors in the Mediterranean Sea. The discovery of multiple anchors at numerous sites confirms it was standard practice to carry several. Some of these anchors were eight feet long and weighed more than 1,500 pounds.

Paul states that there were 276 persons aboard the ship he was traveling on. Ancient reports speak of considerably larger vessels, such as the ship with 600 persons aboard on which Josephus was shipwrecked in the Sea of Adria. After

While shipwrecks in the Mediterranean were not unusual in Paul's time, one can only imagine how terrifying his experience of being shipwrecked off the island of Malta was.

a night of swimming, he and some 80 survivors were rescued by a passing ship.

The ship Paul was journeying on took the traditional sea route to Rome used by vessels of the day. Merchantmen preferred the open sea, which was faster and far from dangerous coastal shoals. However, a direct route was possible only when sailing from Rome to the eastern Mediterranean. Unfavorable trade winds required that the return voyage follow the coasts of Syria and Asia Minor.

As was customary on this route, Paul's ship put into port each night to avoid the danger of being caught in a storm and being blown off course or run aground. The Roman chronicler Lucian describes a voyage along the same route by a Roman general named Petronius.

Interestingly, lighthouses—such as the famous one at Alexandria in Egypt—were a rarity. As a rule, harbors along the coast could offer little assistance to ships traveling by night.

Did Ancient Judeans Sail to America?

Scholars have long believed that, apart from a Viking settlement in Newfoundland, the first visitor to the New World was Christopher Columbus in 1492. However, it appears that a long-forgotten inscription discovered in 1889 threatens to overturn that scholarly consensus. If the stone containing the text is genuine, the inscription is evidence of contact with the New World by mariners from ancient Judea.

The Smithsonian Institution's Institute of American Ethnology was conducting a survey of ancient mounds when it discovered a small inscribed stone in a mound next to the Little Tennessee River some 40 miles south of Knoxville. The mound contained nine skeletons lying in two parallel rows, all facing north except for one that faced south.

An inscription, measuring about 4.5 inches by 1.75 inches, was found under the skull of this skeleton. Also found were a pair of brass bracelets, the remains of jewelry, and some wood fragments—evidence that would later prove crucial in dating the finds.

Eight characters were scratched on the stone, which came to be known as the Bat Creek Inscription. They were initially identified as letters of the Cherokee alphabet, said to have been invented by a part-Cherokee in the 1820s. The only basis for this identification, seems to have been that the stone was found in what was once Cherokee territory.

For nearly 80 years, the Bat Creek Inscription lay forgotten in a drawer at the National Museum of Natural History in Washington, D.C. Then, in the late 1960s, it was observed that the text resembled Phoenician, the basis for the Canaanite and Hebrew scripts.

A photo of the stone was sent to the Semitic languages scholar Cyrus Gordon, who identified the characters as a form of ancient Hebrew known as paleo-Hebrew. The Hebrew language has been written since at least 1500 B.C. The language is still written as well as spoken today. Not only is the word order of the language very different from English, Hebrew is written in a script from right to left.

Because it is a very old language, different dialects of Hebrew have developed over the centuries. All of these dialects have affected the copying and translating of ancient manuscript.

Noting the resemblance to the writing on coins of the First and Second Jewish Revolts against Rome, Gordon dated the inscription to the first or second century A.D. Even more remarkable was what the inscription said. Gordon translated several of the letters to mean "for the Judeans."

So radical was the proposal that ancient Judeans may have visited the New World that for two decades virtually no scholars responded to the challenge posed by the Bat Creek Inscription. That silence could no longer be maintained, however, when new evidence regarding the Bat Creek Inscription became available. This new evidence surfaced when the other artifacts found at Bat Creek were examined.

The pair of bracelets were originally thought to be made of copper, which would not have been unusual for ancient burial mounds. When Gordon announced his findings, however, the Smithsonian Institution analyzed the metal and found it was not copper, but heavily leaded yellow brass composed of copper with approximately 27 percent zinc and 3.3 percent lead.

The 3.3 percent lead content of the brass prompted the Smithsonian to conclude that the bracelets could not have come from the time to which Gordon dated the Bat Creek Inscription. It was believed at the time that Roman brass of the first and second century A.D. never contained more than 1 percent lead.

Subsequently, researchers at the British Museum demonstrated that brass with higher lead contents was indeed widespread in the ancient world. Numerous ancient brass artifacts dated to the first and second century A.D. were found to contain essentially the same composition as the bracelets from Bat Creek.

Significantly, production of brass with the higher lead content, such as that found in the bracelets at Bat Creek, fell off after the second century A.D. This meant that, if the bracelets found at Bat Creek were Judean, they would likely have been produced before A.D. 200. This date coincides with the destruction of Judea by the Roman Emperor Hadrian after the Second Revolt in 135 A.D.

The crucial evidence for dating the findings at Bat Creek were the fragments of wood that were found along with the inscription and the bracelet. The method of radiocarbon dating used in 1970 could not test the tiny fragments found at Bat Creek. In more recent years, a new method of radiocarbon dating has been developed with technology that requires only a few milligrams of carbon.

The Smithsonian permitted the Bat Creek wood fragments to be tested. As it turned out, the sample of material donated was not quite large enough to give as accurate a reading as would otherwise have been possible. However, scientists were able to date the wood to between A.D. 32 and 769.

Since the wood fragments were found along with the bracelets in an undisturbed site, this suggests that the bracelets can be dated to before A.D. 200. This theory agrees with Cyrus Gordon's dating of the inscription to the first or second century A.D.

As the Little Tennessee River is not navigable beyond northern Alabama, the mystery remains as to how voyagers from Judea ended up at Bat Creek. Interestingly, it has been pointed out that the Judeans were not the only explorers to take such a route. Between 1539 and 1543, Hernando De Soto, one of the first explorers in the New World, crossed the Appalachians and traveled down the Tennessee River. The Spaniard is believed to have camped just 12 miles downstream from Bat Creek.

Few scholars accept Cyrus Gordon's theory about ancient Hebrew visitors to the New World. The Bat Creek mound has long since been destroyed by plowing, and we may never know more about the strange and mysterious group of travelers who found their way far into the interior of America and left behind a pair of brass bracelets and a suggestive but undeciphered inscription.

New Testament: Epistles

The Apostle Paul traveled extensively throughout the Roman Empire to spread the teachings of Christ and establish new Christian communities. Determined to keep in contact with the fledgling churches that had formed to minister to them, Paul wrote his famous epistles, which are contained in the New Testament as his letters to the Romans, Corinthians, Galatians, Ephesians, Philippians, Colossians, and Thessalonians. His letters to Timothy and Titus addressed matters of pastoral care.

The wedding at Cana as depicted in stained glass in St. Stephen's church, Stevens Point, Wisconsin.

MISSIONARY TO THE GENTILES

Miracles and Healing

No one was better qualified than the Apostle Paul to be an expert on miracles and healing. Not only had he healed others, but he had experienced the miraculous in his own life. The Book of Acts relates how Paul was badly injured and left for dead:

"Then some Jews came from Antioch and Iconium and won the crowd over. They stoned Paul and dragged him outside the city, thinking he was dead. But after the disciples had gathered around him, he got up and went back into the city" (Acts 14:19–20).

It is not clear here whether Paul had actually expired or not, but either way he must have experienced a miraculous healing. Stoning was a serious business and was usually fatal. But even if he had only lost consciousness, he would have at the least been severely injured.

On another occasion, a young man fell asleep while Paul was preaching (as the text says) "on and on." This young man fell from the third story and was taken up dead: "Paul went down, threw himself on the young man and put his arms around him. 'Don't be alarmed,' he said, 'He's alive!' Then he went upstairs again and broke bread and ate. After talking until daylight, he left. The people took the young man home alive and were greatly comforted" (Acts 20:10–12).

After being shipwrecked on the island of Malta, Paul experienced another miraculous healing from the bite of a potentially lethal serpent. It happened as he was gathering brushwood on the beach:

"...As he put it on the fire, a viper, driven out by the heat, fastened itself on his hand.... But Paul shook the snake off into the fire and suffered no ill effects. The people expected him to swell up or suddenly fall over dead, but after waiting for a long time and seeing nothing unusual happen to him, they changed their minds and said he was a god" (Acts 28:3–6).

We then read that Paul healed the father of the chief official of Malta, along with many others: "After this happened, the rest of the people on the island who had diseases also came and were cured" (Acts 28:9).

Paul believed in healing and experienced healing in his own life and that of others. He also taught the churches in his care to practice healing. In his letter to the church in Corinth, he includes the "gift of healing" in his list of spiritual gifts.

Thus it is all the more puzzling to learn that both Paul and his associates suffered maladies that were not healed. His trusted lieutenant Timothy had recurring stomach problems, for which Paul offered some practical advice: "Stop drinking only water, and use a little wine because of your stomach and your frequent illnesses" (1 Timothy 5:23). A bit of advice about drinking wine seems a pale substitute for physical healing. Why didn't Paul just heal his accomplice?

Paul's inability on occasion to heal the illnesses of others was matched by his own chronic malady, which he called his "thorn in the flesh": "To keep me from becoming conceited because of these surpassing great revelations, there was given me a thorn in my flesh, a messenger of Satan, to torment me. Three times I pleaded with the Lord to take it away from me. But he said to me, 'My grace is sufficient for you, for my power is made perfect in weakness'" (2 Corinthians 12:7–9).

How could it be that, after experiencing such dramatic miracles, Paul could fail to see healing in his own life? There are no easy answers, and Paul's "thorn in the flesh" has truly become a thorn in the side of theologians.

Some try to avoid the issue of why Paul was not healed by suggesting that his "thorn" was a spiritual temptation, not a physical problem. But we read in Galatians that Paul indeed suffered from physical illness: "As

This depiction of St. Paul by painter Lippo Memmi portrays the earnest dedication of the "Apostle to the Gentiles." He is pictured holding his Epistles to Rome and to various churches in Asia Minor.

you know, it was because of an illness that I first preached the Gospel to you. Even though my illness was a trial to you, you did not treat me with contempt or scorn" (Galatians 4:13–14).

The Synagogue

The word "synagogue" is derived from a Greek word meaning "assembly of people." Throughout the world, synagogues are where Jews meet for worship and other religious and social activities.

According to some traditions, the institution of the synagogue was initiated by Moses. However, this is unlikely because worship was initially centered around the Tabernacle and later the Temple in Jerusalem. Throughout the Old Testament, local worship was discouraged. Thus, for example, when Jereboam along with ten tribes seceded from Judea, his establishing of alternative altars at Dan and Bethel was viewed as a further act of rebellion.

Scholars believe the roots of the synagogue can be traced to the period after the Temple was destroyed, and the Jewish people found themselves in exile. Since the Jews could no longer go to Jerusalem to worship, it became necessary to develop another means of worshiping. The synagogue was a place of the reading of the law, prayer, and teaching. It also served a charitable function; if necessary, a visiting Jew could find a place to sleep at the local synagogue.

The synagogue originated when the Jewish people returned from exile in Babylon. It was a gathering place for teaching and social events, as well as a refuge for Jewish travelers.

When the Jews returned to Jerusalem, they continued the institution of the synagogue, even after the Temple was rebuilt. Josephus mentions several synagogues in Galilee where he was stationed as a soldier.

Jesus attended the synagogue in his home town of Nazareth but was rejected when he applied a messianic passage in Isaiah to himself while reading the Scriptures. The Gospels record that, throughout his ministry, he preached and taught in synagogues, where he often encountered opposition.

The earliest excavated remains of a synagogue are at the Dead Sea mountain fortress of Masada. Dated to the rule of Herod the Great (37–4 B.C.), the synagogue probably served the Jewish members of Herod's family, servants, and guests.

By the first century A.D., synagogues had spread from Judea to many places in the known world. The Egyptian-Jewish writer and philosopher Philo attests to the existence of numerous synagogues in Alexandria, and Paul found Jewish synagogues as he traveled throughout the Roman Empire.

In the early days of the Church, some Jews who converted to Christianity remained in their synagogue. However, as time passed they were forced out of the synagogues and began meeting in homes.

Scholars have made various suggestions as to what Paul's ailment was. One prominent theory is that he suffered from a disease of the eyes. We have an indication of this in the same passage where he mentions his "illness," when he says: "For I testify that, had it been possible, you would have torn out your eyes and given them to me" (Galatians 4:15). He commends the church in Galatia for being willing to sacrifice its own eyes for his diseased eyes.

At the end of his letter to the Galatians, he makes the following comment: "See what large letters I use as I write to you with my own hand!" This is another indication that his sight was not good. Some have speculated that his eye problems originated when he was temporarily blinded during his conversion experience on the road to Damascus.

It may never be determined with certainty what Paul's ailment was. But he does tell us that he believes the purpose for his "thorn in the flesh" was "to keep me from becoming conceited because of these surpassing great revelations."

New Testament Cities: Philippi

On his second missionary journey, the Apostle Paul visited the city of Philippi, "a leading city of the district of Macedonia and a Roman colony" (Acts 16:12). There he established a church, which we know from the New Testament book addressed to the Philippians.

Located in the Roman province of Macedonia, Philippi was located approximately 10 miles inland from the Aegean Sea.

It was situated on the Via Egnatia, the main overland route from Asia to the West.

The city was greatly enlarged and developed by Philip II of Macedonia (359–336 B.C.), whose name it takes. Philippi gained fame as the site of a decisive battle in 42 B.C. in which Antony and Octavian defeated Brutus and Cassius.

Excavations conducted at Philippi between 1914 and 1938 may have discovered the site where Paul ministered at Philippi: "On the sabbath day we went outside the gate by the river, where we supposed there was a place of prayer; and we sat down and spoke to the women who had gathered there" (Acts 16:13).

One mile from the city are the remains of a Roman ceremonial arch near the Gangites River. The arch was likely erected when Philippi became a Roman colony. The arch could also mark the *pomerium* or outer limits of the city. Inside the *pomerium* line, certain activities were restricted. Some, like burial, were prohibited for obvious sanitary reasons. The *pomerium* was also used to restrict activities within the city that were deemed unsuitable, such as those associated with foreign religious cults.

Unlike other cities in which Paul evangelized, we find no mention of a synagogue in Philippi. At various times and places in the Roman Empire, Judaism was considered a foreign cult, and it is likely that this was the case at Philippi when Paul arrived. This explains why he found the women meeting down at the river, outside the *pomerium*.

It was at the river that Paul found his first convert: "A certain woman named Lydia, a worshiper of God, was listen-

Philippi, an ancient city in northeastern Greece, was established in 356 B.C. by Philip II of Macedonia. It was a major city on the Roman road connecting Byzantium to the Adriatic.

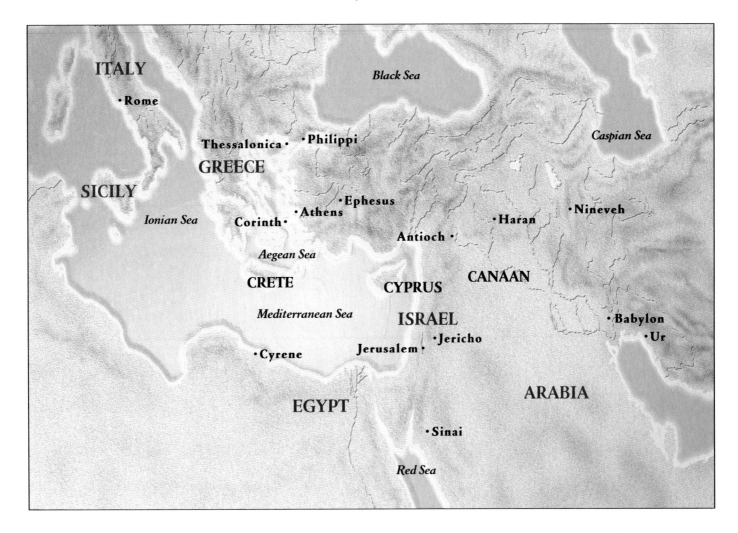

ing to us; she was from the city of Thyatira and a dealer in purple cloth. The Lord opened her heart to listen eagerly to what was said by Paul" (Acts 16:14).

Archaeologists found ample material evidence of a Christian community founded by Paul that thrived for centuries at Philippi. Artifacts discovered there include Latin crosses

Rome, Philippi, Ephesus, and Corinth were among the cities in which Paul evangelized. Here they are shown in juxtaposition with other significant Biblical cities.

dated to the second century, Christian epitaphs from the third century, and two large basilicas from the fifth and sixth centuries.

New Testament Cities: Rome

No city in the ancient world compared in size or grandeur with the city from which the Roman Empire took its name. Pliny the Elder, governor of the province of Bithynia, writes that in A.D. 73 the walls of Rome measured more than 13 miles in circumference. The city was divided into 14 districts and had 265 street intersections with statues dedicated to guardian deities.

Some of the magnificent public buildings of Rome, including the Colosseum, the Pantheon, and numerous temples, can still be seen today. Others, including the Circus Maximus, which held 150,000 people, and the theater of Pompey, which held 40,000, are known only from ancient sources.

While the rich lived in villas on the hills of the city, the poor lived in crowded districts in multistory tenements subject to collapse or fires. Rome had an extensive public welfare system that distributed wheat to most citizens at no cost. Water was also free and abundant, provided by several aqueducts to the city.

The emperor Augustine established police and fire-fighting forces in the city. Arson was considered a particularly evil crime and carried severe penalties. The concern was justified by the fire of A.D. 64, which destroyed an estimated 10 of Rome's 14 districts.

Like many modern cities, Rome had become a melting pot of many nationalities, so much so that its citizens complained that Rome was no longer Roman. The foreigners brought with them their own traditions and religions and found mutual support in their own culturally isolated groups. The Jews would have constituted one of these tolerated underclasses of Rome. Like other foreign groups, they were

The colonnade of the Forum of ancient Rome. The Forum was an open area in a town or city and typically formed the center of judicial and public business.

Rome's Colosseum was built between A.D. 72 and 82. The amphitheater seated 50,000 spectators, who viewed animal hunts, gladiatorial fights, and, when the arena was flooded, mock sea battles.

To an Unknown God

Paul's second missionary journey took him to Athens, the cultural center of the ancient world. There, distressed to see that the city was full of idols, he spent his days evangelizing in the synagogue, the marketplace, or wherever people would listen.

A group of Epicureans and Stoics were sufficiently impressed to invite him to the Areopagus, located on a height overlooking the city. The Areopagus was where philosophers gathered for debate and discussion: "Now all the Athenians and the foreigners living there would spend their time in nothing but telling or hearing something new" (Acts 17:21).

Paul stood up before those gathered at the Areopagus and judiciously began his speech with a point of reference from something he had observed in the city: "Athenians, I see how extremely religious you are in every way. For as I went through the city and looked carefully at the objects of your worship, I found among them an altar with the inscription, 'To an unknown god.' What therefore you worship as unknown, this I proclaim to you" (Acts 17:22–23). He then went on to use the theme of the unknown God to introduce the monotheistic theme of the one true God who is the creator and lord of the universe.

Even though no inscription with precisely this wording in the singular has yet been discovered, it is known that the Greeks were careful to affirm the existence of unknown gods. This was because, being polytheists, they believed in many gods and wanted to ensure they would not fail to acknowledge any.

Ancient sources mention the existence of various altars dedicated to "unknown gods" on the road from Phalerum to Athens and also at Olympia. The Greek writer Diogenes Laertius tells of how, during a plague, the Athenians were advised to sacrifice to "the appropriate god"—in other words, the unknown god responsible for the plague.

The essence of Paul's message to the Athenians is the same one given by Jesus himself in speaking to the Samaritan woman: "You worship what you do not know; we worship what we know, for salvation is from the Jews" (John 4:22).

allowed to build their places of worship. The names of at least 13 synagogues in Rome are known from ancient sources.

An ancient cemetery has been excavated under St. Peter's Basilica. Both St. Peter's Basilica and the original fourth-century church that occupied the site were built in an area that contained pagan mausoleums dated to the second century. Christians were buried in pagan cemeteries until the third century. Although no bones have been uncovered that might be those of the apostle, the continuous reverence of the site indicates that Peter may have been buried here.

Other early material evidence of the Christians of Rome is found in the catacombs, extensive underground burial areas where believers buried their dead and gathered during times of persecution.

Excavations under churches in the city have also revealed homes of the late second and early third centuries that had been transformed into places of worship. These homes were generally located in the poor and populous districts of the city. However, there were also converts to the new faith of Christianity in influential quarters. In his letter to the Philippians, the Apostle Paul writes: "All the saints greet you, especially those of the emperor's household" (Philippians 4:22).

New Testament Cities: Corinth

Corinth was the capital of the Senatorial province of Achaia and a major city of antiquity. Strategically situated on the isthmus between mainland Greece and the Peloponnesus, it controlled commerce between ports on the Gulf of Corinth and the Saronic Gulf.

The Temple of Apollo in Corinth. Seven of the original 38 columns of the Temple, partially destroyed in 146 B.C., still stand.

This platform, or bema, *located in the center of the forum of Corinth, was probably the "tribunal" of Gallio, the proconsul of Achaia. The Apostle Paul was brought before Gallio's tribunal during his year-and-a-half stay in the city.*

Sections of a specially constructed roadway between the two ports, used for transporting boats over land on rollers, can still be seen today. This three-mile route saved ships from an often hazardous 200-mile voyage around the southern end of the Greek peninsula. In 1893, a canal across the isth-mus was completed, connecting the Aegean Sea with the Adriatic.

Excavations at Corinth have shed light on Paul's letters to the church there, and his letter to the Romans, written while he was at Corinth. In the sixteenth chapter of Romans, Paul sends greetings to the Roman church: "Gaius, who is host to me and to the whole church, greets you. Erastus, the city treasurer, and our brother Quartus, greet you" (16:23).

In 1929, a pavement inscription was uncovered that was dated to the latter half of the first century. The original bronze letters were torn out by looters, but the text could still be read: "Erastus in return for his aedileship laid [the pavement] at his own expense." In ancient Rome, an "aedile" was similar to a commissioner of public works.

There is no other officer known to have the name Erastus. Thus it seems fairly certain that this is the same official mentioned by Paul in Romans 16:23. It is likely that Erastus first served as city treasurer before being promoted to aedile. (Erastus was also the name of a member of the Christian church at Ephesus; it is not known if they are one and the same.)

Paul's custom on his missionary journeys was to seek out the Jewish community of a city, which he did on his first visit: "When they reached Ephesus, he left them there, but first he himself went into the synagogue and had a discussion with the Jews" (Acts 18:19). That brief visit to Ephesus bore fruit, for when Paul returned to spend 18 months there in about A.D. 50, a small group of believers had already formed.

A piece of a marble doorway of uncertain date has been found that evidently was part of the Jewish synagogue of Corinth. The restored inscription, written in Greek, reads: "Synagogue of the Hebrews." Another fragment of marble is decorated with Jewish ritual objects: a menorah, palm branches, and citron.

Since the sixth century B.C., Corinth sponsored the biennial Isthmian Games, a Panhellenic festival of athletic contests dedicated to the sea god Poseidon. Paul would have witnessed the opening of the A.D. 51 festival, and in his first letter to the Corinthians, he applies his observations regarding athletics to spiritual self-discipline: "Do you not know that in a race the runners all compete, but only one receives the prize? Run in such a way that you may win it. Athletes exercise self-control in all things; they do it to receive a perishable wreath, but we an imperishable one. So I do not run aimlessly, nor do I box as though beating the air; but I punish my body and enslave it, so that after proclaiming to others I myself should not be disqualified" (1 Corinthians 9:24–27).

It was a message that the Corinthian church, known for its moral and spiritual laxity, sorely needed to hear, and which Paul apparently exemplified in his own life.

New Testament Cities: Ephesus

Ephesus, located at the mouth of the Cayster River on a gulf of the Aegean Sea, was a political and commercial center of Asia Minor. A magnificent avenue 35 feet wide and lined with columns led from the harbor to the center of the city, creating a favorable impression for the visitor.

When the Apostle Paul visited and established a church there in the mid-first century, Ephesus was at the peak of its greatness. Many people chose to live there, and with an estimated population of 250,000, it is believed to have been the fourth largest city in the world. Later, during the reign of the emperor Hadrian in the early second century, the city became the capital of the Roman province of Asia.

Since ancient times, the inhabitants of Ephesus worshiped Artemis, the Greek goddess of fertility, whom the Romans later identified with their goddess Diana. The Temple of Artemis at Ephesus, considered one of the seven wonders of the world, appears on Roman coins of the day.

Artisans in the city prospered through the production of small figurines of the goddess. When Paul visited Ephesus during his second missionary journey, his preaching about the one true God stirred up the polytheistic vendors. One of them, a silversmith named Demetrius, instigated a riot when he called together his fellow tradesmen.

His speech is recorded in the Book of Acts: "'Men, you know that we get our wealth from this business. You also see and hear that not only in Ephesus, but in almost the

The elaborate facade of the temple dedicated to the second-century Roman emperor Hadrian at Ephesus. Hadrian ruthlessly suppressed the Second Jewish Revolt of A.D. 132–135, destroying Jerusalem and rebuilding the city as "Aelia Capitolina."

whole of Asia, this Paul has persuaded and drawn away a considerable number of people by saying that gods made with hands are not gods. And there is danger not only that this trade of ours may come into disrepute, but also that the temple of the great goddess Artemis will be scorned, and she will be deprived of her majesty, which brought all of Asia and the world to worship her.' When they heard this, they were enraged and shouted, 'Great is Artemis of the Ephesians!'" (Acts 19:25–28).

The city was stirred up, and a mob made for the theater, dragging two of Paul's companions with them. The theater of Ephesus has been excavated and is visible today as an imposing tiered edifice that seated 24,000 people. The text aptly describes the chaos that reigned: "Meanwhile, some were shouting one thing, some another; for the assembly was in confusion, and most of them did not know why they had come together" (Acts 19:32).

Fortunately, the magistrate of the city prevailed upon the crowd not to harm the evangelists, who were able to leave the city without further incident. In writing to the church at Corinth, Paul mentions that he "fought with wild animals at Ephesus" (1 Corinthians 15:32). It is not known whether he intends a literal or figurative meaning here.

According to Christian tradition, the Apostle John moved to Ephesus and died there at an advanced age. The city also served as a center for the imperial cult of Rome, which was centered around the worship of the reigning emperor as well as preceding emperors.

At the time John is thought to have resided in Ephesus, the city had a temple and cult dedicated to the ruling Flavian

dynasty, and it is likely that John wrote during the rule of Domitian (A.D. 81–96). Some scholars believe that much of John's use of imagery in the Book of Revelation, such as the worship of the "Beast," is a reference to the imperial cult that was so prevalent at Ephesus.

Traditionally, much of prophecy is understood to have a dual reference, in that the prophet uses the language, imagery, culture, and circumstances of his day to describe events destined to occur far in the future. If so, the "Beast" of the Book of Revelation, who demands worship and instigates a worldwide conflagration, may not only represent a fearful personage from the past, but may also be a symbol of Satan, whose work, according to the Scriptures, is far from completed.

A Radical View of Marriage

The Apostle Paul has long been suspected by theologians of harboring a negative opinion toward the female sex, as well as a repressive view of the institution of marriage. But compared to the culture in which he lived and ministered, Paul's teachings can be seen as nothing short of revolutionary.

Up until the time of the emperor Augustine, Roman society had a utilitarian view of marriage, the purpose of which was to produce heirs to inherit one's property and continue the family name. A husband was fully justified in divorcing his wife solely on the grounds that she was unable to bear children.

The remains of the Odeum, a theater for dramatic performances, at Ephesus. The Apostle Paul and his companions were dragged into the theater by the irate citizens of Ephesus.

In the Roman concept of the *paterfamilias*, the purpose of marital relations was to procreate. Roman men often looked to prostitutes for their sexual satisfaction.

In fact, increasing numbers of men were not bothering to marry. A concerned Augustus decided to redress this trend, and in 18 B.C. he proclaimed new laws that imposed heavier taxes upon unmarried men and women, while granting financial benefits for those who married and had children.

After Augustus' new regulations went into force, more Roman men chose to marry, but without the intention of entering into a monogamous relationship. Prostitution flourished as before.

It is this practice of promiscuity that Paul is referring to when writing to the Church in the Roman city of Corinth: "But because of cases of sexual immorality, each man should have his own wife and each woman her own husband" (1 Corinthians 7:2–4).

Paul's teaching here is a radical departure from established Roman custom regarding the relationship between husbands and wives. It granted hitherto unknown rights to wives and placed them on an equal basis with their husbands. His state-ment that a wife has "authority" over her husband's body must have been greeted with shock by the typical Roman husband, who until then had considered himself free to seek sexual pleasure outside of marriage.

The teaching of the New Testament regarding marriage eventually won the day and set a standard for Western civilization that has lasted for more than 19 centuries. While often taken for granted and increasingly challenged, the ideal of a mutual, monogamous relationship in which two people commit themselves exclusively to each other is still reflected in the marriage vows of lands that have come under the influence of the teaching of the Apostle Paul.

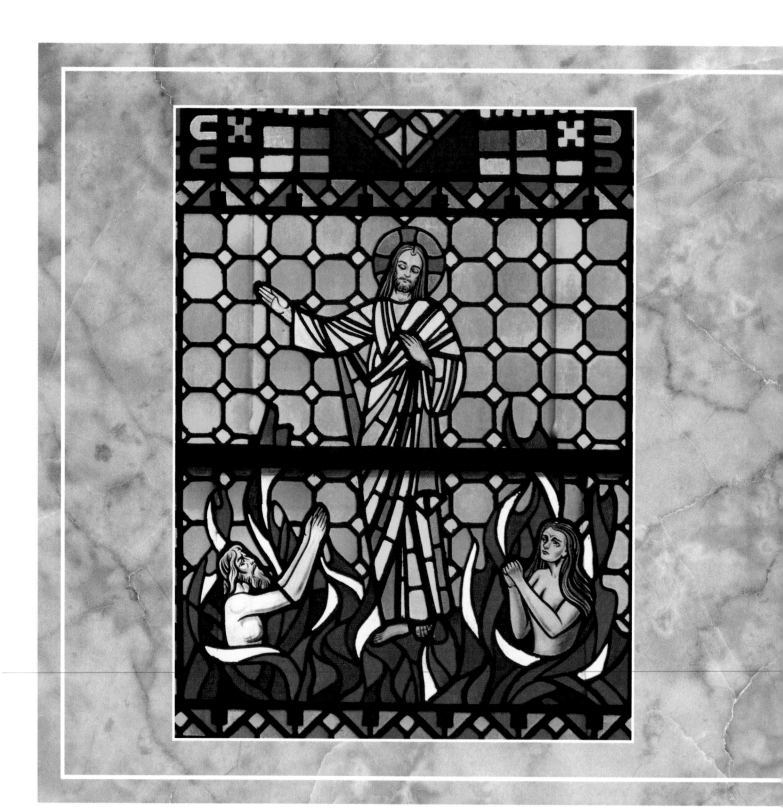

NEW TESTAMENT: THE BOOK OF REVELATION

Addressed to the early Christians of Asia Minor, the Revelation to John, also known as Apocalypse, helped give them the strength to endure their persecution by the Romans by demonstrating God's awesome power and revealing the greater glory that awaited them. Filled with riddles and symbolic imagery, it describes a cosmic cataclysm in which God destroys the forces of evil and raises the righteous to join him in his heavenly kingdom.

A vision of Hell is captured in stained glass at St. Raymond's Cathedral in Joliet, Illinois.

THE MYSTERIES IN PROPHECY

The Seven Cities

The letters to seven churches in Chapters 2 and 3 of the Book of Revelation have long been a source of scholarly controversy. One view is that the churches addressed actually represent seven types of churches that are present in all ages. That is, the strengths and weaknesses mentioned with regard to each of the seven churches can be found in the Christian Church in all ages.

Another view is that the seven churches represent a historical progression, and that each of the churches symbolizes the state of the Church in a different age. The difficulty with this view is that few students of the Bible have been able to agree as to which churches represent which time periods.

A third view is that the seven churches of Revelation refer primarily to churches in the first century, and that the admonitions given to each can be applied to churches and Christians of all ages.

The churches are congregations in seven prominent cities of first-century Asia Minor: Ephesus, Smyrna, Pergamum, Thyatira, Sardis, Philadelphia, and Laodicea. Why these particular churches were chosen is not known. However, the order in which the cities are listed in Revelation corresponds to their actual location on a circuitous route in Asia Minor. This was the likely route used by government messengers and itinerant Christian evangelists and teachers.

Particular characteristics of each city are found in each of the letters. The Ephesians, for example, are commended for their love of the truth, but are urged to remember their earlier love, which evidently had begun to wane. Some commentators suggest the Ephesians had fallen into a comfortable accommodation with the pagan imperial cult prevalent in the city.

Smyrna was a large and prosperous coastal city 40 miles north of Ephesus. The church there is warned about hostile Jews who are called the "synagogue of Satan." Christians were persecuted in the city with the complicity of the Jewish population. The most famous example was Polycarp, one of the first martyrs of the church, who was put to death in Smyrna at the instigation of the Jews of the city.

Some 50 miles northeast of Smyrna lie the ruins of Pergamum, an impressive capital city in the first century. Pergamum is described as the location of "Satan's throne," a possible reference to the fact that the city was the official center for the imperial cult in Asia. One of the most imposing pagan edifices was the great altar of Zeus, which jutted out prominently high on the mountain above.

The overland route continues to Thyatira, a center for manufacturing and marketing. The church there is warned against learning the "deep things of Satan," a possible reference to the pagan guild feasts, which the rest of the city would have participated in. Apparently, a woman known as Jezebel was stirring up trouble in the church at Thyatira and is condemned in the strongest terms.

Sardis, located 45 miles east of Thyatira, had an illustrious history as the ancient kingdom of Lydia. In 133 B.C., the city came under Roman control and was then known for its wealth. However, the church at Sardis comes under severe criticism and is particularly warned to be watchful: "Remember then what you received and heard; obey it, and repent. If you do not wake up, I will come like a thief, and you will not know at what hour I will come to you" (Revelation 3:3). This was a message that the people of Sardis needed to hear, for twice in its history the city was conquered when its defenders were caught off guard.

Thirty miles beyond Sardis lies Philadelphia, the sixth city along the circuitous route. Philadelphia was a prosperous agricultural and industrial center whose main drawback was that it was prone to devastating earthquakes. To the Philadelphians is given the promise of an unshakable city: If they remain faithful, they are told, they will become like an unmovable pillar in the new Jerusalem.

The last city, Laodicea, was the wealthiest city in Phrygia during Roman times. The Laodiceans are criticized for their

The archangel slays the dragon of Revelation, as depicted in Francesco Zuccato's "Vision of the Apocalypse" on the east wall of the Church of St. Mark in Venice, Italy.

spiritual poverty: "Therefore I counsel you to buy from me gold refined by fire so that you may be rich; and white robes to clothe you and to keep the shame of your nakedness from being seen; and salve to anoint your eyes so that you may see" (Revelation 3:18).

Laodicea was famous for its medical school, and one of the medicines produced in the city was an eye-salve made from a substance called "Phrygian powder" and olive oil. It became a fitting illustration of the Laodiceans' spiritual blindness.

An Evil World Leader

*T*he Book of Revelation tells us that at the end of the age a mysterious figure of consummate evil will arise:

"The beast was given a mouth uttering haughty and blasphemous words, and it was allowed to exercise authority for forty-two months. It opened its mouth to utter blasphemies against God, blaspheming his name and his dwelling, that is, those who dwell in heaven. Also it was allowed to make war on the saints and to conquer them. It was given authority over every tribe and people and language and nation" (Revelation 13:5–7).

According to the Book of Revelation, Satan will be chained before his destruction, as depicted here in the Resurrection Window in the St. Lawrence chapel of Strasbourg Cathedral, dated to A.D. 1308–45.

World history is the story of great empires. None of them, however, has been capable of dominating the world's political system to the degree portrayed here.

We read that the Beast of Revelation will also exercise complete authority over the economic affairs of the world: "Also it causes all, both small and great, both rich and poor, both free and slave, to be marked on the right hand or the forehead, so that no one can buy or sell who does not have the mark, that is, the name of the beast or the number of its name" (Revelation 13:16–17).

The Antichrist, or Beast, along with the false prophet mentioned in Revelation chapter 16, will make war with the saints and lead the world in a final rebellion against God. Their leader is Satan, the "great red dragon" mentioned in the twelfth chapter of Revelation.

All the peoples of the world will be commanded to bow before the Antichrist: "And all the inhabitants of the earth will worship it, everyone whose name has not been written from the foundation of the world in the book of life of the Lamb that was slaughtered" (Revelation 13:8).

The Antichrist will have the ability to perform unimaginable feats: "And it was allowed to give breath to the image of the beast so that the image of the beast could even speak and cause those who would not worship the image of the beast to be killed" (Revelation 13:15).

Some biblical scholars believe that the Antichrist is a symbolic reference to the forces of evil. Others conclude that the passages speak of a political ruler who will one day arise and exercise his power over the nations of the world.

The Mark of the Beast

Popular books on the subject of biblical prophecy have abounded with theories as to the identification of the Antichrist.

Some rather wild attempts have been made to connect this individual with a cryptic verse in Revelation: "This calls for wisdom: let anyone with understanding calculate the number of the beast, for it is the number of a person. Its number is six hundred sixty-six" (Revelation 13:18).

The numerical value of more than one prominent political figure's name has been equated to that number. Thus, there are even those who have harbored suspicions regarding former President Ronald Reagan because his full name, Ronald Wilson Reagan, consisted of three groups of six letters. Others suggest that 666 refers to the Social Security number of the Antichrist, or perhaps some computerized identification code of the future.

Few of these various attempts to interpret the meaning of 666 take into account the historical context of the verse in Revelation that speaks about the number. The modern mind may consider it strange to designate someone's name by a number, but those living at the end of the first century, when Revelation was written, would have understood the writer's intention.

The Apostle John was in all likelihood employing Gematria, the practice of discovering hidden meaning in a word by computing its numerical value. This method of inter-

The Lawless One

Christians have traditionally referred to the man of consummate evil who will arise at the end of days to deceive the nations as the Antichrist. However, nowhere in the Bible is the word used to refer to a person. It appears only in the Book of I John in an impersonal sense: "And every spirit that does not confess Jesus is not from God. And this is the spirit of the antichrist, of which you have heard that it is coming; and now it is already in the world" (1 John 4:3).

There are, however, other passages that speak of a personal manifestation of evil yet to come in the future. These would include the "beast" in the Book of Revelation and the "prince" and "willful king" of the Book of Daniel. In addition to these cryptic passages, the apostle Paul gives a fuller description of this mysterious person whom he calls "the lawless one":

"He opposes and exalts himself above every so-called god or object of worship, so that he takes his seat in the temple of God, declaring himself to be God...And then the lawless one will be revealed, whom the Lord Jesus will destroy with the breath of his mouth, annihilating him by the manifestation of his coming. The coming of the lawless one is apparent in the working of Satan, who uses all power, signs, lying wonders, and every kind of wicked deception for those who are perishing, because they refused to love the truth and so be saved. For this reason God sends them a powerful delusion, leading them to believe what is false, so that all who have not believed the truth but took pleasure in unrighteousness will be condemned" (2 Thessalonians 2:4, 8–12).

preting words and texts was not uncommon in the ancient world of the Hebrews and Greeks.

The languages of both the Jews and the Greeks, which used the letters of the alphabet to denote numbers, lent themselves to Gematria.

Some early Christian documents, for example, use 888 for the name of Jesus in Greek. Graffiti on the excavated walls of Pompeii provides further examples of the common practice of assigning numerical values to names. The Jewish rabbis also sought hidden meanings in the Old Testament through Gematria.

Accordingly, the attempts of the early Church to decipher the meaning of the three sixes focused on the numerical value of the names of possible Antichrist candidates. Church father Irenaeus of Lyons, for example, records several possibilities in the Greek language, but seems not to have considered any in Hebrew. The Book of Revelation, however, was written by the Apostle John, a Jew from Galilee. Even though the text of Revelation was written in Greek, the language of the Roman world, John would have been more familiar with Hebrew Gematria than its Greek counterpart.

So it is not surprising to discover that the Hebrew translation of the Greek for *Caesar Nero* adds up to the required

666. This does not necessarily mean that the Apostle John believed Nero was the Antichrist. He may have been pointing his readers to Nero as a forerunner of the coming Antichrist, exhibiting characteristics of the future beast of Revelation.

A Revived Roman Empire?

A popular belief among students of biblical prophecy is that, at the end of the world, the Roman Empire will rise from the ash heap of history. With the Antichrist at its head, Rome will draw the armies of the world into the final battle of Armageddon.

Belief in a revived Roman Empire comes from a prophecy in the Book of Daniel: "After the sixty-two weeks, an anointed one shall be cut off and shall have nothing, and the troops of the prince who is to come shall destroy the city and the sanctuary. Its end shall come with a flood, and to the end there shall be war. Desolations are decreed" (Daniel 9:26).

In this passage, the expression "anointed one" is believed to refer to Jesus, who will be "cut off" or crucified. The text then goes on to state that Jerusalem will be destroyed by "the troops of the prince who is to come." From history we know that the troops mentioned here are the Roman legions that sacked the city in A.D. 70. Who, then, would be "the prince who is to come"? This description is taken to be a reference to the future Antichrist. If so, then he is here identified with Rome.

Additional clues are found in the thirteenth chapter of Revelation: "And I saw a beast rising out of the sea, having ten horns and seven heads; and on its horns were ten diadems, and on its heads were blasphemous names.... And the dragon gave it his power and his throne and great authority. One of its heads seemed to have received a death-blow, but its mortal wound had been healed. In amazement the whole earth followed the beast" (Revelation 13:1–3).

As the chapter in Revelation progresses, a political leader appears who exercises extraordinary supernatural powers and who, according to many scholars, can only be the Antichrist. It has been suggested that the "ten horns and seven heads" may refer to political powers aligned with him.

We have already seen how the Antichrist is connected with Rome in the Book of Daniel 9:26. If that identification is correct—and scholars are by no means of one mind on this issue—then it makes possible the identification of the "ten horns" as 10 kings of a revived Roman Empire.

The efforts to unite Europe politically and economically in recent times caused a furor among some students of biblical prophecy. These students eagerly awaited the tenth nation to join the European Economic Community (EEC), which they expected to be followed by the revealing of the Antichrist. However, those expectations failed to materialize as the EEC reached and then exceeded the magic number of 10 member nations.

One explanation for why the prophetic passages of the Bible defy a common interpretation comes at the end of the Book of Daniel, when the prophet is told: "But you, Daniel, keep the words secret and the book sealed until the time of the

Aerial view of Megiddo, overlooking the Jezreel Valley in northern Israel. The valley is thought to be the future site of the final battle mentioned in the Book of Revelation.

end. Many shall be running back and forth, and evil shall increase" (12:4).

This verse seems to indicate that the meaning of these mysterious passages is being withheld until some future time.

The Last Battle

The Book of Revelation speaks about a final cosmic battle between the forces of good and evil. We read that the "kings of the whole world" will be assembled "for battle on the great day of God the Almighty.... And they assembled them at the place that in Hebrew is called Harmagedon" (Revelation 16:14, 16).

Other translations have the more familiar "Armageddon" instead of "Harmagedon." Many Christians through the centuries have interpreted Harmagedon to mean Mount Megiddo (since the Hebrew word for "mount" is *har*), and have thus located the future battle at the ancient site of the city of Megiddo in the Carmel Mountain Range of what used to be northern Palestine.

Megiddo is strategically located near an important pass overlooking the Plain of Esdraelon. The Via Maris, the major route from Egypt to Mesopotamia, went past Megiddo. In ancient times, whoever controlled the pass controlled the region.

Megiddo has been the site of several important battles in biblical history. It was on the Plain of Esdraelon that Deborah and Barak routed the Canaanite king Sisera and where Jehu struck down Joram and ran King Ahaziah through with a spear in his zeal to destroy the house of Ahab. Later, Josiah would meet Pharaoh Neco II in battle at Megiddo, despite Neco's attempt to avert conflict: "But Neco sent envoys to him, saying, 'What have I to do with you, king of Judah? I am not coming against you today, but against the house with which I am at war; and God has commanded me to hurry. Cease opposing God, who is with me, so that he will not destroy you'" (2 Chronicles 35:21). Josiah would not be dissuaded and persisted at the cost of his own life.

The strategic value of Megiddo has been underscored through the ages. At the beginning of the nineteenth century, Napoleon Bonaparte, who himself fought a major battle against the Turks at nearby Acco, is said to have remarked upon viewing the valley from Megiddo that it would be an admirable location for a battle of cataclysmic proportions. In more recent times, British commander General Edmund Allenby drove the Turks from Palestine during World War I after capturing the pass.

Some scholars, however, reject the identification of Megiddo with the Armageddon mentioned in the Book of Revelation. There is no record of a mountain in either ancient or modern times called "Mount Megiddo." An archaeological mound bearing that name hardly qualifies to be called a hill, much less a mountain.

It has also been pointed out that other descriptions of the future battle center around Jerusalem, in the central highlands, rather than on the Plain of Esdraelon. In the Book of Zechariah we read: "On that day I will make Jerusalem a heavy stone for all the peoples; all who lift it shall griev-

The remains of the gate of the ancient city of Megiddo, built as early as the tenth century B.C. Megiddo was one of four important cities fortified by King Solomon (1 Kings 9:15).

ously hurt themselves. And all the nations of the earth shall come against it" (Zechariah 12:3).

Other suggested translations for "Armageddon" include "mount of assembly," "city of desire," and "his fruitful mountain," all of which are compatible with Jerusalem. One mediating position points out that the battle of Harmagedon is spoken of as taking place in the geographically limited land of Israel. Since the battle is described as involving massive armies, it is conceivable that it would not be confined to any one battlefield. Thus, if the battle spreads from Jerusalem to the Valley of Esdraelon in the north, both interpretations would be satisfied.

Who Are the 144,000?

*I*n Chapter 7 of the Book of Revelation, John witnesses another in a series of visions, this one regarding a mysterious number that has intrigued students of the Bible throughout the centuries:

"I saw another angel ascending from the rising of the sun, having the seal of the living God, and he called with a loud voice to the four angels who had been given power to damage earth and sea, saying, 'Do not damage the earth or the sea or the trees, until we have marked the servants of our God with a seal on their foreheads.' And I heard the number of those who were sealed, one hundred forty-four thousand, sealed out of every tribe of the people of Israel" (7:2–4).

Who are the 144,000, and when does their "sealing" take place? Some scholars take the number literally, based on the fact that this group is described in the text as coming from the 12 tribes of Israel. They are thought to be Jewish converts to Christianity who will evangelize the world.

Others dispute this, pointing out that the original 12 tribes of Israel no longer exist as distinct entities. Ten of the tribes were lost to history in the Assyrian captivity in 722 B.C. The remaining two tribes lost their separate identity much later, after the fall of Jerusalem in A.D. 70.

Still others take this numerical figure to be symbolic. Many people have tried using various mathematical methods in an effort to solve biblical mysteries. The squaring of the number 12 (12 tribes times 12 thousand) is interpreted as a way of emphasizing completeness. For these believers, the number 144,000 symbolizes the generation of faithful who will enter the final turbulent stage of human history when the forces of evil reach their peak. The "sealing" does not mean they will be spared persecution—indeed, the verse that follows describes a vision of a multitude of martyrs in Heaven. Rather, it symbolizes the promise of eternal life in Heaven when their life on earth is finished.

Some scholars believe the figure refers not to all the faithful, but only to the number of martyrs in the last days of human history, during the final conflict with the forces of evil. However, a following passage from the Book of Revelation describes a "great multitude that no one could count, from every nation, from all tribes and peoples and languages" who have come out of "the great ordeal" (Revelation 7:9, 14). According to this passage, it appears that the total number of martyrs exceeds 144,000 and is beyond counting.

Whether the number is to be taken literally or symbolically, it is clear that the ultimate price they pay will not compare to the glories that follow: "They will hunger no more, and thirst no more; the sun will not strike them, nor any scorching heat; for the Lamb at the center of the throne will be their shepherd, and he will guide them to springs of the water of life, and God will wipe away every tear from their eyes" (Revelation 7:16–17).

ANTICHRIST CANDIDATES IN HISTORY

The Minstrel Emperor

By the year A.D. 68, Rome was in turmoil. The enemies of Lucius Domitius Nero, the reigning Caesar for the preceding 14 years, were finally gaining the upper hand. The man whose reign had begun so promisingly had degenerated into a wandering minstrel obsessed with grandiose illusions. He was no longer fit to rule.

In his very first speech to the Senate, Nero had promised a new Golden Age, and for the first five years of his reign he exhibited generosity and moderation toward his subjects. Historians record a long list of noteworthy improvements in the political and social life of Rome, including an end to capital punishment and the blood circuses.

But by A.D. 59, Nero had snapped. He embarked upon a reign of terror that likely resulted in the deaths (among countless others) of the apostles Peter and Paul in Rome.

The notorious fire that ravaged Rome for nine days in A.D. 64 consumed much of the city. Nero was blamed, though he was 35 miles away at the time, at his villa in Antium. A newly established religious sect—Christianity—was also blamed for starting the fire. It was an accusation that Nero encouraged.

The following year, Nero put down a revolt with brutal force, resulting in the deaths of Seneca and the poet Lucan, as well as many others innocent of the conspiracy.

A lesser known side of Nero began to appear, that of an aspiring poet, lyre player, and theatrical performer. He was also deeply attracted to mystical religions. He dabbled in Zoroastrianism, Gnosticism, and perhaps even Christianity (as indicated by a fresco in the Palantine Chapel depicting Nero and the Apostle Paul conversing).

At the end of A.D. 66, smitten by the siren's call from the land of the gods, Nero spent 15 months wandering throughout Greece as a barefoot ascetic, reciting poetry and playing his music. His obsession with mystical religions when the Empire was reeling from revolts in Africa, Gaul, and Spain, not to mention Judea, earned him the contempt of his fellow Romans.

In blissful distraction, Nero occupied himself with composing songs and inventing a hydraulic organ on which to play his beloved music. He laughed at the growing threats to the Empire and at popular discontent at home, claiming, "I have only to appear and sing to have peace once again in Gaul!"

The end was near for the eccentric emperor. Condemned by the Senate to die a slave's death on the cross, abandoned

The remaining head portion of a marble bust of the Roman emperor Nero (A.D. 54–68). Many early Christians believed that 666, the number of the Beast of Revelation, was reference to representation of Nero's name.

That same year he consented to the assassination of Agrippina, his increasingly insane mother who had ruthlessly engineered his rise to power.

even by his Praetorian Guard, Nero fled the city. Arriving at one of his villas outside Rome, and seeing that all hope was lost, Nero stabbed himself and was buried by his Christian mistress, Acte.

Well before Nero's death, the Christians in Rome had begun calling him the Antichrist for his attempts to deify himself by enforcing emperor-worship. The fact that he died virtually alone, in an obscure place, passing from the scene without even a state funeral, gave rise to rumors that the emperor was, in fact, not dead.

There was speculation that Nero had somehow managed to escape east to the Parthians, a dreaded enemy of Rome. From there, he would return to wreak a fearsome revenge on the city that had turned against him.

These rumors, though unfounded, spread rapidly through the Empire and continued even into the next century and beyond. Decrees appeared, allegedly from the hand of Nero, and Roman historians record no fewer than three instances in which impostors arose claiming to be the fallen emperor. One of them managed to convince a large number of Parthians, throwing Achaia and Asia Minor into terror.

The early Christians were influenced by these popular legends about Nero, and many considered him the Antichrist. As time passed, some thought he would rise from the dead to wage war against Rome. This battle would occur at the end of the world, prior to the second coming of Jesus Christ.

The apocalyptic *Ascension of Isaiah*, dated from the end of the first century, echoes this belief: "And after it has been

Nero's Madness Unleashed

The historian Eusebius gives the following account of how the emperor Nero's madness was unleashed against the Christians of Rome:

"When Nero's power was now firmly established, he gave himself up to unholy practices and took up arms against the God of the universe. To describe the monster of depravity that he became lies outside the scope of this present work. Many writers have recorded the facts about him in minute detail, enabling anyone who wishes to get a complete picture of his perverse and extraordinary madness, which led him to the senseless destruction of innumerable lives. . . . All this left one crime still to be added to his account—he was the first of the emperors to be the declared enemy of the worship of Almighty God. . . . So it came about that this man, the first to be heralded as a conspicuous fighter against God, was led on to murder the apostles. It is recorded that, in his reign, Paul was beheaded in Rome itself and that Peter was crucified, and the record is confirmed that the cemeteries there are still called by the names of Peter and Paul" (*History of the Church*, II:25).

brought to completion, Beliar will descend, the great angel, the king of this world, which he has ruled ever since it existed. He will descend from his firmament in the form of a man, a king of iniquity, a murderer of his mother—this is the king of this world."

The description of the Antichrist as "a murderer of his mother" is, of course, a reference to Nero's assassination of his mother in A.D. 59.

The legend of *Nero redivivus* (Nero resurrected) was held by Christian writers long after the first century. Jerome, writing at the end of the fourth century, affirmed that it was still held by some Christians even in his day.

The Imperial Dictator

*I*magine the following scenario: An immensely charismatic and powerful European monarch extends his domain by military force to include much of the former Roman Empire. His army marches on Rome itself, the Eternal City, bringing the Pope into his sphere of influence with a peace treaty.

Next comes the Middle East. He occupies Egypt by force and invades the Holy Land. Marching up the coastline at the head of a powerful army, he invades the land of Israel. His army camps at the very mouth of the plain of Megiddo, the traditional location of the prophetic battle of Armageddon. He journeys to the ancient site of Megiddo overlooking the expansive valley. Looking down from the summit,

he observes that the setting is an ideal site for a battle of epic proportions.

To many students of biblical prophecy, this description reads like a page out of the Book of Daniel or the Book of Revelation. But this scenario is not destined to occur in the future; it played itself out 200 years ago during the reign of Napoleon Bonaparte.

The parallels between the greatest imperial dictator of European history and the biblical description of the Antichrist are amazing. For starters, Napoleon was very nearly an Italian subject, bringing to mind the biblical passages linking the Antichrist with the revived Roman Empire. His mother tongue was a dialect of Italian. His place of origin, Corsica, was an island off the Italian mainland; its language and culture are closely allied with Italy.

After a military education and commission as an artillery officer, Napoleon faltered in his career and was reduced to wandering the streets of Paris at half-pension and without an assignment. As destiny would have it, a fresh opportunity presented itself when Napoleon was called upon for assistance during an uprising in Paris in 1795. He demonstrated strategic genius and decisiveness in suppressing the revolt, and he was rewarded by being appointed commander of the French occupation army of Italy.

The next few years brought dazzling success in a campaign against the Austrians fought on Italian soil. While the defeated Hapsburgs sued for peace, Napoleon turned his attention toward southern Italy. In an epic campaign, his army overcame all resistance on the Italian peninsula and occupied, significantly, the papal states.

Napoleon's conquest of the Vatican territories of the vicar of Rome excited the imagination of students of Bible prophecy. The banishment of the Pope was taken as a fulfillment of the cryptic passage in Revelation 13, which speaks of the Beast suffering a "mortal wound."

Even the numbers seemed to add up. The Beast of Revelation 13 "was given a mouth uttering haughty and blasphemous words, and it was allowed to exercise authority for forty-two months" (v. 5). Forty-two months was taken (somewhat incorrectly) to mean 1,260 days, which was later taken to mean 1,260 years.

When 1,260 years are subtracted from the year of Napoleon's occupation of the papal states, one arrives at the magic number of 538, which happens to be the year of the beginning of papal power. Indeed, there is some justification for this, in that 538 happens to fall within the reign of Justinian, the greatest of the Byzantine Roman emperors.

Napoleon's next military move reads like a page out of the Book of Daniel. He decided to invade Egypt in order to threaten the trade routes of his adversary, England. Accordingly, in 1798 he sailed with his army for Egypt, managing to elude the overwhelmingly superior fleet of Britain's Admiral Nelson. After defeating the Egyptian army in the shadow of the great pyramids, all opposition collapsed and Napoleon's army of 38,000 troops easily won control of the country.

French artist Jacques Louis David's portrait of Napoleon in his study. Napoleon's invasion of Egypt and the Holy Land led many Bible students of his day to conclude that he was the Antichrist.

Trouble loomed for Napoleon when Turkey, within whose Ottoman Empire Egypt was forcibly enrolled, declared war upon France. Napoleon was then forced to march up the Mediterranean coast into Palestine to secure the ports of Jaffa and Acre against the onslaught of the Turkish navy. This appeared to be a stunningly accurate fulfillment of a prophecy in the Book of Daniel: "At the time of the end...the king of the north shall rush upon him like a whirlwind, with chariots and horsemen, and with many ships" (Daniel 11:40).

Napoleon's army occupied Jaffa, but ground to a halt at Acre, which withstood his siege with help from the British fleet offshore. This appeared to fulfill yet another prophecy of Daniel: "For ships of Kittim shall come against him, and he shall lose heart and withdraw. He shall be enraged and take action against the holy covenant. He shall turn back and pay heed to those who forsake the holy covenant" (Daniel 11:30). "Kittim" is the tribal name for the island of Cyprus, and is used to refer to the lands beyond that island kingdom—perhaps, it was thought, as far away as Great Britain.

It seemed as if all the pieces of the puzzle were in place. However, instead of fighting the decisive battle of Armageddon, Napoleon withdrew from Palestine, confounding the hopes of those who hoped to witness the great final battle at the end of time.

Napoleon's fortunes eventually waned until he met his match in the Duke of Wellington at Waterloo in 1815. Shortly afterward, he was sent into exile. Another possible Antichrist had failed to live up to the grand expectations of prophecy enthusiasts.

Il Duce

*I*n the midst of the two World Wars that dominated the first half of the twentieth century, a political and military leader emerged on the European continent who occupied the attention of prophecy teachers and their followers for

Italian dictator Benito Mussolini was suspected of being the Antichrist because he ruled from Rome, thought by some students of biblical prophecy to be the future capital of the Antichrist.

more than a decade. Their focus was centered not on Germany's Adolf Hitler, as we might expect, but on his fellow dictator to the south, Italy's Benito Mussolini.

Out of the tumult of the first World War rose the ex-schoolteacher who preached a fiery brand of nationalism and promised the revival of an Italian empire. This caught the attention of prophecy watchers, who believed that the Antichrist would arise out of a "revived Roman Empire." All eyes were on *Il Duce* ("the leader").

Mussolini was appointed premier in 1922. Two years later, following a rigged election won by terrorizing the opposition, his Fascists finally obtained a majority in the Italian cabinet. Mussolini promptly dissolved all rival political parties and inaugurated a one-party state.

Evidence was not long in coming that linked *Il Duce* with the Beast of Revelation. It seemed as though he fit the role of the egotistical, bombastic leader uttering "proud words and blasphemies" (Revelation 13:5) who was expected to rise out of Rome. Furthermore, with his signing of the Lateran Treaty and the Concordat of 1929, Mussolini was seen as joining forces with the Roman Catholic Church.

Mussolini's invasion of Ethiopia in October of 1935 caused some excitement among prophecy enthusiasts. On the one

hand, it constituted a downward thrust into a region bordering the Middle East, which could be taken as a distraction preceding a thrust up into Israel for the Battle of Armageddon. It was also noted, in Ezekiel 38, that Ethiopia is an ally of Gog, who will lead an invasion of Israel.

In the end, however, it became clear that Mussolini did not possess the necessary military prowess of the Antichrist. His ineptness as a commander in one military campaign after another eventually disqualified him from consideration.

Long before Mussolini was unceremoniously shot by Italian partisans in 1945, the "revived Roman Empire" of his pompous rhetoric had crumbled before the advancing Allied forces. Another nominee for the title of Antichrist had failed to live up to expectations.

In the decades to follow, there would be no shortage of candidates for the biblical Antichrist as students of the Bible sought to identify this ominous personage. Even today, as the new millenium approaches, there are many who believe that the conflagration of Armageddon prophesied in the Bible cannot be far off, followed by the return of Jesus Christ and a new era of peace upon the earth.

But the enigma remains, as Jesus himself said that none but the Father knows the time of his return.

ABOUT THE BIBLE

The earliest books of the Bible were written approximately 3,500 years ago; the last were written a little less than 2,000 years ago. Also, in what today would be considered an editorial nightmare, the 66 Books of the Bible were written by about 40 different authors.

The first part of the Bible, customarily called the Old Testament, is made up of 39 books translated from Hebrew and Aramaic, the ancient languages of the Jews. Most were dictated by their authors to professional scribes. Tradition holds that Ezra (whose story is told in the Book bearing his name) compiled those 39 books, but there is no evidence to prove this.

The Apocrypha (which means "hidden") were accepted by the early Christians. They contain wisdom, history, and visionary writings; since they are no longer considered part of Holy Scriptures, many Christians do not accept them as authoritative.

The New Testament was written over a span of about 50 years during the first century A.D. It was recorded because of the needs of the Early Church. As Jesus had done, his followers used the 39 books of the Hebrew Scriptures. Additionally, however, there were now first-hand accounts of the life of Christ, which spread through the rapidly growing church. As eyewitnesses began to die, there was a growing need to record the life and ministry of Jesus. It became necessary to write these accounts down. Thus we have Matthew, Mark, Luke, and John.

Matthew and John were among Jesus' original 12 disciples, whereas Mark and Luke were not. They traveled with St. Paul and wrote what they heard from the eyewitnesses. These four Books—known as the four Gospels—as well as letters written by Paul and other apostles, bolstered the Early Church. During the third and fourth centuries, the New Testament was formally established. It was very similar to the New Testament as we know it today.

BOOKS OF THE OLD TESTAMENT

Genesis	Joshua	1 Kings	Nehemiah
Exodus	Judges	2 Kings	Esther
Leviticus	Ruth	1 Chronicles	Job
Numbers	1 Samuel	2 Chronicles	Psalms
Deuteronomy	2 Samuel	Ezra	Proverbs

Ecclesiastes	Ezekiel	Obadiah	Zephaniah
Song of Solomon	Daniel	Jonah	Haggai
Isaiah	Hosea	Micah	Zechariah
Jeremiah	Joel	Nahum	Malachi
Lamentations	Amos	Habakkuk	

BOOKS OF THE APOCRYPHA

Tobit	3 Maccabees	Baruch	Prayer of Azariah and the
1 Maccabees	Wisdom	Psalm 151	Song of the Three Jews
Judith	4 Maccabees	1 Esdras	Susanna
2 Maccabees	Sirach	2 Esdras	Bel and the Dragon
Additions to Esther	Prayer of Manasseh	Letter of Jeremiah	authors

BOOKS OF THE NEW TESTAMENT

Matthew	2 Corinthians	1 Timothy	2 Peter
Mark	Galatians	2 Timothy	1 John
Luke	Ephesians	Titus	2 John
John	Philippians	Philemon	3 John
Acts	Colossians	Hebrews	Jude
Romans	1 Thessalonians	James	Revelation
1 Corinthians	2 Thessalonians	1 Peter	

AUTHORS

Old Testament

Genesis	Moses
Exodus	Moses
Leviticus	Moses
Deuteronomy	Moses
Numbers	Moses
Joshua	Possibly Joshua, Phineas, Eleazer, Samuel, Jeremiah, or one of Joshua's elders
Judges	Uncertain
Ruth	Uncertain
1 Samuel	
2 Samuel	Samuel possibly wrote part of 1 Samuel
1 Kings	
2 Kings	Possibly Ezra, Ezekiel, or Jeremiah
1 Chronicles	
2 Chronicles	Possibly Ezra
Nehemiah	Nehemiah
Esther	Attributed to Mordecai
Job	Uncertain
Psalms	Attributed to David, Solomon, Asaph, and the sons of Korah, among others
Proverbs	Solomon and other wisdom writers
Ecclesiastes	Solomon or a Jewish sage
Song of Solomon	Possibly Solomon
Isaiah	Isaiah
Jeremiah	Jeremiah
Lamentations	Attributed to Jeremiah
Ezekiel	Ezekiel
Daniel	Daniel
Hosea	Hosea
Joel	Attributed to Joel
Amos	Amos
Obadiah	Obadiah
Jonah	Attributed to Jonah
Micah	Micah
Nahum	Nahum
Habakkuk	Habakkuk
Zephaniah	Zephaniah
Haggai	Haggai
Zechariah	Zechariah
Malachi	Malachi

Apocrypha

Tobit	unknown
Judith	unknown
Wisdom of Solomon	unknown
Sirach (Ecclesiasticus)	Joshua, son of Eleazar

Baruch .... unknown	Philippians .... Paul, the apostle
1Maccabees .... unknown	Colossians .... Paul, the apostle
2Maccabees .... unknown	1 Thessalonians .... Paul, the apostle
	2 Thessalonians .... Paul, the apostle
	Philemon .... Paul, the apostle
New Testament	1 Timothy .... Paul, the apostle
	2 Timothy .... Paul, the apostle
Matthew........................ Matthew, the apostle	Titus .... Paul, the apostle
Mark............................. John Mark	Hebrews............................... Unknown
Luke .... Luke	James.................. James, the brother of Jesus
John .... John, the apostle	1 Peter .... Peter, the apostle
Acts .... Luke	2 Peter .... Peter, the apostle
Romans .... Paul, the apostle	1 John .... John, the apostle
1 Corinthians..................... Paul, the apostle	2 John .... John, the apostle
2 Corinthians..................... Paul, the apostle	3 John .... John, the apostle
Galatians .... Paul, the apostle	Jude .... Jude
Ephesians........................ Paul, the apostle	Revelation........................ John, the apostle

Time of Events and Writing

Time of Events Old Testament				
	Joshua .... 1230–1200 B.C.	2 Chronicles ...... 1000–586 B.C.
	Judges .... 1200–1070 B.C.	Ezra .... 538–428 B.C.
	Ruth .... 1375–1050 B.C.	Nehemiah .... 458–432 B.C.
Genesis .... 2000–1650 B.C.	1 Samuel .... 1200–1070 B.C.	Esther .... 460 B.C.
Exodus .... 1325–1225 B.C.	2 Samuel .... 1200–1070 B.C.	Job .... unknown
Leviticus .... 1325–1225 B.C.	1 Kings .... 970–586 B.C.	Psalms .... throughout
Numbers......... 1325–1225 B.C.	2 Kings .... 970–586 B.C.	Israel's history
Deuteronomy.......... 1230 B.C.	1 Chronicles ...... 1000–586 B.C.	

TIME OF EVENTS AND WRITING

Proverbs . . . . .during/after Solomon's reign	Judith . . . . 200 B.C.	Acts. . . . . 60–85 A.D.
Ecclesiastes. . . . . uncertain	2 Maccabees . . . . 200 B.C.	Romans . . . . Around 57 A.D.
Song of Solomon. . . 971–931 B.C.	Additions to Esther. . . . . 200 B.C.	1 Corinthians . . . . 54–57 A.D.
Isaiah . . . . 790–722 B.C.	3 Maccabees . . . . 200 B.C.	2 Corinthians . . . . 55–58 A.D.
Jeremiah . . . . 627–586 B.C.	Wisdom . . . . 200 B.C.	Galatians. . . . . 47–57 A.D.
Lamentations . . . probably 586 B.C.	4 Maccabees . . . . 200 B.C.	Ephesians. . . . . Early 60s A.D.
Ezekiel. . . . . 593–571 B.C.	Sirach. . . . . 200 B.C.	Philippians. . . . . Around 54 or early 60s A.D.
Daniel . . . . 605–536 B.C.	Prayer of Manasseh. . . . . 200 B.C.	Colossians . . . . Early 60s A.D.
Hosea. . . . . 790–715 B.C.	Baruch . . . . 200 B.C.	1 Thessalonians. . . . . . 50–51 A.D.
Joel . . . . uncertain	Psalm 151 . . . . 200 B.C.	2 Thessalonians . . Early 50s A.D.
Amos . . . . 790–722 B.C.	1 Esdras. . . . . 200 B.C.	1 Timothy . . . . About 63–66 A.D.
Obadiah . . . . uncertain	2 Esdras. . . . . 200 B.C.	2 Timothy . . . . About 67 A.D.
Jonah . . . . 793–753 B.C.	Letter of Jeremiah . . . . . . 200 B.C.	Titus . . . . Unknown
Micah. . . . . 750–722 B.C.	Prayer of Azariah and the Song of the	Philemon. . . . . 62 A.D.
Nahum . . . . uncertain	Three Jews . . . . 200 B.C.	Hebrews. . . . . Before 70 A.D.
Habakkuk . . . . 612–597 B.C.	Susanna. . . . . 200 B.C.	James . . . . .Possibly early first century A.D.
Zephaniah . . . . 640–609 B.C.	Bel and the	
Haggai . . . . 520 B.C.	Dragon Authors . . . . 200 B.C.	1 Peter . . . . 64 A.D.
Zechariah. . . . . 520–515 B.C.		2 Peter . . . . Uncertain
Malachi . . . . 430 B.C.		1 John. . . . . Early 60s A.D.
		2 John. . . . . Early 60s A.D.
Time of Writing Apocrypha	**Time of Writing New Testament**	3 John. . . . . Early 60s A.D.
		Jude . . . . 67–80 A.D.
	Matthew . . . . 60–80 A.D.	Revelation . . . . 95 or 96 A.D.
Tobit. . . . . 200 B.C.	Mark. . . . . 60–70 A.D.	
1 Maccabees . . . . 200 B.C.	Luke . . . . 60–85 A.D.	
	John . . . . 60–100 A.D.	

EPILOGUE

Because so many people regard the Bible as the Word of God for one of the world's largest and most powerful religious groups, it is universally mysterious. There is a certain force we attribute to things of a spiritual nature, a force that invokes musings charged with eerie background music and a mist rising out of nowhere. It is most likely we are confusing the true, awesome power of God with something Hollywood once generated merely for the sake of entertaining us.

While this confusion may at first seem to border on blasphemy, it is actually a double-edged sword. On the one hand, elaborate computer enhancement of things that go bump in the night may *seem* far more magnificent than the simple workings of God. But the truth is that the cinematic scenes are cheap counterfeits of truly marvelous wonders from an omnipotent God. If indeed the Red Sea did part, it would have been far more dramatic than anything Cecil B. DeMille could have conjured up. Should you ever behold the handiworks of God as embellished by special effects, rest assured that God, unassisted, is capable of far more wondrous and powerful deeds.

Even the modest, uneducated, most-obscure personages of the early Bible were aware of the power and puzzles hidden within the Kingdom of God. Daniel, the Old Testament prophet who was cast

Moses is a central character in the Old Testament. It was through him that God communicated His Ten Commandments and showed His mighty power.

into the lions' den, could interpret dreams with such authority that kings and queens spoke of his abilities. The Bible records a conversation that Daniel had with his king (Nebuchadnezzar): "No wise men, enchanters, magicians, or diviners can show to the king the mystery that the king is asking, but there is a God in heaven who reveals mysteries, . . ." (Daniel 2:27-28).

We on earth cannot conceive of what God can do because his power is so elusive. But this inspires two logical questions. Did God purposefully provide clues to the profound secrets contained in Scripture? And does he want us to study the Bible and carry out his marching orders based on what we read? Some might answer that God does not want us to delve too deeply—similar to God forbidding Adam and Eve to eat the fruit of the Tree of Knowledge. Others believe that God gives us insight and talents just so we *can* pursue all that is written in his word. Yet others think he wants us to simply be in awe of him and the profound mystery that surrounds him.

And so, we go to the greater mystery: Who wrote these words considered Holy Scripture, and why? Are they divinely inspired? The Bible is replete with action, adventure, drama, and love. It contains the full range of human emotion. It would be unnatural *not* to ponder whether the Scriptures are the stuff of God, or the stuff of allegory, poetry, and late night dreams. Whether you accept them as

divinely inspired is an intensely personal decision. By studying the mysteries described within our pages, you could find yourself closing in on your own answer to this question.

Mysteries of the Bible unraveled many previously inexplicable parts of Scripture. We began with the location of the Garden of Eden, and ended with the meaning of the divine revelation to St. John on the Isle of Patmos. Through aerial photography; down-in-the-dirt archaeological digs with brushes and spoons; and hi-tech sonar, radar, and carbon-dating equipment, new information continues to be gathered every day. *Mysteries of the Bible* employed and explained that up-to-date information to shed light on secrets previously thought to be too complex or too rooted in antiquity to solve. Occasionally, too, it appears that the only explanation seems to fall within the realm of a miracle from an all-powerful God.

To close this authoritative and thought-provoking book by writing "The End," would be trite and inaccurate. There is no end to the secrets hidden and mysteries posed within the Bible—nor to the solutions we can entertain as new and more-sophisticated equipment is developed. Perhaps, then, it is better to end this passage by saying . . . Amen.

INDEX